The Life and Works
of
Lili Boulanger

The Life and Works
of
Lili Boulanger

Léonie Rosenstiel

Rutherford • Madison • Teaneck
Fairleigh Dickinson University Press
London: Associated University Presses

© 1978 by Associated University Presses, Inc.

Associated University Presses, Inc.
Cranbury, New Jersey 08512

Associated University Presses
Magdalen House
136–148 Tooley Street
London SE1 2TT, England

Library of Congress Cataloging in Publication Data

Rosenstiel, Léonie.
    The life and works of Lili Boulanger.

    Bibliography: p.
    Includes index.
    1. Boulanger, Lili, 1893–1918. 2. Composers—
France—Biography.
ML410.B7727R7   780'.92'4 [B]   75-18244
ISBN 0-8386-1796-4

To my parents
Who helped make dreams into reality

PRINTED IN THE UNITED STATES OF AMERICA

Contents

Foreword

October 1, 1975

Dear Léonie,

I am very moved by the devotion with which you have undertaken the study of Lili Boulanger's music, the delicacy of your intelligence, your sensibility. The seriousness of your approach brought me to give you the entire liberty to develop the subject you have treated with such respect. May your readers find out all that is implied in these pages by your penetrating mind and understanding heart.

Nadia Boulanger

Preface

This is the first comprehensive study of the life and works of Lili Boulanger. In the 1930s two articles about her were published —one in the United States, the other in Holland. Paul Landormy's article in *Musical Quarterly* (16:1930) has almost inevitably appeared in bibliographical listings of scholarly articles about the composer ever since, and Eduard Reeser's two-part article in *De Muziek* (7:1933), has become the principal source for most later works on the subject. The fact remains that both of the above writers derived most of their data from the poet Camille Mauclair's 1921 article, "La Vie et l'oeuvre de Lili Boulanger," which was published in the August issue of *La Revue Musicale*. His essay, while written with great literary polish and sensibility, is impressionistic rather than scholarly, and contains numerous inaccuracies. Reeser had announced that his published work was only a preliminary survey of the material, and that he planned to use it as the basis for a larger study. His project never came to fruition, however.

The most recently published material on Lili Boulanger to appear in scholarly sources is the article on the Boulanger family by Jacques Chailley, which was included in the 1971 supplement to *Die Musik in Geschichte und Gegenwart*. It, too, cites Reeser, Mauclair, and Landormy as the best available scholarly source materials, and, consequently, perpetuates some of their inaccuracies.

The fact that Lili Boulanger won the Prix de Rome for musical composition, and actually was the first woman to do so, would not itself be justification enough for devoting a full-length study to her life and works. If her compositions themselves did not show a steadily growing mastery of musical techniques and evidence that her own finely honed intelligence was at work—a faculty that provided the basis for such artistic growth—such a study would be an exercise without meaning. This composer also held an important place among her contemporaries. Lili Boulanger's accomplishments during her life were considered newsworthy, and her peers and professors clearly felt that both her musical and personal qualities were extraordinary.

Lili Boulanger stands squarely within the French tradition and is greatly indebted to such composers as Debussy, especially in her early works. In the course of her brief lifetime, she also developed a personal style. This, added to the musical vocabulary of her era, and combined with frequent use of sacred texts and works by Symbolist poets such as Francis Jammes and Maurice Maeterlinck helped her to achieve a quality of expression and power based on the use of harmony for tonal effect but tending more and more to polytonality in her later works, especially the *Psalms* and the *Pie Jesu*. The suppleness of line and imaginative use of instruments are characteristics of her style from the beginning and show, even in her early works, the composer's subtle feeling for texture and timbre. Although she worked in a wide variety of genres, Lili Boulanger's main contributions are in the area of vocal music—both sacred and secular—and, above all, in the sacred compositions she completed during the last two years of her life.

My own interest in Lili Boulanger was sparked when, as a violin student at the Juilliard School, I was first given her *Nocturne* to perform in 1962. The published score contained the composer's dates of birth and death, and standard music reference works provided little additional information. The late Louis Persinger, then a master teacher at Juilliard, kept my interest alive by discussing the period and its ambience with me in depth after I became a pupil of his. I was unable to obtain any substantially new information until I could establish contact with Mlle Nadia Boulanger, the composer's sister and only surviving relative.

Until she granted me her complete cooperation, all primary source materials had remained out of reach of researchers. Earlier studies, therefore, had had to rely mainly on secondary sources. Under such circumstances, it is surprising that the previous articles contained as few errors as they did. This study, on the other hand, has relied almost entirely on hitherto unavailable primary sources. It has included library, archival, and field research, personal interviews, and extensive correspondence with surviving friends and acquaintances of Lili Boulanger, as well as with her sister.

I was fortunate enough to have been given access to personal correspondence, manuscripts, official and family documents, as well as memorabilia of all kinds. In the process of securing the necessary primary information, which could not be obtained in any other way, I was obliged to travel to many places where Lili Boulanger had stayed during her lifetime. These included Paris, Gargenville, Compiègne, Bayonne, Arcachon, Biarritz, St. Raphaël, Nice, and Mézy (in France), Florence and Rome (in Italy), Bad Kreuznach and Frankfurt (in Germany), Scheveningen, Wittebroecke, and The Hague (in The Netherlands).

In the course of my research, not only were numerous biographical details clarified and previous errors corrected, but also considerable light was shed on the reasons why Lili Boulanger composed particular works when she did. Interviews with those who had known her also helped to explain the associations that certain of her compositions had in the composer's own mind.

Special thanks are due to M. Balthus (Count Balthassar Klossowski de Rola), Director of the Académie de France à Rome, and to M. J. Mathieu, General Secretary of the Académie, for permitting me personal access both to the Villa Medici itself and to its private archives, and for their assistance in relocating the portrait of Lili Boulanger by Pierre Bodard, which is part of the Villa's permanent collection. The staff of the French Embassy in Rome, and particularly MM. Mallet and Mattei and the Countess Corti, were most cooperative in suggesting other sources of archival material.

Mme Larnaudie-Laffitte of the Académie des Beaux-Arts of the Institut de France in Paris was exceedingly helpful in giving me free access to the Academy's private as well as public records. M. Antoine Terrasse of Fontainebleau, Mlle Robert of the Conservatoire National (Paris), M. J.-M. Nectoux of the Bibliothèque Nationale (Paris), and Mme E. Lebeau, formerly Head Librarian of the Music Division of the Bibliothèque Nationale (Paris), were instrumental in making it possible for me to locate some difficult-to-find material.

I am also grateful to Mlle Jeannine Auboyer of the Musée Guimet in Paris, and to Professors André Bareau and Jean Filliozat of the École pratique des Hautes Études for providing me with background information on Suzanne Karpelès, and to the Venerable Kosgoda Sobhita, also of the École pratique, for attesting to the authenticity of the text of the *Vieille prière bouddhique* set to music by Lili Boulanger. M. Dousset and Mlle Dunan of

11

the Archives Nationales were also helpful, as was Mlle Lilian Hérisson of the Société des Auteurs, Compositeurs et Éditeurs de Musique in Paris.

Thanks are also due to the following professors at Columbia University: to Professors Patricia Carpenter and Edward Lippman, who encouraged me to undertake this project, to Professor Hubert Doris, who first made it possible for me to contact Mlle Nadia Boulanger directly, and to Richard Taruskin, who translated my correspondence with the Lenin Library in Moscow. Mrs. W. H. Johnstone of Boston kindly placed at my disposal the archives of the Lili Boulanger Memorial Fund of Boston.

I wish also to thank Mlle Monique Legrand of Saint-Germain-en-Laye, who made it possible for me to meet the late M. Henri Büsser. The latter, a centenarian who had known the Boulanger family since before the birth of both Nadia and Lili, had conducted the first performance with full orchestra of Lili's cantata *Faust et Hélène,* in November 1913, as well as the concert of her works given at the Envois de Rome concert in 1921.

Throughout the years that this work has been in progress, I have been indebted to M. François Lesure, the Head Librarian of the Music Division of the Bibliothèque Nationale in Paris for his insightful comments and very helpful suggestions, and for having generously placed at my disposal all of the resources at his command that might possibly prove of help to my research.

There are some without whose full help and patient coopera- tion this work could not have been undertaken. Chief among these is Mlle Nadia Boulanger, who granted me many hours of her time both in Fontainebleau and in Paris, and who made available to me hundreds of documents in her possession. Without her au- thorization, my access to the Villa Medici and the Académie des Beaux-Arts, as well as to many other primary sources, would not have been possible. A special note of appreciation is due to Mlle Boulanger's assistants, Mlles Annette Dieudonné and Cécile Ar- magnac, and to her secretary, Mme Diana Ferenczfy, for their thoughtful cooperation throughout this project. Mlle Boulanger also made it possible for me to contact others who had known Lili Boulanger personally. I especially appreciate the generous thoughtful help given to me by the late Mme Miki Paronian of Nice during the days she spent with me in her villa answering my myriad questions, and revealing to me the human side of Lili Boulanger, which she wanted very much to have me include as an integral part of my study. Mme Mireille Apostol of Paris, Mme Renée de Marquein of Nyons (Drôme), MM. Paul Paray of Monaco, Jules Piel of Paris, and the late Marcel Grandjany were also most cooperative.

English translations of all passages quoted in the text are my own. Musical illustrations from the copyrighted and published scores of *Nocturne, Renouveau, Les Sirènes, Attente, Reflets, Hymne au Soleil, Le Retour, Pour les Funérailles d'un Soldat, Soir sur la Plaine, Cortège, D'un Jardin Clair, D'un Vieux Jardin, Dans l'immense Tristesse,* and *D'un Matin de Printemps* are reproduced with the kind permission of Mlle Nadia Boulanger; those for *Faust et Hélène, Clairières dans le Ciel, Psalm 24, Psalm 129, Psalm 130, Vieille Prière bouddhique,* and *Pie Jesu* are given with the permission of Éditions A. Durand et Compagnie (Paris). Examples from unpublished scores not otherwise copyrighted are here used with the kind permission of Mlle Nadia Boulanger. Appendixes A–S contain transcriptions of supporting documents and extended passages in their original language. Appendix T contains a chronological list of the published and unpublished works of Lili Boulanger. Appendix U gives basic biographical data on selected people who played significant roles in the life of the Boulanger family.

My special thanks go to Professor Gordana Lazarevich of the University of Victoria (British Columbia) for her valuable suggestions in the final preparation of this manuscript.

I am deeply indebted to Professor Denis Stevens of the University of California at Santa Barbara for introducing me to many of the humanistic dimensions of musicology that have proved so necessary in the completion of this study, as well as for reading the manuscript at its various stages of completion.

Lili Boulanger has been the subject of ongoing debate for more than half a century. Although it is not possible to discuss all the sources in a volume of this size, I have tried to present and analyze representative contemporaneous and current opinions, both published and unpublished, concerning her and her work, in order to give a balanced picture of this gifted and controversial composer.

Acknowledgments

I would like to thank the following for permission to use material for which they hold the copyright:

Académie de France à Rome, for permission to quote from the *Livre d'inscription des pensionnaires*, MS, p. 77, and for permission to quote the inscription on the verso of Bodard's portrait of Lili Boulanger, which is now in the possession of the Académie.

Archives Nationales de France for permission to quote from the semester records of the Conservatoire National for the years 1912 and 1913.

Mademoiselle Nadia Boulanger, for permission to quote from published and unpublished music by Lili Boulanger, from our interviews, from her unpublished letters to me, and for authorizing the publication of family photographs and other personal memorabilia.

Mademoiselle Annette Dieudonné, for permission to quote from a letter to me.

Durand et Compagnie, Paris, for permission to use musical examples from the following works of Lili Boulanger: *Faust et Hélène, Clairières dans le Ciel, Psalm 24, Psalm 129, Psalm 130, Vieille Prière bouddhique, and Pie Jesu*.

Mr. U. P. Ekanayake, for permission to include the Sinhalese version of the *Maitri Bhavanava* from his edition of the *Buddhist Manual for Novices*.

Librairie Plon, for permission to cite passages from Henry Lapauze, *Histoire de l'Académie de France à Rome*, vol. 2, Paris: Librairie Plon, 1924.

15

Madame Renée de Marquein, for permission to quote from her unpublished letters to me.

Maître Paul Paray, for allowing me to cite a passage from an unpublished letter to me.

Monsieur Arsène Paronian, for permission to reprint an illustration from *En Recueillement* by the late Madame Miki Paronian, and to use a photograph of her.

Saturday Review, for permission to reproduce sections of Marc Blitzstein, "Music's Other Boulanger" (May 1960).

The Life and Works
of
Lili Boulanger

1

The Boulanger Family

The Boulanger family has been an active part of the Parisian musical scene since the first awards ceremony at the Conservatoire National in 1797. It was on October 24 of that year that the prizes for the preceding year were given to the winners. It was a gala occasion.

> The distribution of the prizes of the Conservatoire de Musique for the courses of study for year V[1] was made in the beautiful hall of the Odéon Theater on the 3rd of Brumaire, in the presence of the executive members of the Directoire, the Ministers, the Diplomatic Corps, the Institut national des Sciences et Arts, and public functionaries. The whole hall—lavishly illuminated and perfectly decorated—was filled with a huge number of citizens and elegantly dressed women. The view was magnificent. The Directoire came in about seven in the evening. It was welcomed with warm applause. Immediately, the concert began.[2]

During the course of this concert, Frédéric Boulanger, then a nineteen-year-old cello student of Levasseur, performed as a soloist in a work of Bréval. The concert itself was long and varied, including works of Gluck, Salieri, Cherubini, Méhul, and Viotti. After the concert,

> The Minister of the Interior, charged by the Directoire with the distribution of the prizes, praised music in general without, however, neglecting to recall the particular influence exerted by this beautiful art in the course of our revolution.

After his speech began this distribution of prizes impatiently waited for by the students, and which was watched with the greatest interest by the spectators. Each prize-winning student was called aloud by the secretary of the Conservatoire and led by his teacher to the Minister of the Interior who offered him his award.[3]

The first prize in cello for the year 1797 was given "To Citizen Frédéric Boulanger, aged 19 years, born in Saxony, student of Citizen Levasseur. *Prize, a cello.*"[4]

But this Dresden-born musician[5] did not carry on an active career as a cellist only. He joined the faculty of the Conservatoire in 1816 as a vocal coach, continuing in that capacity until 1820.[6] In 1820, after the assassination of Jean de France, Duc de Berry, by Louis-Pierre Louvel, a harness-maker, Boulanger composed a commemorative song, setting verses of Desaugiers.[7]

During this entire period, Frédéric Boulanger was also a musician in the King's Chapel, as he proudly indicates on the cover of the published music,[8] as well as professor in the École Royale de Musique.

Marie-Julie Hallinger was born in the Department of the Seine on January 29, 1786. She, too, attended the Conservatoire National, and in 1809 won first prize for voice. The following year she carried off the first prize in *Comédie lyrique.* Two years later she joined the Théâtre de l'Opéra-Comique as a regular member of the company.[9] She had made a great reputation for herself even as early as the time of her debut in 1811. Before that, she had already become known as "gifted with a very beautiful voice and possessing a brilliant and facile vocal execution. . . ."[10] It was said that she was such a sensation at her first performance at the Opéra-Comique, that

> called back by great cries after the performance, she was led back onto the stage . . . to receive the noisy proofs of the public's satisfaction. Such was the eagerness of the Parisians to hear her that the administration of the theater prolonged her debut for an entire year.[11]

By the time of her first success, Marie-Julie Hallinger had already married Frédéric Boulanger. She used either the name Mme Hallinger-Boulanger, or, more usually, Mme Boulanger as her professional name throughout her career.

On September 16, 1815, a son, Henri-Alexandre-Ernest, was born to the couple. Both the Boulanger and the Hallinger families

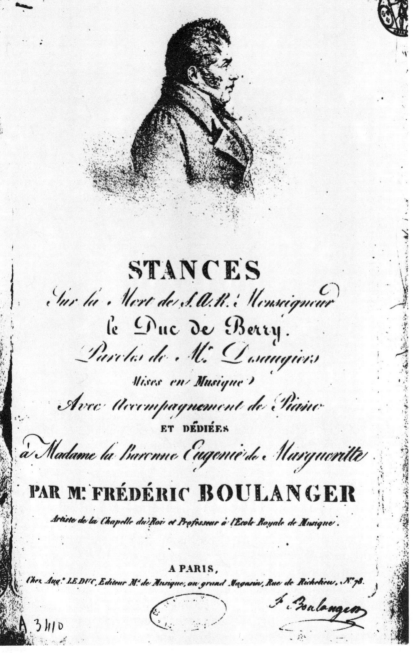

Figure 1. Title page of Frédéric Boulanger's *Stances. . .*, auto-graphed by the composer. *Courtesy of the Département de la Musique, Bibliothèque Nationale, Paris.*

Madame Boulanger.

Figure 2. Mme Boulanger as she appeared in the 1830s, at the height of her popular success at the Opéra-Comique. *Courtesy of the New York Public Library Music Division.*

were extremely active in Parisian artistic life, and from his earliest youth the boy was in contact with dramatic and musical artists of the first rank, as well as poets, playwrights, artists, and intellectuals. Ernest Boulanger "was linked by his mother to the world of musical theater—Boïeldieu, Halévy, Auber—and by his uncle, the great actor Frédérick Lemaître, to the world of the theater. . . ."[12] Madame Hallinger-Boulanger was herself linked to the theater through her sister, Sophie, a leading actress at the Théâtre de l'Odéon. It was Sophie, in fact, who made Lemaître part of the Boulanger family by marrying him. They had met while playing opposite each other in melodramas at the Odéon, and "a host of actors and actresses from the Boulevard theaters were invited to the wedding,"[13] which took place on October 10, 1826. In this type

Figure 3. Title page of Ernest Boulanger's cantata *Achille. Courte of the Département de la Musique, Bibliothèque Nationale, Par*

of artistic household, Ernest was exposed to the most distinguished literary lights of the time—Alexandre Dumas, Eugène Labiche, Eugène Scribe, and Eugène Sue, to name just a few.[14]

Madame Boulanger had become a great favorite among the general public who frequented the Théâtre Feydeau.

> To the charm of her singing was joined an acting style both natural and full of comic verve. A happy combination of gaiety, sensitivity and finesse gave to her dramatic talent a character all its own. She played best of all soubrette and servant roles, and the habitués of the Théâtre Feydeau remembered for a long time her talent in characters as different as the soubrette of the *Evénements imprévus* and the servant of the *Rendez-vous bourgeois*.[15]

Madame Boulanger continued her professional activities throughout Ernest Boulanger's childhood.[16]

Like both his father and mother before him, Ernest Boulanger attended the Conservatoire National, then known as the Conservatoire de Musique. By the time he was nineteen years old, he had studied with Halévy and LeSueur. In 1835 Ernest Boulanger won the Prix de Rome competition. The announcement issued by the Conservatoire in its bulletin of the prizes awarded for 1835 reads as follows:

Composition.
First Grand Prize in Musical Composition, taken at the Académie royale des Beaux-Arts of the Institut de France, by M. BOULANGER (Henri-Alexandre-Ernest), of Paris, age twenty.[17]

In his speech in honor of the occasion, the Duc de Choiseul congratulated the entire Conservatoire, terming it the finest in Europe. He then went on to recall the institution's recent losses—the deaths of Boïeldieu and others, the retirements or leaves of absence. Finally, he observed that these losses would not irreparably damage the Conservatoire itself. "The students of the Conservatoire will be the proof of it, and this very year gives us more than hope."[18] First on his list of the accomplishments of Conservatoire students over the past year was that of Ernest Boulanger, whose family name, the Duke reminded his audience, was already dear to the arts.[19]

Although it had been a great honor for Ernest Boulanger to win the Prix de Rome, the year 1836—the first one he spent at the Villa Medici as part of his prize[20]—was not completely untroubled. True, his Prix de Rome gave him the right to live in the Villa Medici during the Directorship of Dominique Ingres, and to meet with such other artists as Hippolyte and Paul Flandrin, as well as such other composers as Ambroise Thomas, but there were two problems that year. The first was relatively petty. By May 15 the intervention of the French Ambassador to Rome had been necessary to put a stop to the "nocturnal attacks which menaced the *pensionnaires* and domestics of the Villa."[21] There was another problem far more serious than that, however.

A few months later, the architect Famin was stopped at Anagni under the pretext that he was without a passport, and was dragged off to prison, handcuffed, guarded by five mounted policemen. M. de La Tour-Maubourg[22] demanded an apology from the Holy See. At his request, the guilty Vice-Prefect of police was discharged and was incarcerated for a month in the Castel San'Angelo, and the functionary's colleagues were advised by official circular of his disgrace. This commanding officer [i.e., Sub-Prefect] had, perhaps, the semblance of an excuse: the fear of cholera was terrorizing the peninsula, and each foreigner seemed to the Italians to be the plague incarnate.[23]

Happily, the Villa Medici itself escaped the worst of the Italian cholera epidemic of 1836, which wrought havoc in the rest of Rome. Ingres maintained order and managed to keep the *pensionnaires* as calm as possible under the circumstances. But he could not keep them from falling prey to a mysterious fever that had attacked all of them to some extent by the end of 1836.[24] The *pensionnaires* were even more impressed by his courage, knowing that he was not himself in good health, and admired the fact that

24

the Director continued his own artistic activities as if nothing had happened.

But in 1837 another cholera epidemic menaced Italy. It had become the policy of the Academy not to evacuate the Villa Medici in times of disease, but three of the pensionnaires—the engraver Bridoux, the painter Hippolyte Flandrin, and Ernest Boulanger—were allowed to go to Florence, which was then safe from the disease.

> The other *pensionnaires,* grouped around Ingres, began to regret their courage when the terrifying, unexpected death of Sigalon came. The unfortunate man was returning from Paris. Sunday, he had dined at Ingres's house, full of health, in fact happy to be alive, after the success of his copy of the *Last Judgment,* which won for him other important commissions. Having caught cholera on Monday, he died the following Thursday, August 18th. Late at night on the 18th to the 19th, Simart, panic-stricken, believing himself to be a prey to cholera, came to wake up Bonnassieux,[25] who succeeded in calming him. Becoming a prey to terror in his own turn, Bonnassieux passed on the same dread to his comrades. It was only a false alarm. But it was enough to decide the *pensionnaires* to reclaim their passports.[26]

The Academy in France, however, refused to permit a mass exodus of *pensionnaires* at that point, and the terrified artists were required to stay in the Villa and await the end of the epidemic. It did nothing to calm their nerves when six of the nuns in the convent next door died—at almost the same time—of the same disease. For those of the *pensionnaires* most frightened by recent events, Ingres prescribed a most singular remedy: the reading aloud of a chapter from Plutarch![27]

During 1842 Ernest Boulanger began to win a considerable reputation in Parisian musical circles. His one-act opera, *Le Diable à l'École,* was given its premiere by the Opéra-Comique on January 17 of that year. This work, with a libretto by Scribe, produced a favorable impression,[28] and he followed it with another one-act opera, *Les Deux Bergères,* which was given its premiere by the Opéra-Comique on February 3 of the following year.

During these years, Ernest Boulanger remained extremely close to and fond of his mother. He was a tall man, with brown hair and dark, intense eyes,[29] and every night, on his return from the opera, he lifted his mother up in his arms to greet her.[30] Only a month after Mme Boulanger's retirement from the Opéra-Comique after thirty-four years there, Ernest Boulanger had yet another one-act comic opera premiered by this company, on May 28, 1845. His first three-act opera, *La Cachette,* received its premiere there on August 10, 1847.[31]

After her retirement from the Opéra-Comique, Mme Boulanger was given a pension from the Société des Acteurs. A little over five years later, she ruptured a blood vessel and died quite suddenly, on July 23, 1850.[32] Marie-Julie Boulanger was then sixty-four years old.[33]

His mother's death did not stop Ernest Boulanger from continuing to be extremely active in the world of music. He began to work with the librettists Michel Carré and Jules Barbier, and Barbier became a particularly close friend of his.[34] Boulanger also wrote numerous works for the large choral groups that were then the rage in Paris and published a number of operettas that were never performed.[35] His first opera with M. Carré was the one-act work *Le 15 Août au champs* in 1852. There followed *Les Sabots de la Marquise* in 1854, in which Carré and Barbier collaborated on the libretto,[36] and once again the two librettists worked together on Boulanger's *L'Eventail,* which was presented first at the Opéra-Comique on December 4, 1860.[37]

Raïssa, Princess Mychetsky, was born in Saint Petersburg, Russia, on December 19, 1858.[38] She was raised according to the fashion then most acceptable among the Russian nobility. That is, as a young child, she was taught German, French, and Russian simultaneously by her nurse.[39] Having persuaded her parents to permit her to go to France to complete her education, the princess saw Ernest Boulanger conduct.[40] A gifted singer, she took lessons from him[41]—Ernest Boulanger had become a professor of voice at the Conservatoire beginning in 1871—and married him in Saint Petersburg, at the Église du Régiment des Chasseurs de la Garde du Corps, on September 16, 1877. The Head Chaplain, Paul Favorsky, officiated.[42]

During her years of studies in Paris, Raïssa, Princess Mychetsky, had been under the guardianship of a good friend of her family, Mademoiselle Louise (Loulou) Gonet, whose family had also been close friends of the Mychetskys in Saint Petersburg.[43] In fact, Henri Gonet, the father of Louise, had been a witness at the wedding of Ernest Boulanger and Raïssa Mychetsky.[44] Ernest Boulanger was then sixty years old; his bride was nineteen.

Meanwhile, Ernest Boulanger had continued to compose operas.[45] Judging by the good comments it was given in the Clément and Larousse *Dictionnaire des Opéras, Les Sabots de la Marquise* was, on the whole, a well-received work. The authors commented:

The music is pleasant. The romance sung by the Marquise . . . recalls quite happily the old style. The air *Vive le veuvage* is vulgar, but the soubrette's couplets, *Aimons qui nous aime,* are charming. We will recall again the hunting song sung by the Baron; it is well worked-out and ingeniously imitative, as well as the scenic duet sung over lunch. As for the couplets sung by Nicolas, they were applauded for their broadly comical eccentricity.[46]

Boulanger's other operas were *Don Quichotte,* a five-act work first performed on May 10, 1869, and *Don Mucarade,* a one-act opera also produced on May 10th, six years later. Both had librettos by Barbier and Carré, and both were premiered by the Opéra-Comique.[47] Even in the short *Don Mucarade,* the *Dictionnaire des Opéras* found some congenial features, a duet and a bass aria that had what it called "a frank gaiety and a facile melody."[48] But not all observers of the musical scene admired M. Boulanger's easy way with melody. The *Annales du Théâtre et de la Musique* for 1875 state that the music is, in the opinion of the critic, "as old as the play."[49] That critic further complains that Ernest Boulanger's melodies are too facile, and that this work "has everything needed to go to join the other works of M. Boulanger," that is, in limbo.[50] The critic further suggested that Ernest Boulanger could console himself for the reception his opera had received in the knowledge of the future achievements of his singing students at the Conservatoire National. The negative reactions of some of his critics did not prevent Ernest Boulanger's achievements from being recognized by the French government. In 1870 he was named a Chevalier de la Légion d'Honneur, and eleven years later he became an Officer d'Académie.

Madame Ernest Boulanger became a Roman Catholic, and adapted to life in France by becoming a part of her husband's social circle. Among those she came to know as Ernest's closest friends were the Bouwens van der Boijen family, Charles Gounod, Massenet, and those of his colleagues still remaining from the Villa Medici, as well as—to a lesser degree—Camille Saint-Saëns. William Bouwens van der Boijen was a remarkable man. While in France during the War of 1870, he had become a French citizen out of sympathy with French suffering during the siege of Paris. An architect, he was responsible for the Crédit Lyonnais building in Paris, among others. His son, Richard, and his daughter, Marthe, also were close to the Boulanger family, and so, after their birth, were his grandchildren, Hélène and Jean. The Bouwens home on the rue de Lota was a social gathering place. Until the family was decimated during World War I, soirées were held there—frequent evenings of amusements, music-making, and practical jokes, in which the Bouwens were often joined by the Boulangers as well as their other friends who had gone there to enjoy the relaxed and fun-loving atmosphere.[51]

In 1885 a daughter was born to Ernest and Raïssa Boulanger. They named her after her paternal grandmother, Nina Juliette Boulanger. But she did not long survive. Exactly fifteen months later, on April 16, 1886, Juliette Boulanger died.[52]

A year later, another daughter was born to the Boulangers in their apartment on the rue Maubeuge. Juliette-Nadia Boulanger was born on September 16, 1887. She was conscious very early of her father and his friends. In fact, one of her strongest memories of early childhood is the last visit Charles Gounod paid to his dear friend Ernest Boulanger in 1893.[53]

Figure 4. Ernest Boulanger in the late 1890s. *Courtesy of the New York Public Library Music Division.*

It can thus be seen that members of the Boulanger family were active in the fields of music and the theater. Their involvement with music can be traced back to Frédéric Boulanger and Julie Hallinger in the late eighteenth and early nineteenth centuries respectively. The world of the theater was part of the family tradition both by blood in the person of Julie's sister Sophie and, later, also of her husband, the great actor Frédéric Lemaître. These associations, as well as those stemming from a sense of continuity of family traditions, surrounded Ernest Boulanger from his earliest youth, permitting him natural, easy access to artistic circles in Paris. His own abilities earned for him a reputation as an accomplished musician, and the friendships he formed with other artists while at the Villa Medici after winning the Prix de Rome in 1835, were warm and lasting ones. For her part, Raïssa, Princess Mychetsky, who became Ernest's wife, was both well educated and musically gifted. Their first child died in infancy, but their second, Nadia, was exposed to a very high level of general culture, and especially to music of all sorts, even as a very young child, just as her father had been. Once again, the Boulanger family, its social circle, and its cultural tradition provided fertile soil in which the talent of the new generation could take root and flourish.

2

Early Life: To Age 16

Marie-Juliette Olga (Lili) Boulanger was born in the Boulanger family's apartment at 30 rue La Bruyère on August 21, 1893, with the father of harpist Lili Laskine as the attending physician. Christened in honor of her paternal grandmother, just as her parents' firstborn daughter had been, she was surrounded from her earliest days with artists, intellectuals and gifted amateurs. The Boulangers and their circle of friends and neighbors provided an environment ideally suited to the early development of Lili's artistic and intellectual abilities.[1]

Even as a baby, Lili showed inquisitiveness, intelligence, alertness, and an enthusiasm for life. Some of these qualities are evident in family photographs of her from this period.[2] Lili's eyes were large and strikingly intense for one so young, a fact that sometimes led total strangers to notice her in public places when she was still young enough to travel in her nurse's arms.

In 1895 M. Boulanger, Lili, and her nurse were taking the train from Paris to Munich to meet Mme Boulanger and Nadia, who had just returned from visiting relatives in Russia. In the train a stranger stopped to look at Lili, and remarked to M. Boulanger, "With eyes like that, she will either give you much joy or much worry."[3] From her earliest days, Lili seems to have had the kind of personality that simultaneously startled, charmed, and attracted others.

Ernest Boulanger was a warm and affectionate father, in spite of the difference in age between him and his children. Although

Figure 5. Lili Boulanger with her nurse in the Boulanger family's apartment at 30 rue La Bruyère.

he never spoke about his own father, Frédéric, he did speak frequently and warmly about his mother, and Nadia and Lili grew up to have a sense of communion with and attachment to the past. However, M. Boulanger seemed to have an empathy with Lili that Nadia felt she did not completely share.[4] When Lili was still a young baby, M. Boulanger placed her in Nadia's arms one day and asked her to promise to take care of her younger sister and to be responsible for Lili's welfare. The experience so profoundly impressed Nadia that she still speaks of it.[5]

The Boulanger family traveled frequently. Although William Bouwens had become a French citizen during the war of 1870, he maintained close ties with his native Holland. The Boulangers spent time there with him and his family on several occasions before Ernest Boulanger's death in 1900. These visits to the area around the Hague, notably Scheveningen and Wittebroecke, impressed young Lili, and Wittebroecke especially remained a fond memory to her.[6]

Summers prior to 1905 were usually spent in Trouville, where the family lived in a house at 4 rue de Londres. It was there that

Figure   6. Lili Boulanger at Trouville (ca. 1899).

the Boulangers became acquainted with the writer Paul (Tristan) Bernard and his children, one of whom, Étienne, was later to become a specialist in the treatment of tuberculosis.[7] The two families also saw each other from time to time during the rest of the year.

In the course of his career as an opera composer, Ernest Boulanger had become a close friend of the librettist Jules Barbier. The latter's granddaughter, Mme de Meyenbourg, owned her own villa in St. Raphaël on the French Riviera. Mme de Meyenbourg was a highly cultivated and intelligent person, an *Agrégée* in mathematics. The two families spent time together at her villa, remaining on close terms for some years after the death of M. Boulanger.[8]

Significant aspects of Lili's development appeared early, and, from the time she was a toddler, they became inseparably woven into her existence. She showed a great interest in the music she heard constantly all around her. At the age of two, she was already singing melodies by ear.[9] During this same year, she contracted such a severe case of bronchial pneumonia that Dr. Leudet, who treated her, was not at all sure she would survive. Lili's recovery was not complete. Almost all of her resistance to illness was destroyed, and she spent the rest of her life in precarious health, suffering from a combination of recurrent attacks of intestinal tuberculosis, as well as other infectious diseases to which she was exposed.[10]

In addition to being sisters, Nadia and Lili shared mutual interests. They also shared the same room when they were young, spent much time together, and exerted a strong emotional influence over each other.[11] Nadia was always deeply attached to her younger sister, and frequently took Lili to audit her music lessons when Lili was well enough to attend. This habit, which began with Nadia's earliest musical studies in the mid-1890s, may help to account for the intense dedication to music that Lili was later to develop to such a high level. With consistent exposure to music and examples of dedication to art from among her friends and relatives, she internalized at an early age the values of persistence and conscientiousness and diligence.

By 1898[12] Lili was auditing, however sporadically, the harmony classes of Auguste Chapuis at the Conservatoire National. The organ classes of Louis Vierne followed in 1899. As early as 1900, Lili tried to put into practice what she had heard in Paul Vidal's accompaniment classes.[13] Lili's notebooks and musical exercises from this period seem to have disappeared or been destroyed, so it is impossible to know exactly how much she consciously absorbed during her visits to these classes. But, because she was alert and interested, it is safe to assume that at least some of what was said there remained with her and probably facilitated her later rapid progress.

In spite of her frequent bouts with illness, Lili was an affectionate child with an active sense of humor. She reveled in the atmosphere of camaraderie and warmth, and greatly enjoyed the practical jokes that prevailed among the Boulanger family, their friends, and neighbors.[14] This gaiety was shared with only her closest friends, however, and most of those who knew her superficially found her an intense but extremely serious child.[15]

Like many other French intellectuals of the nineteenth and early twentieth centuries, the Boulangers were also interested in exoticism—the attraction of different customs and faraway places. Although the family was devoutly Catholic, Loulou Gonet[16] could bring the Orient alive for them. Her visits to the Boulanger household often brought with them tales of exotic places and art forms. She was a personal friend of the great Indian poet Rabindranath Tagore, and her descriptions of his poetry recitals were especially vivid. It was through her, too, that Lili later became acquainted with the Karpelès family, after hearing about them and their travels for years from Loulou. They spent a great deal of time in the Far East—Suzanne Karpelès was later to found the Royal Library of Phnom Penh—and it was from Suzanne that Lili received the French translation of an ancient Buddhist prayer, which she later set to music.[17]

In addition to piquing their curiosity, Loulou also exercised a strong moral influence over the two Boulanger sisters, since her almost constant presence and complete freedom of the house—she had assisted at the births of both Nadia and Lili—made her a dynamic part of their lives. She was considered part of the family. Those who knew her described her as "goodness personified."[18]

If Ernest Boulanger was ill, he kept the knowledge of it from his two daughters. It must have seemed strange to them both when, on April 13, 1900, he suddenly called his dear friend Théodore Dubois to his apartment on rue de La Bruyère and commended Mme Boulanger, Nadia, and Lili into his protective care. But life appeared to continue normally in the household. The next day, M. Boulanger called the twelve-year-old Nadia to him. They argued aesthetics for a time, and Nadia noticed nothing out of the ordinary about her father. Then, in the middle of a sentence, Ernest Boulanger died. The shock of his death was deeply felt by both girls, but perhaps even more by six-year-old Lili, who had been her father's favorite.[19]

Lili found solace in her deep religious belief, in the certainty Catholicism gave her that she would one day rejoin her father.[20] Nevertheless, his death marked her deeply. She turned eventually to composition, even though she had no formal training in it. Not surprisingly, the poem she chose to set had as its theme death and grief, and Lili gave it the intimate form of a solo song. The composition itself no longer survives: it was among those early

34

works that Lili later destroyed herself after she had had some musical training. All that remains of this song to a text of Eugène Manuel are four pages of sketches for it in a composition notebook that Lili used occasionally over a period of years to record the fugitive ideas that darted through her mind. She probably completed the composition about 1906.[21]

In 1900 Nadia Boulanger met André Caplet, a fellow student in the class of Paul Vidal. He and the Boulangers became close friends, and although Caplet was quite a bit older than Lili, he often played with her when she was still a small child.[22] When he tried to catch a boat across the Channel from Trouville to England, Caplet generally missed it. On such occasions, he stayed at the Boulanger's home there until he could get another passage.[23]

Lili's health continued to be a problem. Other doctors tried to help, but without lasting success. Lili's personality charmed and attracted them, and they became anxious to make her as well as possible. Two other doctors from the period before Mme Boulanger moved with her daughters to 36 rue Ballu in the autumn of 1904 were Professor Moizart and Dr. Brocq. The latter had originally been Nadia's doctor when she was a young child. He had become a close family friend, and played a great part in the moral development of both sisters.[24]

As a result of her extremely uncertain health, Lili was rarely able to complete the projects she started. Both her musical studies and her schooling were erratic before 1909. During these years, Mlle Léonie Nègre was in charge of Lili's general education.[25] Lili became extremely fond of her, and customarily referred to her as "dear Mlle Nègre."

For a year or so, Lili also went when she could to the Cours Dieterlen on the rue du Colisée, but she was unable to attend regularly.[26] During this period, she studied mathematics with her godfather, William Bouwens. Her own first music lessons were in solfège, and, significantly, her teacher was the same one who had taught Nadia in 1896—Mme Roy-Got.[27] There followed lessons in violin from Fernand Luquin, cello lessons from Fernande Reboul, harp lessons from Marcel Tournier and Alphonse Hasselmans, and piano lessons from Mme Hélène Chaumont. Lili did not continue any of these studies for very long; her extremely uncertain health during those years made sustained effort impossible, a state of affairs that she deeply regretted and that continued to frustrate her all her life.[28]

The various lessons were not entirely without result, however. Lili did learn to play the violin, cello, harp, and piano. In addition, she was a student of Marcel Tournier, while the Opéra-Comique, for whose orchestra he was the harpist, was rehearsing for the premiere of Debussy's *Pelléas et Mélisande* in 1902. Lili, therefore, was in a favored position—she was given the opportunity to preview the work.[29]

During her studies with M. Luquin and Mme Chaumont, Lili played in a number of student recitals. Her first public performance was as a violinist on September 5, 1901, when she played Godard's *Berceuse* and Gounod's *Prière* at a musical Mass (Messe

Figure 7. Program of the first public performance in which Lili Boulanger participated.

en Musique) at Notre Dame du Bon Secours in Trouville. Lili had then just passed her eighth birthday. The next extant program shows that, as part of a recital of Mme Chaumont's piano students, Lili played Beethoven's C♯-minor Sonata in the Salle Érard on February 7, 1904. On March 26 of the following year, Lili again took part in Mme Chaumont's students' recital. This time, she played Schumann's *Berceuse*.[30]

Experiences such as these undoubtedly helped young Lili to develop poise and stage presence, as well as the ability to convey musical ideas to an audience.

Lili's circle of friends included a wide variety of people and encompassed a range of ages. There was often informal music-making in the Boulanger household, and Lili sometimes took part. At the age of six, she had already read at sight Fauré's "Une Prière," with the composer at the piano.[31] Lili enjoyed sight-reading, and her musical explorations ranged from the sixteenth-century masters through Bach, the French clavecinists, Mozart, Chopin, Schumann, Wagner, Fauré, Debussy, and Mussorgsky. These were by no means exclusive tastes, and she also read much organ music. Frequently, Lili improvised on the piano or the organ.

Meanwhile, Lili continued to accompany Nadia to classes whenever she could. By 1901 she was sitting in on the classes of André Gédalge, Fauré's assistant. In 1902, at Alexandre Guilmant's organ class, she met Marcel Dupré, who was to become a good friend of the family,[32] and, years later, to perform publicly with Lili.[33] That same year Lili also audited some of Gabriel Fauré's composition classes. At that time, Roger Ducasse had become both Fauré's assistant and his favorite student. In the course of time, Ducasse became "like an older brother to Nadia and Lili."[34] Fauré often permitted Nadia to replace him at the great organ of the Madeleine, and these proceedings excited both Lili's curiosity and her enthusiastic interest.[35] In Fauré's class the sisters also met and became friendly with Alfredo Casella, Charles Koechlin, Georges Enesco, and Florent Schmitt, as well as—in a more impersonal way—Raoul Laparra and Maurice Ravel.[36]

Nadia did not neglect music history classes in the course of her years at the Conservatoire. Consequently, Lili sometimes accompanied her sister to the lectures given by Louis Aubert. Both sisters were extremely impressed with the brilliance and erudition of Bourgault-Ducoudray, whose history classes they also attended. In addition Lili went regularly to the classes of Maurice Emmanuel, "as if she had been an officially registered student."[37]

Lili was as anxious to develop herself intellectually as she was eager to make use of her musical ability. Such an ambition is hardly surprising, since the circles in which the Boulanger family was accustomed to move were the élite of the artistic, intellectual, and diplomatic society of that era. Under these circumstances, a person not well-versed in general culture, languages and history would be placed at a decided disadvantage. Her health had made it impossible for Lili to attend classes or to study regularly the way she would have liked. So Lili embarked on a reading program of her own that was to continue for the rest of her life, and tried to learn as many languages as she could. Mme Boulanger spoke Russian, French, and German fluently, along with a little English and Italian.[38] During Ernest Boulanger's lifetime, however, she had refused to speak Russian to her two daughters because their father did not speak it. After his death, she did begin to talk Russian in the house. Lili, who was always more home-bound than Nadia, picked up enough Russian so that she could carry on conversations intelligibly, and later on she even taught herself to write a sort of phonetic Russian using the Cyrillic alphabet.[39] In addition to her attempts at Russian, Lili also learned some English and Italian.[40] Undoubtedly the fact that Mme Boulanger had a Russian maid helped Lili in her efforts to learn that language. Some of her closest friends were also partly Russian, and Lili often practiced her Russian with them, too.[41] To expand her knowledge of literature and philosophy, Lili read as many of the classics as she could. As a young child, she enjoyed fairy tales, but later her favorite writers came to include Aeschylus, Sophocles, and Euripides, as well as later authors such as Shakespeare, Pascal, Racine, Poe, Daudet, Tolstoi, Claudel, Maeterlinck, and Jammes.[42]

Meanwhile, the Boulangers were broadening their circle of friends. A whole new horizon was opened to all three of them as a result of Nadia's final examinations at the Conservatoire in 1904. Following the advice of Théodore Dubois—who had counseled her to remain a student one year more (if not for his sake, then in memory of her father)—Nadia continued on at the Conservatoire. Raoul Pugno, who was on her jury in the spring of 1904, was so impressed with Nadia's work that they met and became close friends. He, his wife, his daughter Renée and, later, her husband Georges Delaquys, became intimate friends of the Boulangers. Raoul Pugno and Nadia often played duets together both privately and publicly. They also later composed pieces jointly, including a number of songs, "Les Heures Claires," and "La Ville Morte."[43]

As soon as she left the Conservatoire, Nadia began to teach pupils of her own. Some, like Cella Delavrancea-Lahovary, she had known from her days at the Conservatoire—in this particular instance, from the piano lessons of Hélène Chaumont.[44] Nadia was only sixteen when she started to teach—younger, in fact, than some of her first pupils. Her seriousness and dedication more than offset her youth.[45] The majority of her pupils never became close friends of Lili, but there were some exceptions: Suzanne Vidal, who was already one of Lili's closest friends, Mina Vaurabourg, and Renée de Marquein. Generally, Nadia's students knew Lili only superficially, if at all, since they did not see her very often. Among this group were Annette Dieudonné, Germaine de Manziarly, and Cella Delavrancea. Lili's charisma was, if anything, even stronger than it had been in her infancy, and those students of Nadia who saw her, however briefly, were quite struck by her personality. "I remember quite vividly the few times I saw her, coming to the salon where I was taking my lesson . . . (she was always so fragile . . .) ."[46] It was during this period that Lili moved from the room she had shared with Nadia to another in a separate wing of the apartment, a small room down a long corridor from the main rooms, close to the kitchen and the bath.[47] Each sister had begun to develop her own circle of friends in addition to the ones they had in common, and from this time on they spent considerable time separated from each other while still in the same apartment. Each was engaged in her own projects.[48]

Because of their friendship with the Pugno family, the Boulangers no longer summered at Trouville. Raoul Pugno had a large group of friends and students who congregated in Hanneucourt, a small hamlet located several miles from the nearest railroad station in Gargenville, and, in the summer of 1904, the Boulangers joined them there. The first summer, they rented a house, but later they bought a group of three buildings, known as "Les Maisonettes," just around the corner from Pugno's home.

Artistically, Hanneucourt was a bustling center, and so was the area around it. About the same distance from Juziers as Hanneucourt was from Gargenville lay the hamlet of Le Mesnil and the country home of the poet Paul Valéry and his family. Mme Valéry loved music. She was a talented pianist and took lessons from Pugno. The Boulangers became acquainted with the whole family, although Paul Valéry and his oldest son usually remained behind in Paris. Mlle Gobillard, the sister of Mme Valéry, and her constant companion, was an accomplished painter. The Valérys' second son, François, shared his mother's love of music.[49] The house next to them was occupied by the Rouarts, whose son, Paul, became a music editor and the Director of the Strassbourg festival.[50]

Both of these families became close friends of the Boulangers. Paul Vidal frequently joined the artistic community at Gargenville.[51] Suzanne Denis-Vidal was one of Lili's closest friends and remained so until her death.[52]

At Gargenville many artists met: Eugène Ysaye, Jacques Thibaud, Joseph Hollman, Fernand Pollain, Wilhelm Mengelberg, Maurice Léna, Paul Vidal, Gabriele d'Annunzio, Emile Verhaeren, and still others from among the innumerable friends who were part of the circle of friends of M. and Mme Pugno and of Mme Ernest Boulanger. The Pugno-Ysaye sessions were the most famous, but, above all, there was an incomparable atmosphere surrounding the genial being who was Raoul Pugno —with a ceaseless amassing of books, of pictures, of objets d'art, a real interchange among extraordinary people and things, constant changes even in the places, buildings, arrivals, departures, etc . . . also in the "atmosphere" of Mme Boulanger—so witty, with such remarkable energy, and who knew how to create an environment where everyone felt at ease.[53]

Lili's musical gifts and accomplishments at an early age surprised people of Pugno's circle and even Pugno himself. "More than once, passing in front of the house and hearing music, Raoul Pugno believed that Nadia was at the piano when, to his great surprise, it was Lili who was improvising. . . . Raoul Pugno became attached to the little girl while she was becoming a close friend of his daughter, Renée. . . ."[54]

In a vain attempt to cure Lili's illness, Mme Boulanger took her to various spas. During August of 1905, for example, she accompanied her daughter to Frankfurt and Bad Kreuznach in Germany, and in September they went to Mürren, Lausanne, Geneva, Interlaken, and Zurich in Switzerland.[55] Nadia, who was already working, but was still considered too young to be left alone, generally stayed either at the home of the Bouwens on rue de Lota or with the Vidals on such occasions.[56] Nadia received frequent letters and postcards from her sister, who took her illness as a matter of course, and sometimes commented on her musical activities and the reactions of others to her.[57]

While retaining many of their old friends, the Boulangers were constantly making new ones. Some resulted from their move to 36 rue Ballu. The apartment building itself was a beehive of artistic activity. In the apartment above the Boulanger household lived the Dourgnon family. M. Dourgnon was an architect, and his daughter, Mireille, was two years younger than Lili. They and some of the other tenants had been astonished when they saw a large organ being moved up the stairs and into the fourth-floor apartment the Boulangers were about to occupy.[58] But what interested Mireille more than anything else was the arrival of a potential playmate. She lost no time in introducing herself to Mme Boulanger. Soon she had met Lili, and the two girls saw each other frequently after that. They spent more time in the Boulangers' apartment than in the Dourgnons' fifth-floor rooms. At the time, Lili asserted a kind of mock-authority as the older of the two, making sure that most of their meetings took place in her

Figure 8. Façade of the building at 36 rue Ballu, where the Boulanger family has lived since 1904. *Photo: L. Rosenstiel.*

home. This state of affairs also assured her both of having more energy to spend with Mireille, and of always having someone near who knew how to help her if she suddenly became ill. Her usual gaiety and good humor concealed from Mireille any pain or discomfort Lili might be feeling. At this time, Lili also had an elaborate doll with a complete wardrobe, and coming to the Boulanger apartment gave Mireille another chance to play with this treasure —of which she was a bit jealous.[59] Other tenants in the building included Georges Caussade, the Vidal family, the music critics Dézarnaux and Marie-Louise Bousque, as well as the kindly Dr.

41

Grenier who lived in the next apartment to the Boulangers.[60]

All three Boulangers were fond of animals and took their pets with them whenever possible. Mme Boulanger had a toy terrier, Jippy, of whom she was very fond, and Lili herself had two dogs. The first, Kitchill, was a longhaired Pomeranian whose name, derived from Malay, had been suggested by Georges Caussade. When it became evident that Kitchill was seriously ill, Mme Boulanger gave her daughter a Great Pyrenees dog, Fachoun, whose breed Lili had admired at a dog show in Biarritz when she was taking the cure there in 1903. Although he was gentle with the family and their pets, Fachoun was quite contentious when it came to animals outside the Boulanger household. Lili never walked him alone. Sometimes Katia, Mme Boulanger's Russian maid, would accompany her, interposing herself between Fachoun and any other animal he chose to try to attack.[61] His size and strength made him difficult for Lili to control. More frequently, her close friends—Suzanne Vidal, Renée de Marquein, Mireille Dourgnon or, later on, Miki Piré, would join her on these walks.[62] Sometimes, in Paris or at Gargenville, Lili would go riding with one or more of her friends in the family's cabriolet, drawn by their horse, Manis.[63]

Lili's love of nature and her enjoyment of it were often frustrated by the illnesses that kept her indoors a good part of the time. Whenever possible, she took long walks with her friends, but being out-of-doors sometimes led to further troubles with her health. There was constant conflict between Lili's desire to escape from what she came to view as the prison of her ill health and her recognition of the practical medical necessity of avoiding possible exposure to the diseases against which her weakened system had no immunity. These problems and Lili's reactions to them formed a pattern of stimulus and response that eventually caused emotional repercussions for her. It was her practice—encouraged by her mother—to avoid habitual physical contact with others.[64] Undoubtedly, this state of affairs added to her acute feelings of isolation, which expressed themselves in Lili's letters to those who shared her full confidence and trust. As early as 1906, she complained to her godfather, William Bouwens, that her health had not changed for the better. She had been tired on New Year's Eve, and had also been confined to the house for some time—a situation that made her extremely unhappy.[65]

One psychological consequence of this was her strong emotional identification with the heroine of Maurice Maeterlinck's play, *La Princesse Maleine*.[66] Like Maeterlinck's heroine, she spent a great deal of time separated from those she loved and from activities she enjoyed. By that time, too, Lili had experienced the death of members of her family—her baby sister in 1898, her father in 1900, and her beloved Aunt Lisa Kondrakieff in 1906.[67] In addition to these emotional shocks, she had to contend with her own physical problems, and could therefore identify with similar problems in others. So the story of the frail, pale young Princess Maleine, who is left alone by the destruction of her father's kingdom, who finds her fiancé engaged to marry another princess, who despite every effort is unable to overcome the social and psychological pressures brought to bear on her by malevolent forces beyond her control, and who gradually wastes away and dies, impressed Lili deeply. She identified with the Princess Maleine, for she felt that she, too, had a tragic destiny.

Before the end of 1909 Lili Boulanger had already shown considerable interest in musical composition, but as with most of her other interests, she had been unable to take lessons or to work at it consistently. It may have been partly in imitation of Nadia that Lili worked during those years on various musical projects. Most were religious in nature, and probably reflected in equal measure her own devout Catholicism, her familiarity with religious texts and ritual resulting from her faithful attendance at Mass, and the music and musicians that had impressed her so deeply— Alexandre Guilmant, Louis Vierne, Charles-Marie Widor, Gabriel Fauré, and her sister Nadia, for example. Significantly, Lili was extremely excited by the premiere in 1904 of Florent Schmitt's *Psalm 47*. Written in Rome during his tenure there as a winner of the Prix de Rome in composition, it was first performed in Paris with Nadia Boulanger at the organ. Lili followed every rehearsal with rapt attention.[68]

Lili's own works in the period between Ernest Boulanger's death and 1909 included, in addition to *La Lettre de Mort,* four psalms: two for soloist and orchestra (Psalms 131 and 137) in 1907; and two for chorus and orchestra (Psalms 1 and 119) in 1909. In 1908 she had written an *Ave Maria* for voice and organ. Evidently, Lili's attraction to the field of composition was increasing, as can be seen by the number of compositions on which she worked during that year—more than in any previous year. In addition to the two psalms already mentioned, sixteen-year-old Lili also completed a setting of Corinthians 1:13 for chorus and orchestra, and *Cinq Études pour Piano*. A fifth work, *Apocalypse,* for soloists, chorus, and orchestra was never completed. All of these compositions Lili later destroyed after she had had rigorous mu-

43

Figure 9. Members of the Gargenville circle (1908). Among those present are: the Dourgnon family; Mme Chaumont; the Pugno family; Dr. Parenteau (see chapter 3); Magda Tagliaferro; the family of M. Caressa, the French luthier; Mme Boulanger, and Nadia and Lili Boulanger.

sical training. She did not show them to her friends or family, and they were never performed.[69]

As a young child, therefore, Lili Boulanger enjoyed a warm relationship with both parents, but more especially was considered to be her father's favorite. Ernest's affection for his younger daughter gave her a sense of belonging and importance in spite of her already very precarious health. Lili's musical gifts became apparent quite early, and she was given the opportunity to accompany her sister Nadia to the latter's classes at the Conservatoire. Deeply moved by her father's death in 1900, Lili became very attached to his memory. Her own musical studies were sporadic until 1910. Both her talents and her interest were real, but her desire to learn to play various instruments—harp, violin, piano, and organ—was frustrated by her recurrent ill health. Despite the uncertain state of her health, Lili became a member of an active social and prominent artistic circle in which she formed deep friendships and was respected by those who knew her well as much for her personal warmth and intelligence as for her musical abilities.

3

Intensive Studies: Ages 17-19

After Lili's sixteenth birthday, Mme Boulanger began to worry about her younger daughter's lack of any clearly defined objectives in life, for although Lili had shown a real aptitude for music, she had never directed enough of her energy into any one field long enough to master it completely. In 1909, at the age of sixteen, Lili was no longer a child. She was a properly brought-up young lady, and since her state of health made life uncertain and marriage impossible, the only thing for her to do was to choose an occupation in keeping with her abilities and concentrate on it until she had achieved any long-range goals she might set for herself. Besides, the Boulanger family at that time consisted of three women. What if something should happen to either Mme Boulanger or Nadia? What would become of Lili then? Mme Boulanger put these questions to Lili one day when the family was together, and Lili's answer was almost instantaneous. She wanted to study composition. Specifically, Lili wanted to win the Prix de Rome as her father had done in 1835,[1] and to bring back to the family the prize that had just eluded her sister Nadia in 1908.[2]

Having made her commitment to composition, Lili began to take her work extremely seriously. Now that she had immediate and long-term goals, her life had acquired both direction and purpose. Without a doubt, Mme Boulanger's insistence that her daughter "learn to do something really well"[3] was an excellent idea. It provided Lili with the means to decide her own future as much as possible, and to show her family, her friends, and, above

46

all, herself, that she was capable of being considered a contributing member of the artistic and intellectual community in which she lived. In other words, it gave Lili the chance to develop a positive self-image—although it is unlikely that anyone at that time and place would have expressed it in this way. Lili's physical dependence on others, especially her immediate family and their servants, was often total, but she enjoyed complete intellectual and artistic autonomy.

All of Lili's formal lessons in harmony, counterpoint and composition were considered to be strictly between her and her instructors, Georges Caussade and Paul Vidal, and she alone determined the speed of her own progress. It has often been inferred that Lili was, somehow, Nadia's "creation," and that it was really Nadia who was the creative power.[4]

An examination of Lili's extant harmony, counterpoint, fugue, and composition workbooks, as well as her autograph manuscripts, and a consideration of the circumstances of her life during this period help to refute any such claims. Of the fifteen workbooks, only one—a book containing lessons in fugue that begins with the date July 3, 1911, and ends on October 11 of the same year— carries the title "With Nadia." None of the others has the name of Lili's teacher listed on the cover, and in no case do any surviving manuscripts contain a notation indicating that Nadia was the first person to view the completed composition. This is significant, because Lili was generally extremely meticulous in her work. For example, the original maunscript of *Pièce courte pour flûte et piano,* which was later published as *Nocturne for violin (or flute) and piano* is very carefully annotated at the end as follows: "Lili Boulanger/composed September 24th and 25th, 1911/Shown to Caussade the 25th and 26th—/Shown to class Friday the 27th/sent to Nadia November 3, 1911."

It would be completely unrealistic to ignore the fact that Nadia herself was extremely busy with her own pupils by the time Lili began to study music seriously, on December 10, 1909.[5] That year, Nadia was already the assistant in Henri Dallier's organ class at the Conservatoire,[6] in addition to her other teaching activities, performing commitments and work as a composer. She did not—nor could she—give all this up to teach her younger sister, since Nadia was the main support of her family during these years.[7] Therefore, those who assume that Lili's achievements are in some way the result of Nadia's hard work do both sisters a disservice.

From what remains of Lili's homework books, it is obvious that she was anxious to learn as much as she could about music

Figure 10. Final page of the holograph flute and piano score of Lili Boulanger's *Nocturne*, indicating both the dates of composition and the dates on which it was shown to various people.

as quickly as possible. The harmony lessons that Georges Caussade gave her followed the same rigorous pattern as those given in the Conservatoire, using the harmony treatises of Dubois and Reber.

By mid-February of 1910, she had already completed one entire notebook. As was also customary at the Conservatoire, all her exercises were written in four parts and in the four traditional clefs: soprano, alto, tenor, and bass. By the time Lili began to study counterpoint with Caussade in April of 1910,[8] she was already well into her third harmony notebook. Usually she took daily lessons, including weekends and holidays. During the summer, or when either she or Caussade was out of Paris for any reason, Lili made it a practice to send her homework to him for correction. Sometimes Lili recopied these correspondence lessons into her permanent bound notebook, sometimes she did not. But the lessons proceeded systematically and, by March of 1911, Lili had filled eight notebooks, had completed all of the required work in the Dubois treatise, and had begun to work on the more advanced Lenepveu exercises. Meanwhile, her counterpoint studies were also proceeding rapidly. The first entries in her third counterpoint notebook, beginning June 12, 1911, show that she was already starting to work with fugue subjects. There is some overlap in subject matter between this workbook and her first fugue notebook, the first entry there being dated June 15, 1911.[9]

It was during this same summer that Lili spent a little time studying with Nadia. On the basis of the surviving evidence, this was the only period during which Lili actually took any sort of formal lessons from her sister. It may have been because Lili felt that she needed additional help with her work in fugue, and because consultation with Caussade by mail would take longer; a notation in her counterpoint notebook indicates that he was in Brussels during these months.[10]

Lili's illness, meanwhile, seemed to be allowing her a little respite, and she took full advantage of it. During the summer of 1911, which the Boulangers spent at Hanneucourt, Lili became friendly with Miki Piré, who was then a piano student of Raoul Pugno. Miki rapidly became Lili's closest friend and confidante. "My little Miki," as Lili came to call her friend, was vivacious, outgoing, and a talented pianist. Miki had spent her early life in St. Petersburg. Her mother was Russian, her father French. She spoke Russian, German, and French fluently, and Lili was delighted to try out her Russian on her new-found friend. The word *little* when applied to Miki Piré was not just a term of endearment: it was a statement of fact as well, for Miki was less than five feet tall, while Lili, already taller than Nadia, was at least five-and-a-half feet tall. Miki was Lili's frequent companion in the cabriolet on the roads near Gargenville, and sometimes, in 1912,

Georges Caussade, Lili's friend as well as her teacher, joined them. With Miki, Lili discussed her hopes and fears for the future, her feelings for her family, music, and literature, but rarely her own compositions. It was Miki who first gave Lili a copy of the Francis Jammes poems she later set to music as the song cycle *Clairières dans le Ciel.*[11]

Lili did not go out alone. This was the result, in part, of her extreme sense of propriety, which dictated that a well-brought-up young lady should not leave the house unaccompanied.[12] But it was probably also conditioned by her long experience with illness, and her need to have someone nearby who could at least run for a doctor if necessary.

Gargenville was a lovely country area, and the Boulangers, especially Lili, became very much attached to it. "Les Maisonnettes" was not just a summer place, but a true second home. Good friends like the Pugnos were close by, and even the local people of Hanneucourt, the carpenters and stable attendants and servants, made Lili feel welcome.[13] In general, Lili shared warm relationships with the family's servants, and even became the godmother of Fernande Lhomme, the daughter of one of their domestics.[14] The servants saw in Lili a protector, for Mme Boulanger frequently treated them as though she were still in pre-Revolutionary Russia—a habit no doubt stemming from her girlhood—while Lili defended their lapses and helped to mediate disputes and soothe hurt feelings.[15] Her conciliatory ways had made her a favorite among the servants even as a child. In 1908, for example, Nadia became ill with whooping cough while in Gargenville, and Lili was sent to stay with friends nearby to prevent her from contracting the disease. Katia, the family's Russian maid, who had never learned to write French, taught herself enough so that she could write Lili a postcard telling her that her presence was missed in the household. Strangely, this postcard was not delivered until the following year, and arrived with indications that it had literally gone as far afield as China! An odd itinerary indeed for an item mailed from Gargenville whose destination was the same village.[16]

Those unacquainted with the precariousness of Lili's health were sometimes shocked at the lengths to which Mme Boulanger was willing to go to protect her younger daughter from exposure to infectious diseases. One Easter the Dourgnon family had been invited to spend the holiday with the Boulangers at "Les Maisonnettes." They had arrived, and all was well until it was discovered that Mireille had suddenly developed swollen glands. As soon as Mme Boulanger found out about Mireille's condition, she whisked

Lili back to Paris, since she could not be sure what Mireille had, and, therefore, whether Lili could catch it. This incident remained a mystery to Mireille until years later, after Lili died, when their mutual friend, Suzanne Vidal, finally explained to her the nature of Lili's illness. In an era when all children were expected to contract a variety of "childhood diseases," Mme Boulanger's extreme concern with Lili's health undoubtedly seemed strange to people who did not know the reasons behind it.[17]

During these years, Lili's sense of humor and her practical jokes continued to make themselves felt among her friends and neighbors, and she enjoyed more and more the social evenings, the dinner parties and bridge parties, the dances and costume balls, and musicales that she attended whenever her strength permitted.[18] Lili also enjoyed teasing her friends. One day, for example, she ran up to Mireille's apartment and announced breathlessly that something horrible had happened. She had ruined the piano cover with ink. Mireille was horrified. The shawl had been so beautiful, and now it was ruined. She rushed downstairs with Lili to survey the damage and see if she could help Lili get it clean before Mme Boulanger came home. From a distance, the spot was enormous. But from close up, it was—colored isinglass.[19] There were frequent costume balls at Gargenville and in Paris. Sometimes Lili dressed in regional French costume, sometimes in the flowing gown and wimple of medieval nobility.[20] Among her close friends she was admired for her gaiety and courage. But even in these few years when she was relatively well, there were always doctors nearby—Dr. Cuche went from his home in nearby Melun to treat Lili when she was in Gargenville, and Dr. Marfin, who treated her when she was in Paris, became one of her regular physicians in 1910.[21]

In her zeal to prepare for the Prix de Rome competition, Lili worked not only on harmony, counterpoint, and fugue, but—simultaneously—also on composition itself. The first book of sketches is an unnumbered workbook, some of whose entries are dated as early as October and November 1909. It contains all that remains of the still earlier composition, *La Lettre de Mort*. All of the 1909 entries in the early part of this book are identified as having been written in Gargenville. Some, however, are not dated —the opening measures of a quartet, a study for the "Amen" of Lili's last work, the *Pie Jesu*, the vocal line for Psalm 129, fragments of *Thème et Variations pour piano*, and even some very early sketches for *La Princesse Maleine*. Lili kept this book, apparently, for use mainly when she was away from 36 rue Ballu, since

Figure 11. Lili and Nadia Boulanger dressed as Alsace and Lorraine for a costume ball in Gargenville (ca. 1910).

even most of the later entries—1913 through 1917—are listed as having been written elsewhere.[22]

Some of the material in Lili's earliest composition notebook overlaps with her first formal notebook of this type. Both contain sketches for cantatas. Practice in setting the kinds of texts that would be required of her by the Prix de Rome competition itself would be absolutely necessary if she wanted to be successful in this grueling competition. So, in addition to the works she ultimately wanted to complete either for herself personally or for her classes at the Conservatoire, Lili carefully and systematically schooled herself—with the help of Georges Caussade and Paul Vidal, and even, sometimes, Raoul Pugno—for the work of setting the type of formal poetry used in previous competitions. Generally these were assigned to her as homework by Georges Caussade, and were reviewed by him at Lili's private lessons. Sometimes, however, it was Raoul Pugno who saw Lili's work first. In the case of the first scene of the cantata *Frédégonde*, for example, there is a notation in Lili's handwriting at the end of the manuscript, which indicates that it was completed on September 23, 1911, shown to Pugno on the twenty-fourth, but not shown to Caussade until October 14.[23]

Figure 12. Final measures of the first scene of *Frédégonde*, indicating the dates of composition and the dates on which it was shown to Pugno and Caussade.

Lili's first formal composition notebook contains sketches for two cantatas—*Bérénice* and *Maia*. Its title indicates its contents as fragments of cantatas and piano compositions. In fact, this is not entirely accurate, since two other works, a solo song based on Verhaeren's "Les pauvres"[24] and a composition entitled "Triste semble," are in this same book, and a separate sheet containing four measures of a sonata for violin and piano was inserted into this notebook, but there appears to be no composition for piano solo anywhere in it. None of these works was completed.

While Lili enjoyed learning for its own sake, she also enjoyed sharing her knowledge with her friends, and she never stopped playing, singing, and exploring the musical literature. In addition to the musicales in Gargenville at Pugno's home and at "Les Maisonnettes," Lili frequently made music with and for her friends and relatives in Paris. Mireille liked to listen to Lili play the piano.

As she put it, "Listening to her, I realized that I was not a pianist."
On the other hand, when Mireille was practicing, Lili would
frequently go upstairs to invite her to come down to the Boulanger's and play, and Mireille often left her work to do so. Once
in a while, Lili would help Mireille's younger brother a little
with his piano studies. He was very proud of the distinction of
being her only "pupil," and in later years his wife used to tease
their children, telling them to listen to their father and not to
argue with him, because, after all, "He studied with Lili Boulanger."[25] Lili later dedicated some of her compositions to the
Boulanger family's friends with whom she and the rest of the
family enjoyed playing music. Marie-Danielle Parenteau, the
daughter of Nadia's oculist, became the dedicatee of the *Nocturne*
for violin and piano that Lili composed in 1911. M. Jules Griset,
the industrialist, gifted amateur cellist and director of the Chorale
Guillot de St. Brice—the man to whom Saint-Saëns had dedicated
his second cello sonata—became the dedicatee of Psalm 24.[26] And
it was to the violinist Yvonne Astruc, who frequently played
music at the Boulangers' home with her husband, the pianist
Marcel Ciampi, that Lili later dedicated *Cortège*.[27]

The Boulangers continued to do considerable traveling. In
addition to their frequent trips to and from Gargenville, Lili and
Mme Boulanger spent some time every year on the Riviera—
generally in the winter—visiting the Piré family in their villa,
the "Castel Piré," in the Mont-Boron section of Nice. Because of
the pressures of her teaching and performing schedules, Nadia
frequently could not accompany them, however.[28]

The traditional Prix de Rome competition was both a physically and an emotionally taxing experience:

> The Prix de Rome Competition took place in two rounds:
> an elimination round (*concours d'essai*) and a final round
> (*concours définitif*).
> The elimination round consisted in putting the contestants
> in isolation (*mise en loge*) for five days, in the Palace at Com-
> piègne, for the composition of a fugue on a subject given to the
> contestant during the competition as well as of a setting for
> chorus and orchestra of an assigned text.[29]

In the competition itself, the first round ended with the selection of the candidates who were to be permitted to enter the
second and final round of the competition.

> Six candidates were then retained for the Final Round which

lasted one month and also took place at Compiègne. It consisted this time of composing a cantata for soloists and orchestra on an assigned text. . . . The work was judged, first by the jury of the musical division of the Académie des Beaux-Arts of the Institut de France, then, in a formal session by all the sections of the Institut which finally awarded the prize. This prize carried with it the right to a sojourn at the Villa Medici in Rome, as well as to a monetary stipend.[30]

The poetry used for both the *concours d'essai* and the *concours définitif* of the Prix de Rome competition varied widely in form and subject from year to year. Frequently the text for the *concours d'essai* was drawn from a source—a romantic drama, perhaps—that would permit the candidate to demonstrate his or her ability to convey one or more moods. Always the texts for both parts of the competition were in rhymed verse. The poetry chosen was relatively contemporaneous to the year in which the competition was held, and, in the late nineteenth and early twentieth centuries, ran the gamut from the full-blown Romantic drama of Musset to the moderate Symbolism of Samain. As the style and the form changed from year to year, so also did the quality of the texts themselves. A Grandmougin or a Gilles could hardly be considered on the same level as a Samain, a Delavigne, or, certainly, a Musset. In all cases, the contestant was expected to create a musical whole out of a poetic fragment. Even in the *concours définitif* there was the principle of creating the illusion of wholeness out of what was, in fact, only a part of a poetic drama. By being given several scenes to work with, however, and a dramatic situation, the contestant was supposed to show how well he could create and sustain character and dramatic tension. The subjects for the final round of the Prix de Rome competition were almost always great historical, traditional, or mythological conflicts, ranging from medieval history to the Trojan War to the Faust legend.

In her musical studies, Lili was actively preparing to meet the requirements of the Prix de Rome competition. Her practice in writing fugues would help her with one part of the *concours d'essai*. The chorus with orchestral accompaniment and the cantata would be treated separately as part of her work in composition.

There appear to be no surviving, completed manuscripts of *Bérénice* or *Maia*.[31] But Lili's second composition notebook, subtitled "Sous Bois," is just the sort of orchestrally accompanied chorus required of contestants in the Prix de Rome competition's preliminary round.[32] This is not a book of sketches: it is a fair copy of a completed manuscript, a setting of a poetic text by

Philippe Gille that Lili composed in four days—August 25 to 29, 1911—and recopied into this book on September 25, 1911.[33] However, the fact remains that it was really an exercise, and, although Lili did complete it, it was never performed, even privately.[34]

With the competition sequence as a guide, Lili's next major composition was a cantata, *Frédégonde*, a setting of a poem by Charles Morel, for which sketches and completed sections exist in chronological order in the workbook entitled *III/Cantata II/Frédégonde*. It was begun September 17, 1911, and completed October 3 of the same year. Later on in the same book there are sketches for the opera project that had already fired Lili's imagination—*La Princesse Maleine*. Obviously Lili was not neglecting her own compositional interests while preparing for the competition, even though at that time (1911–12) she had not yet received Maeterlinck's permission to use his play as the basis for an opera libretto.[35]

Turning once again to Lili's preparation for the *concours d'essai* for the Prix de Rome competition, her fourth book of compositions contains fair copies of two accompanied choral works, *Renouveau* and *Les Sirènes*. The first Lili designates as "Chorus No. 2," the second, as "Chorus No. 4." Both were completed during the autumn of 1911. The text of *Renouveau* was apparently copied out on October 31, 1911, but the piece was not finished until November 8—Lili kept track of her progress by indicating carefully in her notebook the dates when she worked. Therefore, although it looked as if she had taken more than the required time with this work, her entries indicate that she composed it on November 1, 5, and 8, and recopied it on the ninth, thus keeping her work within the prescribed time limit. On the other hand, there is only one date for *Les Sirènes*—Friday, December 8.[36] A notation in Lili's handwriting indicates that she was also working on corrections for a composition entitled "Soleils de Septembre" at this time. It was probably the companion piece to the other two and formed the third chorus. This work seems to have been destroyed later by Lili.

Meanwhile Lili had continued to audit classes at the Conservatoire whenever she could. This, too, is evident from her notebooks and manuscripts. In her workbooks she makes a distinction between lessons (i.e., private lessons with Georges Caussade) and *envois* (correspondence lessons with Georges Caussade), and between *envois* and class lessons (lessons that she audited at the Conservatoire). She habitually indicated *envois*, listed them by date, and sometimes recopied them into her permanent notebook.

Material discussed at a lesson generally had the notation "at the lesson" alongside it. But on those rare occasions when Lili could go to the Conservatoire, there is either the indication "for the class" or "at the class," followed by the date. In Lili's first book of fugue, for example, there are numerous exercises spanning the period from June 19, 1911 to December 2, 1911, but only once—on October 25—does the notation "for the class" appear. She must have attended two classes at the Conservatoire that week, because the autograph manuscript of *Pièce courte pour flûte et piano* carries her indication that it was shown to the class (i.e., the composition class) on Friday, October 27, 1911.

Lili's next fugue notebook, a group of rough copies, suggests that she took an examination on January 9, 1912. This interpretation is confirmed by the fact that her admission to the Conservatoire—signed by Gabriel Fauré, who was then Director—is dated January 10, 1912, and mentions her having passed the provisional admission examination. This document states, in part:

> I announce to you that you are admitted to the Conservatoire National de Musique et de Déclamation as a Composition student. . . . Students are first admitted only provisionally. Their unconditional admission is not declared until the semester examination that follows.[37]

In no sense did Lili's admission to the Conservatoire mean the end of her private lessons with Georges Caussade. Her third Fugue Notebook (January 31, 1912, to April 25, 1912) shows that she was still working on the material necessary for both the *concours d'essai* and the *concours définitif*. The compositions themselves are not in this workbook, but a definite schedule for the completion of such pieces is mentioned.

By February 22 Lili's notations show that she was already beginning the orchestration of *Les Sirènes*. *Renouveau* is listed as having been corrected on March 11, and *Frédégonde* was corrected on March 11 and 14. In mid-March, Lili Boulanger made her debut as a composer at one of Mme Boulanger's soirées in the family apartment on rue Ballu. The critic Mangeot, who was there, reported the event for the magazine *Le Monde Musical*.

> What a crowd at Mme Boulanger's! Mme Bathori was singing, or, rather, giving a recital there of Debussy and Ravel. Mlle Nadia Boulanger was at the Pleyel with Raoul Pugno performing pieces by Saint-Saëns, Nicolaieff, and Debussy's *Little Suite*, quite small, actually. The organ spoke in the person of Franck—

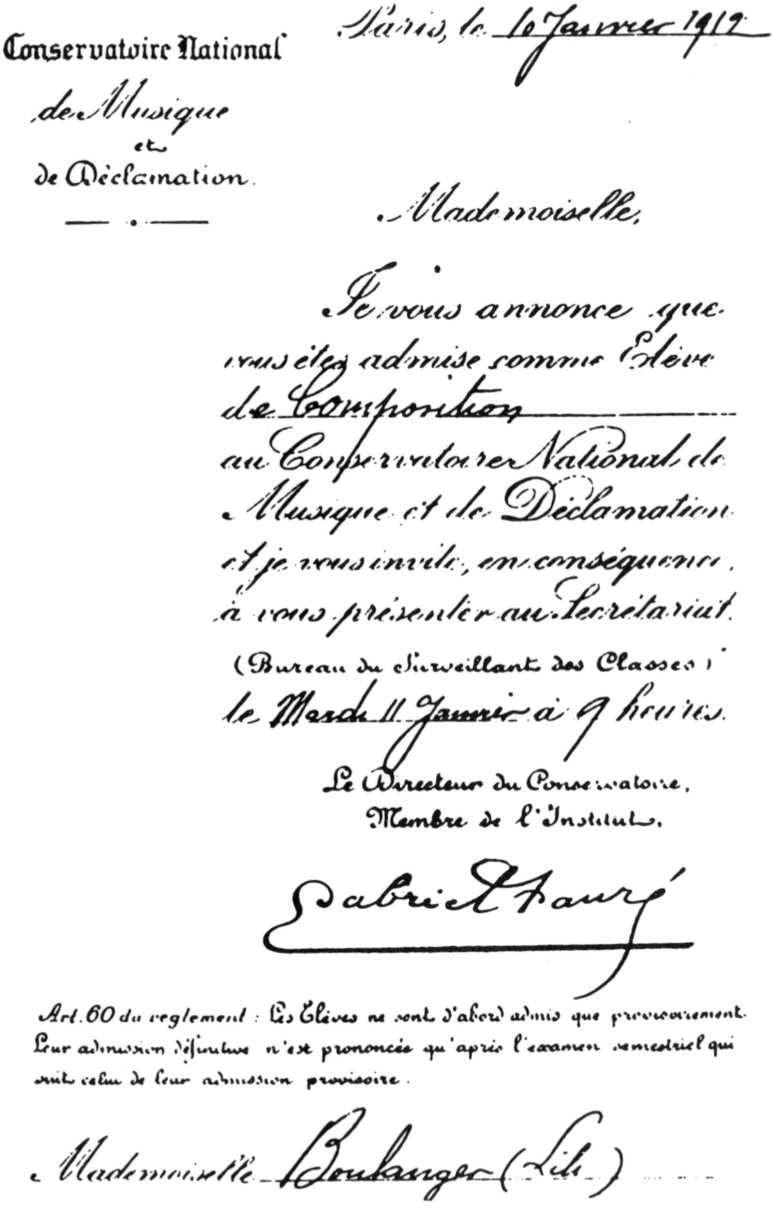
Conservatoire National
de Musique
et
de Déclamation

Paris, le 10 Janvier 1912

Mademoiselle,

Je vous annonce que vous êtes admise comme Élève de Composition au Conservatoire National de Musique et de Déclamation et je vous invite, en conséquence, à vous présenter au Secrétariat (Bureau du Surveillant des Classes) le Mardi 11 Janvier à 9 heures.

Le Directeur du Conservatoire,
Membre de l'Institut,

Gabriel Fauré

Art. 60 du règlement : Les Élèves ne sont d'abord admis que provisoirement. Leur admission définitive n'est prononcée qu'après l'examen semestriel qui suit celui de leur admission provisoire.

Mademoiselle Boulanger (Lili)

Figure 13. Lili Boulanger's certificate of admission to the Conservatoire Nationale de Musique.

César, august and venerable. But the anticipated novelty of the evening was the compositorial debut of the "little sister," Lili Boulanger, whose chorus of the Sirens already shows a firm grounding in technique and whose vocal quartet *Renouveau* has great freshness of inspiration. Mlles Brothier and Sanderson, and Mm. Paulet and Tordo had to repeat it.[38]

As the reviewer indicated, the apartment was, indeed, crowded. In addition to those already listed as performing, a full chorus had sung under the direction of Louis Aubert. Lili herself was the pianist for her own two compositions. Mme Boulanger had made of this a gala occasion, and had even issued programs for the part of the evening devoted to Lili's works.[39]

After this performance, Lili left for the Riviera. Nevertheless, she continued to work at the orchestration of *Les Sirènes*.[40] Her unnumbered fugue notebook dated simply "1912–1913" contains a long list of social engagements for her time in the South, including a visit to the casino at Monte Carlo, a lunch and dinner with friends, and a visit to an oceanographic museum in Monaco. Lili's development as a human being as well as a composer was by no means being neglected.

In addition to the works already mentioned, Lili's third fugue notebook contains references to other compositions she wrote in preparation for the Prix de Rome competition. These seem to have disappeared. On April 17 and April 23, for example, there are entries indicating that she was working on an otherwise unidentified chorus entitled "Pendant la Tempête," and on April 25 mention is made of a "new chorus"—"Soir d'été." Between these two sets of entries is the notation for April 18, 1912, indicating her work on a previously unmentioned piece, Maeterlinck's *Attente*.[41]

Although Lili had been ill early in April—the date April 9 in her 1912–1913 notebook is followed by the statement that she was too sick to take her lesson in Gargenville that day—she continued to work in preparation for the competition. After April 27 there are no further dated entries in Lili's workbook until July 7, 1912. Against all advice, Lili decided to attempt the Prix de Rome competition in 1912.[42] She was ill during the competition, but tried to complete both the fugue and the chorus.[43]

Her compositions for the *concours d'essai* are certified by the Curator of the Palace of Compiègne to have been given to him on May 13, 1912, at eleven o'clock in the morning by Lili Boulanger, then listed as having occupied Loge 19.[44]

The manuscripts themselves show evidence that her physical condition became progressively worse during the five days of the competition, since the fugue has a much surer and stronger hand

Figure 14. Receipt for Lili Boulanger's *concours d'essai* for the 1912 Prix de Rome competition. *From the Bibliothèque du Conservatoire, courtesy of the Département de la Musique, Bibliothèque Nationale, Paris.*

than the chorus. A contemporary account describes the elimination round of the competition in 1912 as follows:

> It was last Wednesday that the aspirants for the Prix de Rome went to Compiègne to be shut away in the palace and undergo the preparatory round. Rarely will such a large number of contestants have come together: there were supposed to be fifteen. Only fourteen presented themselves, among them a young girl, Mlle Lily [*sic*] Boulanger, younger sister of Mlle Nadia Boulanger who entered the competition three years ago and carried off the second prize. . . . It was from ten to noon Wednesday that the dictation of the words of the chorus and the fugue subject took place. The jury, composed of the delegation from the Institut de France, included MM. Saint-Saëns, Th. Dubois, Paladihle [*sic*], Widor, assisted by M. d'Estournelles de Constant, Chief of the Bureau of Theaters at the Under-Secretariat of Beaux-Arts and of M. Arsène Alexandre, Curator of the Palace of Compiègne. By formal order of M. Saint-Saëns, the subject of the chorus was kept a complete secret beforehand. We point out that the contestants in isolation [*logistes*], who find at the

60

palace the most comfortable lodgings, are also the object of strict surveillance to avoid any communication with the outside, even with their family. Since 1809, it has been the security guard of the palace who have performed this duty. The contestants will leave the palace on Monday the 13th. The choice of the six contestants admitted to the final round will take place on May 14th. For the final round they will go into isolation again on May 23rd.[45]

Although Lili withdrew from the competition because of illness, this fact was never made public. The semester records at the Conservatoire also contain the notation that Lili had been unable to take the examination in Paul Vidal's class in the spring of 1912. She became ill at the examination.[46] Actually, the nature of Lili's illness remained a completely private matter, known only to her family and closest friends. Just before this recurrence, however, she had been extremely successful in the fugue class of Paul Vidal at the Conservatoire, and a report of the final examinations for the spring of 1912—dated May 6—lists her as "very gifted" and comments that she "works successfully."[47]

All that was known to the public, however, was that she had been unsuccessful in her first try for the Prix de Rome. Evidently the 1912 competition did not produce a great number of outstanding scores. As reported in *Le Ménéstral* on May 18:

> The jurors of the Prix de Rome met Tuesday at the Conservatoire to judge the preliminary round. In spite of the extraordinary number of contestants . . . the results were so poor that the examiners did not feel justified in letting the full number of aspirants—six—enter the final round, and they permitted only four into the *concours définitif*.[48]

After the final judging of the cantata, it was decided that no Grand Prix de Rome in composition would be awarded for the year 1912. As a result, two became available—a First and a Second First Grand Prize—for distribution the following year.

Lili was ill that summer, a fact that became apparent even to a slight acquaintance. Albert Spalding, the famous American violinist, had recently met Raoul Pugno, and the latter had brought him to Gargenville.

> I had met the Boulangers at Pugno's house at Gargenville outside Paris. The mother, sturdily built, had a deep voice of unexpected baritone timbre. . . . Mme Boulanger's French was fluent and expressive, blanketed with the rich sauce of a Slavic

accent. . . . The daughters were both comely: Nadia, tall and
dark with . . . large, penetrating eyes illuminated by a finely
disciplined intelligence; Lili, slight, fair, and frail, looked like
the lost princess of a Maeterlinck play next to Nadia's healthy
vitality. It was evident even then that the flame of Lili's talent
was likely to overtax her meager physical resources.[49]

Later that summer Pugno and Spalding met in Russia, where they
were to give joint recitals, and the conversation turned again to
the Boulanger sisters. "Nadia Boulanger and her younger sister,
Lili, would, he declared, be talked of long after he, Pugno, had
shuffled off this mortal coil. He planned to bring Nadia with him
soon to introduce her to the Russian audience."[50]

Resuming her work early in July of 1912 (the first entry in
Lili's fourth fugue notebook is dated July 7, 1912) , Lili returned
to her intensive preparation for the Prix de Rome competition.
In addition to the fugue plans themselves, by mid-August she had
also finished two works for chorus, *Hymne au Soleil*[51] and *La Nef*

Figure 15. **Opening measures of the holograph piano-vocal score of**
Hymne au Soleil.

légère. There appear to be no extant copies of *La Nef légère,* and
all that survives is the indication that Lili was in the process of
making corrections on it on August 21. By August 17, 1912, Lili

was already finishing the final corrections for the *Hymne au Soleil* and had begun to work on *Pour les Funérailles d'un Soldat*. A choral work with baritone solo, it was originally assigned to her by George Caussade as a composition exercise. Lili did not finish it until October 13.[52]

Figure 16. Lili and Nadia Boulanger in the cabriolet, talking to an unidentified friend before attending the baptism of Lili's godchild Madeleine Delaquys in Gargenville (summer 1912). See chapter 4.

Lili still enjoyed going out in the cabriolet with her friends, and during the summer of 1912 she, Miki Piré, and Georges Caussade went out riding together one afternoon. They were delayed by a rainstorm and returned three hours late, after dark, to find that their absence had caused panic at "Les Maisonnettes." Raoul Pugno was there trying to comfort Nadia, who had begun to believe that her younger sister had met with an accident.[53] In fact, Nadia's state of mind that evening so touched Lili that she vowed to Miki that she would never worry Nadia again by coming in late.[54]

By early September Lili had begun to have trouble with her feet and legs, and was frequently in severe pain. In a letter written to Miki Piré from Gargenville on September 11, 1912, Lili told her friend that her left foot was extremely painful, so much so that she had nearly fallen. The doctor had already seen her on September 7.[55]

At that time, Mme Boulanger had already left to take the cure in Marienbad. She was not expected back for at least three weeks, but Nadia, Suzanne Vidal, and the daughter of Henri Dallier were all staying with Lili. Lili closed this letter with a plea to her friend to answer her in French, since her last letter, which had been in Russian, had had to be read to Lili by Mme Boulanger.[56] Lili's physical condition worsened as a result of a bicycle accident she suffered while in Gargenville, in which she hurt her knees.[57] These physical problems and their attendant pain help to explain the fact that there are no entries in Lili's notebooks between the end of August and October 13, 1912.

After her return to Paris in October, Lili corrected the score of *Pour les Funérailles d'un Soldat*. At that time she also chose other choruses to work on, but, unfortunately, did not record their names in any extant workbook. The entry simply states that October 17, 1912, would be the day she would select from among the choruses—presumably, again, those previously used for the Prix de Rome competitions—the ones that she would set to music.

Health continued to be a severe problem for Lili throughout October and November of 1912. Nevertheless she took lessons at home, sometimes even indicating the precise times in her notebook.[58] By October 30 she had started the orchestration of *Pour les Funérailles d'un Soldat* while she continued to work on fugues.[59] After November 27 there are no further entries in this workbook.

There appears to be a break of several months between late November of 1912 and the next entries in Lili's workbooks. To return to the "1912–1913" Fugue Notebook mentioned earlier,[60] consecutive, dated entries do not resume until April 9, 1913. This is an unusually long period of time without notebook indications, considering Lili's dedication and extreme conscientiousness. One answer may be found in her worsening physical condition which had forced her to consult doctors more frequently, beginning with the summer of 1912.

Once again, Lili's letters to Miki Piré provide some explanation. By Sunday, November 25, Lili had been examined by a specialist, a Dr. Ménard, who gave his findings to Dr. Brocq on the twenty-seventh. In his opinion, the best thing for Lili would be for her to leave Paris as soon as possible for Berck, on the desolate Pas-de-Calais coast, for physical therapy.

Figure 17. Opening measures of the holograph piano-vocal score of *Pour les funérailles.*

On November 29, 1912, at 7:15 in the morning, Lili was to leave Paris to make the trip by train. Although she realized the medical necessity for this, she was, nevertheless, extremely unhappy about going to Berck.[61] As she usually did when she was weak, Lili wrote this letter to Miki in pencil. In all probability, she was not strong enough to use a pen. The envelope, too, is in the same faint pencil.

The morning after her arrival at the Hôtel de Russie in Berck-Plage, she wrote to Miki, describing her first impressions of Berck. Evidently, there had been such terrible weather that it was impossible to go out at all. Lili was depressed by the fact that there were so many invalids at Berck—all in wheelchairs—but was consoled somewhat by the presence of Mme Boulanger, who, as she wrote Miki, was planning to stay there with her for several days.[62]

The pervasiveness of the somber atmosphere and the inclement weather preyed on Lili's sensibilities. Because of the weather, there was nothing to do but sit inside and look at invalids, and the fact that her friends were not there did not alleviate the feelings of isolation from which Lili was suffering. By 12:10 P.M., she was still busily at work on her letter to Miki in spite of Mme Boulanger's desire to go to lunch. She closed the letter hastily, begging Miki for a long letter to give her the spirit to carry on, and asked to be remembered to Miki's parents. There is no caution to Miki in this letter not to write in Russian, possibly because the presence of Mme Boulanger would—at least for the time being—make such a restriction unnecessary.

By December 10 Lili had moved on to the *Family-House*.[63] Mme Boulanger had left that morning, taking with her the personal maid who had accompanied them to Berck. In addition to her previous sense of separation from her accustomed friends and activities, and to the desolateness of the place, the departure of her mother and the maid[64] had plunged Lili into a mood of deep melancholy. All this she admitted to her friend, apologizing for the tone of her letter, which ends abruptly with the decision that she had no right to speak any further on such a depressing subject.[65] Despite her emotional upheaval, the stay at Berck appears to have done Lili some good physically—up to that point at least—since both this letter and the preceding one were written entirely in ink.

The same mood of bleak despair is to be found in her next letter to Miki, dated Wednesday, December 18. After thanking her for the letter she had received, Lili begged Miki to tell her everything that was troubling her, because in Miki's letter she had sensed that all was not well with her, either. Confiding to Miki that what she wanted most in life was to return to Paris as soon as possible, she told her friend that her only means of taking her mind off her own problems was the arrival of the mail, which brought with it the thoughts of everyone who was dear to her, and made her feel a little closer to them emotionally in spite of the fact of her physical isolation.[66]

Lili wrote her friend again later the same day. A letter from Miki had arrived at the hotel while Lili was out walking, and she was anxious to answer it. Happily she reported that her health had improved so noticeably and her knee was so much better that she had already fixed the day of her departure from Berck for December 30, in the hope that one additional week would be enough to return her to good health. The prospect of spending Christmas there alone, however, was in no sense a pleasant one. But she was willing to accept the emotional pain for the sake of her health, especially since it would give Nadia such pleasure to see her well. Even so, she felt that her emotional strength might fail her. She reminded Miki once more what pleasure her letters gave her, and hoped that Miki would write her so often that she would not even have the time to be unhappy.[67]

On Christmas day Lili wrote once more to Miki Piré. Lili was suffering from a deep and inexorable sense of loneliness. Mme Boulanger had come to spend Christmas with her in Berck, but Lili still felt keenly her isolation from those closest to her. Although Lili and her mother were on good terms, she was not on quite such intimate terms with Mme Boulanger as she was with Nadia and Miki, for example. Mme Boulanger had tremendous nervous energy, and Lili found it tiring.[68]

Lili missed Nadia, Miki, her other close friends—even her dog! She had a strong desire to surround those she loved with her affection, but still she sometimes felt that others did not entirely understand her. She believed that they saw her as merely amusing and superficial, when in fact she was sensitive and felt things very deeply. Once again, this need to confide in Miki ended in Lili's displeasure with herself for letting her letter take on such a note of sadness on a holiday. She closed with the customary greetings, wishing Miki were not so far away in Nice.[69]

There is a sensibility in all of these letters, a perceptiveness that belies Lili's youth and lack of worldliness. Some of the sentiments she expressed could have been the product of a romantic adolescent. But taken as a whole, these letters reveal an extremely sensitive nature, conscious of its own needs as well as those of others, and also aware—sometimes painfully so—both of physical necessity and reality, and of the emotional effects that might be produced by particular statements or actions.

It is possible that Lili did not work at musical composition while she stayed at Berck. Although there is no indication of her having attended any composition classes at the Conservatoire during the entire autumn semester, Paul Vidal's comments on his impressions of Lili and her work in the end-of-term examination of his composition class do appear in the permanent record of the Conservatoire classes for that year. His report, dated January 30, 1913, states that she is a gentle person—suffering, unfortunately, from poor health—who does "very intelligent work."[70]

One work that may have helped persuade Paul Vidal to make these observations about Lili is the orchestrated version of *Pour les Funérailles d'un Soldat*. According to an indication on her own autograph score, Lili finished the orchestration on January 30, 1913.[71] This composition and the vocal quartet *Renouveau* were presented by Lili as part of her semester examinations. They were performed at the Conservatoire on Tuesday, February 11, 1913, at 8:45 P.M., as part of the Salon des Musiciens Français. Lili herself played the piano accompaniment for *Renouveau*.[72]

In describing the end-of-term examination for the composition students at the Conservatoire, *Le Ménéstral* said:

> We note the success of Mlle Lili Boulanger, a student of G. Caussade and P. Vidal, who has received the Prix Lepaul [*sic*] after an examination of great brilliance, and the right to be performed in the orchestra class. Two choral works, *Pour les Funérailles* and *Le Printemps* earned her this particularly flattering reward. Mlle Lili Boulanger is the younger sister of Mlle Nadia Boulanger, who won the Second Grand Prix de Rome. Mlle Lili Boulanger will compete for this prize in her turn, this year.[73]

Evidence of the fact that Lili worked very hard on her musical studies during the month of January is to be found in a letter (postmarked February 6, 1913) to Miki Piré. Beginning with an apology to Miki for not having written sooner, Lili goes on to explain that she had been forced to work late into the night all that month to finish her orchestration. (Undoubtedly the score referred to is *Pour les Funérailles*). Because of these missed hours of sleep, Lili had to guard her remaining rest zealously, thus making it impossible for her to write Miki at all.[74] The envelope itself has been addressed by another hand—possibly Nadia's. This fact, added to the lack of heading and amenities in the letter, as well as the minuteness of Lili's handwriting compared to other letters when she was feeling relatively well, seems to indicate that Lili was at least very tired, if not actually in pain when she wrote this letter.

The months of January and February were busy ones for Lili Boulanger that year. In addition to the compositions she prepared for her semester examinations at the Conservatoire, two of her other works were performed only two days later by the

Société Chorale d'Amateurs. *Les Sirènes* and *Hymne au Soleil* were presented by this group on Thursday, February 13, at nine o'clock in the evening.[75]

After almost two months of frenetic activity, it is hardly surprising that Lili might need some time to rest. During March of the same year, Lili and Mme Boulanger spent time with the Piré family in Nice, staying at the Castel Piré from March 13 through March 25. Although there are no extant dated entries in Lili's workbooks for this period, she frequently sightread music and improvised on the upright piano, which was kept near the room she slept in, on the second floor of the Castel Piré.[77] It is possible, of course, that some of the undated material in her composition workbooks was actually composed during this period. On the other hand, considering Lili's recent, very intensive work, she may have spent this time on the Riviera simply resting for the next stage of her taxing efforts toward preparing for the Prix de Rome competition of 1913.

By April 9 Lili was again at work on fugal techniques, and on this date entries resume in her "1912–1913" Fugue notebook. She took a lesson the next day, and again on Sunday, April 13, at which time Lili made the notation that she was to present a cantata, *Alyssa,* as part of her lesson. Apparently no copy of this work has survived. Between April 9 and April 15 Lili worked every day, consistently, but instead of an entry for April 16, there is the indication that she was too ill to take her lesson that day. The next entry is dated April 22, and, once again, there are entries for each day until the twenty-ninth of that month.[78]

Lili spent only the first days of May in Paris,[79] before leaving to go into seclusion in Compiègne with the rest of the Prix de Rome aspirants. Her work at the Conservatoire during the spring term earned Lili the enthusiastic praise of Paul Vidal. In his report for the Conservatoire dated May 5, 1913, he describes her as an extraordinary person, unfortunately suffering from poor health.[80]

Tuesday, May 6, 1913, was the day set by the Institut de France for the dictation of the fugue subject and the words of the chorus to the contestants in musical composition for the Prix de Rome who had gathered in Compiègne.[81] The first round of the competition that year was described by the magazine *Le Monde Musical.*

Thirteen contestants went into seclusion at the Palace of Compiègne for the elimination round of the Rome competition, which consists, as is known, of an orchestrated chorus and a fugue.

We saw again this year the second prize winners from the last competitions: Marc Delmas, who is on his seventh try, Mignan on his sixth, and Delvincourt on his fifth. If for no other reason, the perseverance of these musicians is already worth rewarding. They have an even greater right to hope this year that the Institut will be able to dispose of *two* First Grand Prizes.

M. Scotto enters seclusion also for the fifth time; MM. Saint-Aulaire and Dupré for the fourth time; MM. de Petzer, Laporte and Mlle Lili Boulanger (sister of Nadia Boulanger) for the second time. The "tyros" are MM. de Lapresle, Grandjany, Tournié, and Mlle Guillot.

MM. [*sic*] Dupré, Mlle Lili Boulanger, MM. Marc Delmas, Mignan, and Delvincourt were admitted to the final round.[82]

Lili Boulanger had given her *concours d'essai* to M. Alexandre at Compiègne on May 12 at 11 A.M.[83] Having been admitted to the

Figure 18. Receipt for Lili Boulanger's *concours d'essai* for the 1913 Prix de Rome competition.

final round of the Prix de Rome competition (as a result of the judging of the chorus and fugue at the Conservatoire at 9 A.M. on Tuesday, May 13, 1913), Lili would be expected to enter seclusion again at Compiègne at 10 o'clock in the morning on May 22.[84]

One of the most striking features of the announcements of Lili's attempts at the Prix de Rome, and, indeed, of publicity about her at all times, is the constant coupling of her name with that of her older sister, Nadia. In addition to the fact that such an identification would help readers to place Lili more easily—Nadia was already widely known as both teacher and performer, and had been one of the first women admitted to the Prix de Rome competition in musical composition—Lili herself encouraged such references. She and Nadia were extremely close, and they identified with each other to the extent of using joint visiting

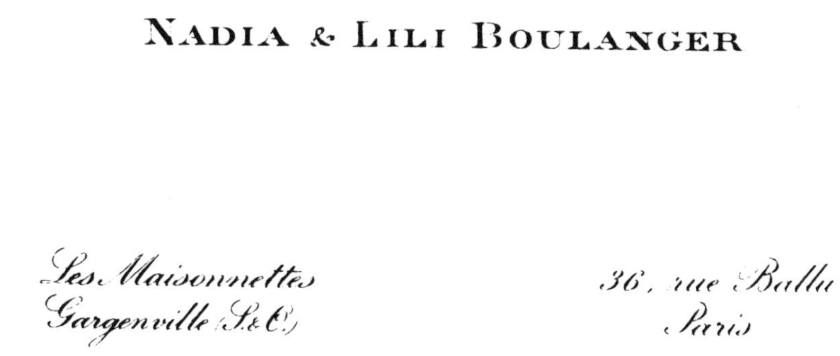

NADIA & LILI BOULANGER

Les Maisonnettes
Gargenville (S.&O.)

36, rue Ballu
Paris

Figure 19. Joint visiting card of Nadia and Lili Boulanger.

cards.[85] Both Nadia and Lili were carrying on an artistic tradition which had been a part of the family since the eighteenth century. It was a tribute to their family to have produced two gifted musicians in one generation, and they were delighted to let it be known.

Even before she had completed the second stage of the Prix de Rome competition in 1913, Lili Boulanger was a celebrity in her own right. Not only had her debut as a composer been reviewed by a widely read music magazine, but the mere fact that she was admitted to the final round of the 1913 competition was considered so newsworthy that a picture of her appeared in *La Vie Heureuse* on June 13 with the following caption:

About the same time four years ago, Mlle Nadia Boulanger earned a Grand Prix de Rome in music—the first time it was given to a woman. Mlle Lily [sic] Boulanger, her sister, has just gone into seclusion, in her turn, for the same competition. All women will admire this continuity of vocation and ability.

71

and will wish that an equally happy continuing success be joined to it.[86]

The French public—or at least, magazines carrying news of the achievements of notable French women—was just as happy to acknowledge ongoing artistic talent in one family as were the Boulangers themselves.[87]

But having earned admission again to the Palace of Compiègne made Lili Boulanger's achievement newsworthy to the French-speaking artistic world at large, not just to magazines catering to women's interests. In 1913 only five out of a possible six aspirants had qualified for the final round of the competition. Thus, simply being one of the five finalists was, in itself, noteworthy. The French magazine *Musica* took this point of view, and its frontispiece for the month of June 1913 is devoted to a group portrait of four of the five finalists standing before the door of the Institut de France: MM. Delvincourt, Delmas, and Mignan, and Mlle Lili Boulanger. In this picture Lili appears frail and tired, but is, as always, dressed with impeccable elegance.[88] Not only was Lili almost six years younger than the next-youngest contestant,[89] but this was also her first experience participating in the taxing final stage of the Prix de Rome competition, for the other finalists had all attempted this part of the competition at least once before. These factors alone would have combined to make Lili's achievement notable even if she had not been one of the first women ever allowed to compete in this last portion of the contest.

The period of seclusion for the final round of the Prix de Rome competition lasted from May 22 until June 21: exactly one month. During that time contestants would have to produce two com-pleted scores—a piano score and an orchestrated version of the same score. Even in her race against time during this hectic month, Lili still kept track of her work and noted her progress. The original piano score of her cantata *Faust et Hélène* indicates that she finished it on Sunday, June 15, 1913, at seven o'clock.[90] This meant that she had only one more week to complete the orchestral version. At best, these competitions were grueling, nerve-wracking affairs, even for someone in perfect health. Lili was not, and the rigors of the preliminary round had taken their toll. She was not well at all during the final round of the competition, and, after she had completed the score herself, her friend Marcel Dupré—himself a contestant—gallantly helped her to write out the fair copies for presentation to the jury.[91]

Although no communication from the outside world was al-

Figure 20. Frontispiece of *Musica* for June 1913.

lowed to reach the contestants at Compiègne, they were permitted
to write letters. On May 30 Lili sent Miki Piré a picture postcard
taken of her and Nadia outside the gates of the Palace of Compiègne before she had entered seclusion for the final round of the
competition in 1913. Lili had not heard from Miki in some time
(Miki Piré was at that time visiting in Russia, where her father
had business interests) but wished her friend an enjoyable stay

Figure 21. Final measures of the holograph piano-vocal score of
Faust et Hélène.

in Russia. Once again Lili was going to be shut away from the
world—this time as part of the competition—and the prospect did
not appeal to her. This time, too, she felt sad and alone, isolated
from her closest friends.[92]

There were two weeks between the completion of the cantatas
at Compiègne and the date of the final judging of the cantatas at
the Institut de France. Lili took advantage of this time to go to the
seashore for a rest. By June 24 she was already in Dieppe. The
trip had been difficult for her, but Raoul Pugno, who accompanied
her on the train, had surprised her by finding just the right words
to cheer her in spite of all her problems. After their arrival, they
found the hotel unsatisfactory. Lili had already moved to another

Figure 22. Picture postcard of Lili and Nadia Boulanger outside the Palais de Compiègne before the 1913 Prix de Rome competition.

Figure 23. Envelope in which picture postcard of the Boulanger sisters was mailed, addressed both in French and in phonetic Cyrillic script by Lili Boulanger.

one when she first wrote to Miki, who was then staying at the Boulangers' house in Gargenville.[93] Lili reminded Miki about the coming concert[94] and asked her to try to be there with Madame Piré.[95] Lili remained in Dieppe at least until June 27, when she sent a postcard to Miki.[96]

Lili returned to Paris for the judging of the cantatas, which took place at the Institut de France on Saturday, July 5.[97] This was an important day for Lili. With her friend Miki Piré she went first to place flowers on her father's grave in Montmartre Cemetery before going to the Institut.[98] Lili had never lost the feeling of closeness to her father, and her vocation as a composer reinforced that bond.

In 1913 the Music Section of the Institut de France included MM. Gustave Charpentier, Théodore Dubois, Émile Paladilhe, Gabriel Fauré, and Camille Saint-Saëns. The final judgment, however, was to be made by all the sections of the Institut des Beaux-Arts, together. "The performance of the cantatas took place in the Great Meeting Hall of the Institute where, in addition to the members of the jury, a certain number of listeners who were not members of the Institute were admitted."[99] At noon the day before, a private performance had taken place at the Conservatoire, with only the members of the Music Section, the President, Vice-President and Permanent Secretary, and three supplementary jurors in attendance.[100]

As for the public performance and the final judging of the cantatas on July 5, 1913, various accounts survive. Émile Vuillermoz, who was there, reported the event for *Musica* in his article entitled "War in Laces," which appeared in the August issue.

Several months ago, in this column, I warned musicians of the imminence of the "pink peril": events have not hesitated to prove me right. Mlle Lili Boulanger has just triumphed in the last Prix de Rome competition over all its male contestants. and has carried off, on her first try [i.e., her first time as a finalist]. the First Grand Prize with an authority, a speed, and an ease apt to seriously disturb the candidates who, for long years, cried tears and sweated blood while laboriously approaching this goal. Do not be fooled: this deed stands on its own merits. Not only did the gallantry (?) [sic] of the judges not intervene to facilitate her victory, but it could be said that they were stricter with this young girl of nineteen than with her competitors. The misogyny of the jury was known. The entry of an Eve into the earthly paradise of the Villa Medici was dreaded by certain patriarchs as the equal of total catastrophe. The precedent established by the sculptors [Mlle Lucienne Heuvelmans, a sculptress, had won the Prix de Rome in 1911, and was already living at the Villa Medici] did not calm their agitation. It was, then, with an unmerciful attention that the female's cantata—which took on in this atmosphere the bravery and the peril of a feminist discourse—was heard. And it required all the crushing weight and indisputable superiority of this woman's work to triumph over the students' homework that surrounded it.

Gallantry, besides, has not found its resting place in musical contests. The frail grace of Mlle Lili Boulanger only moved the spectators who were touched at the group formed by the contestant and her sister united at the piano in an attentive and affectionate collaboration. The heat of battle made her young male rivals, devoured by ambition, insensitive to this poetry.

Perched on the piano like jockeys over the necks and withers of their horses, the daring composers spurred on the accompanists, and lashed out at the performers with desperate gestures and a disordered mimicry. . . .

And it was then that the superiority of the eternal feminine appeared to the observers. Compared with her impassioned comrades, too obviously led to believe that "their time had come," the young girl, who had a right to every bit of impatience and nervousness, showed the most perfect sang-froid. Her modest and simple mien, her eyes lowered on the score, her immobility during the performance, her complete willingness to give her excellent performers free reign—she did not once let herself beat time or indicate a nuance—all contributed to her cause, otherwise excellently defended, and showed up the masculine puerility. Truly it is a sad time for the sex that considers itself strong. If the China dolls of music decide to vie with him for official laurels, he is lost before he starts. . . .

. . . Until now, woman, who knew how to bring such a personal and delicious form of sensitivity to the other arts, who created grace, suppleness, and force in the poem and the novel, who even gave us the taste of a certain precision in truth and a sort of courageous cynicism in sincerity, did not find the means of expressing herself in music. Does not the present harmonic and orchestral technique suit her? Will she have to wait for a congenial woman creator to forge a new style for her? Has she not yet discovered the lode that only she will know how to mine? Time will tell. . . . The cantata competition is not a test of composition in the artistic sense of the word. It is a contest, and in a contest Eve has nothing to fear from Adam. All her qualities serve her and assure her of victory. Then let us salute Mlle Lili Boulanger today, with the resigned heroism that "those who were about to die" saluted Caesar.[101]

77

Lili's cantata had been third on the program—preceded by those of Delvincourt and Delmas, and followed by those of Dupré and Mignan. As M. Vuillermoz has pointed out, Lili fired the imagination of the audience. Other writers confirm this sense of community between the young contestant and those present at the Institute that day. Her youth, demeanor, manner of dress, and, certainly, the musical values of her cantata combined to create this empathy.

> The July 5th meeting at the Institute remains memorable: as early as the performance of the first pages, an atmosphere of wonder was created, and everyone felt himself in the presence of a revelation. The three singers (Mme Croiza, David Devriès, Henri Albers), and Nadia Boulanger at the piano, were directed by Lili Boulanger, standing near the piano, a slim shadow in a white dress, so simple, calm, serious and smiling, such an unforgettable image. . . .[102]

After all five cantatas had been heard, the President of the Academy officially thanked the performers who had given their time and energy to the presentation. Then all of the voting members of the Académie des Beaux-Arts retired to an adjoining room to reach their final verdict. Due consideration was given to the results of the preceding day's deliberations of the Music Section, which had been held at the Conservatoire. This preliminary judgment could have been overturned by a joint vote of all the sections of the Academy. On July 4 Lili Boulanger had received a simple majority of the votes of the Music Section: five out of a possible eight.

According to the report given to the joint sections of the Academy on July 5, 1913, the reasons for proposing Mlle Boulanger as the candidate for the First Grand Prize were, "Intelligence of subject. Correctness of declamation. Sensitivity and warmth. Poetic feeling. Intelligent and colorful orchestration. A remarkable cantata."[103]

The merits of the other candidates were also considered, and mention was made of their records and any other prizes they had previously won in competition. There was no further discussion. Then the thirty-six voting members of the Academy who were in attendance at this closed session voted for the contestant who would be the laureate in musical composition for 1913. This time Lili Boulanger received an overwhelming majority—thirty-one out of thirty-six. "Consequently," reads the transcript of the proceedings for July 5, 1913, "the First Grand Prize is awarded to

Figure 24. Sketch by Dagnan-Bouveret of Lili Boulanger at the Institut de France during the judging of her cantata on July 5, 1913, as reproduced in the article by Vuillermoz. See chapter 4. *Courtesy of the Département de la Musique, Bibliothèque Nationale, Paris.*

Mlle Boulanger (Marie-Juliette), student of M. Paul Vidal, Born in Paris, August 21, 1893."[104]

The results of the final judgment were not at all those anticipated. In fact, they could not have been predicted from the ranking of the *concours d'essai* less than two months before. In the preliminary round, Marcel Dupré had emerged in first place, followed by Lili Boulanger, Marc Delmas, Edouard Mignan, and Claude Delvincourt, in that order.[105] The final voting on the cantatas put Lili Boulanger in first place, followed by Claude Delvincourt, who was awarded the Second First Grand Prize, and then by Marc Delmas, who was given the First Second Grand Prize. The Institute decided to distribute no other awards in the Prix de Rome competition for 1913.[106]

Lili Boulanger's cantata had produced a sensation.

Mlle Lili Boulanger gave us one of the most beautiful cantatas that has been heard in many years (with the exception of Paul Paray's). Her work is completely superior and captured everyone even at first hearing. The prelude, the prologue of Mephistopheles, the dialogues, Faust's song when he sings an ode to Helen, first heroically, then stamped with an exquisite poetry and tenderness, the very successful descriptive orchestrations, Helen's air, the duet of loving expression, finally . . . the extremely poignant trio, the especially successful end with Mephisto's lamentations as he carries off the body of Faust, make this cantata a work absolutely beyond compare.

We must congratulate Mlle Lili Boulanger for having, at her age, such an ability, such a sense of the stage, a touching musicality, turn by turn caressing and despairing, rude and supple, and the innate ability to see and attain exactly the right means of expression. Her cantata was the revelation of the day.[107]

The jury's deliberation had taken forty-five minutes,[108] and their decision had set a new precedent: from then on women composers would be admitted to the Villa Medici. This turn of events surprised—even stunned—the general public. Mangeot, the critic, had asked Lili only four years before whether she was planning to follow the same path as her sister Nadia. Her answer at that time was, "Oh, no! If I have a good enough voice, I would rather sing." But, having known her, he was not surprised at her triumph at the Prix de Rome competition. He had, he said, been one of those fortunate enough to hear her early works performed, and no one who had would be surprised by the present great success of Lili's cantata. In the biographical sketch of her written for *Le*

Figure 25. Lili Boulanger at the organ in the living room of her family's apartment in Paris, shortly after winning the Prix de Rome. *Courtesy of the Département de la Musique, Bibliothèque Nationale, Paris.*

Monde Musical,[109] he congratulates himself and his magazine for having recognized Lili Boulanger's ability fifteen months before her talents began to be appreciated by the world at large. M. Mangeot also recalls the fact that, although Lili Boulanger would be the first woman composer to be admitted to the Villa Medici, two others—her sister Nadia in 1908, and Hélène Fleury in 1904, had already earned a Second Grand Prize.[110]

81

An analysis of Lili's musical development prior to her winning the Prix de Rome in 1913 shows that, after deciding to become a composer, she pursued her musical studies with extreme dedication and a strong sense of purpose. She brought to this project all her mental and physical forces, and was able to complete a very rigorous private course of training in harmony and counterpoint with Georges Caussade—the same course that was given at the Conservatoire—between January 1910 and October 1911. This sequence of study normally took several years. While acquiring her musical education in this way, participating in her usual social activities and continuing to make new friends, Lili was also trying her hand at composition, especially after she began to study fugue formally in 1911. Although she experienced a slight respite from her illness, she still had to guard her health zealously, and recurrent bouts of illness sometimes prevented her from achieving all that she might have achieved had she been in good health, as is borne out by the records of the Conservatoire.

In March 1912 Lili made her official and well-received debut as a composer. Having been too ill to complete her examinations at the Conservatoire, or to complete the competition for the Prix de Rome in 1912, Lili spent part of the summer resting to recuperate and gather her energies for the 1913 competition. The illness that had attacked her during the 1912 competition, added to her new physical problems, made the rest of the year extremely painful for her. In fact, her health made it necessary for her to spend the month of December that year in the then bleak seaside resort of Berck for physical therapy—isolated from her family and closest friends. But Lili managed to recover enough to complete the orchestration of *Pour les Funérailles d'un Soldat* during January 1913, and to present a brilliant examination for her end-of-term work in Vidal's composition class at the Conservatoire, an accomplishment that earned her the Prix Lepaulle from the Conservatoire for 1913. Following this, Lili spent some time at the home of Miki Piré in Nice resting from her concentrated work, and, finally, emerged triumphant from the Prix de Rome competition in 1913.

4

After the Prix de Rome:
Ages 19-24

Winning the Prix de Rome in music made Lili Boulanger an international celebrity almost overnight. By July 7, 1913, accounts of her triumph in the competition with the cantata *Faust et Hélène* had already reached the United States. In fact, the *New York Times* and *Le Temps* carried this news on the same day, and later in the year a copy of the score was even requested by the Municipal Library of Perm, Russia.[1]

With her close friend, Renée de Marquein, Lili made the customary duty calls to thank all the members of the Institut after she won the Prix de Rome. As always, Lili was elegantly dressed—this time in a navy blue suit bordered in lighter braid, and a large black hat ornamented with feathers. She made a striking figure, tall and slender, with chestnut hair and brown eyes.[2] The visits themselves were short, and were merely meant to convey the candidate's gratitude at having become the laureate.

But the Prix de Rome was not the only prize given to Lili Boulanger in 1913. By virtue of her having been admitted to the final stage of the competition, she automatically shared the prize of the Fondation Yvonne de Gouy d'Arsy with the other finalists and the winner of the First Prize for Fugue (at the Conservatoire).[3] In addition, Lili earned the Prix Lepaulle for 1913, for her compositions *Renouveau* and *Pour les Funérailles d'un Soldat*. Ac-

Mademoiselle !

La Bibliothèque publique Municipale de Perm, fondée en l'année 1831, comprend près de 50000 volumes et est une des Bibliothèques Municipales les plus importantes et les plus anciennes de toute la Russie. La Bibliothèque de Perm est une Bibliothèque centrale et la plus grande de l'Oural, en outre elle sert spécialement aux 3731000 habitants du Gouvernem. de Perm. En 1908 la Bibliothèque ouvrit une section musicale, qui se compose de partitions musicales, de livres et de journaux musicaux, etc... Mais la Municipalité ne peut affecter à l'extention de la section musicale, que des sommes peu importantes. Tandis que pour la propagation de la culture musicale il est nécessaire de recueillir pour la Bibliothèque le plus possible de littérature musicale. C'est pourquoi, le Comité Directeur de la Bibliothèque, prenent la liberté de Vous prier de faire don généreux à la Bibliothèque de

la partition d'orchestre de la Votre cantate "Faust et Hélène" et autres Vos belles œuvres,

et en général de toutes écrits, éditions musicales, catalogues, journaux etc... dont Vous voudriez dessaisir au profit de notre Bibliothèque.

S'excusant le Comité Vous remercie.

Membre du Comité à la Section Musicale
Directeur-Bibliothécaire V. Benesff

28 Novembre 1913

PERM. (Russie).

Figure 26. Request from the Municipal Library of Perm, Russia, for copies of Lili Boulanger's *Faust et Hélène* and any of her other works she might be willing to send them.

cording to the terms of the bequest, this recompense was to be given "to a young musician having produced during the year an exceptional work in any genre."[4] Thus, Lili Boulanger won three major awards in 1913, the Prix Yvonne de Gouy d'Arsy, the Prix Lepaulle, and the Prix de Rome.

On the same day that Lili received her awards from the Conservatoire, an article about her appeared in *Les Hommes du jour* in which, while retracing her career up to that point, including the recently extremely successful performance of *Faust et Hélène* at the Institut, the author felt justified in remarking ". . . I say and proclaim with unshakable assurance, that Lili Boulanger will be a great woman musician, or, rather, a great musician: that is obvious."[5] In spite of all her attainments, he cautioned her not to be spoiled by the attention now focused on her, and to continue to grow artistically.[6] This article was accompanied by a sketch of Lili by Raiéter, which appeared on the magazine's cover.

By the twentieth of July, two other French periodicals had found her achievement worthy of mention. The July 15 issue of *Femina* printed a picture of her with Nadia, with a caption[7] remarking on her winning the Prix de Rome.[8] Paul Loisel's article—accompanied by pictures of the three Prix de Rome competition winners of 1913—appeared in *Comoedia Illustré* on July 20. As with so many others, M. Loisel saw in Lili's success a triumph for women's rights. "Feminism has just carried off a great victory," he wrote, "which has been impatiently awaited since the day when women were permitted to compete for the Prix de Rome in Music . . . this is the work of the energetic and delicate Mlle Lili Boulanger."[9] He then speculated on the part Nadia might have played in Lili's musical development, and, finally, recalled the accomplishments of Ernest Boulanger, who, he reminded his readers, had also won the Prix de Rome in music.

Throughout the summer of 1913, news items about Lili Boulanger and her singular achievement continued to find their way into periodicals on both sides of the Atlantic. Mangeot had written a biographical sketch of Lili for the July 15 and 30 double issue of *Le Monde Musical*. The same issue had contained an account of the July 5 cantata performances at the Institut. It also carried a special portrait of Lili on its cover, and a reproduction of one page of the manuscript of her *concours d'essai*.[10]

On July 31 the *Musical Leader*, a widely read American magazine, printed the following, under the title "A Remarkable Young French Woman Prize Winner":

DOUZIÈME ANNÉE. Numéro 131

AOÛT 1913

MUSICA

ABONNEMENTS

Pierre LAFITTE & C⁰, éditeurs, 90, Champs-Élysées, Paris

Xavier LEROUX, rédacteur en chef

LES LAURÉATS DU PRIX DE ROME DE COMPOSITION MUSICALE

Figure 27. Frontispiece of *Musica* for August 1913. *Courtesy of the Département de la Musique, Bibliothèque Nationale, Paris.*

A woman, Lilli [*sic*] Boulanger, the 19-year-old daughter of a singing professor at the Conservatoire, has won the Grand Prix de Rome, this being the first time in 110 years of its history that a woman has won the much-sought-after prize. To show its value, such men as Berlioz, Bizet, Gounod, Massenet, Debussy and Charpentier have been some of the distinguished winners of it. "Faust and Helen" is the name of the composition that won Miss Boulanger the honor.[11]

The August issue of *Musica* devoted its frontispiece to Lili Boulanger and Claude Delvincourt. The feature article, written by Émile Vuillermoz, centered around Lili's recent triumph in the Prix de Rome competition. A pen-and-ink sketch of Lili by Dagnan-Bouveret, made while Lili was directing her cantata at the Institut, was also reproduced in the article. Further on in the same issue, amid photographs of the other contestants, their performers, and the President of the Académie des Beaux-Arts, there is a reproduction of another sketch of Lili during the performance at the Institut—this one by François Flameng, who made the sketch on his tally sheet.[12]

Through Paul Gentien, then head of the Ricordi Company branch office in Paris, Lili met Tito Ricordi, just after she won the Prix de Rome competition. Gentien was very anxious to sign her to an exclusive contract, and, on August 1, 1913, Lili did, indeed, sign just such a contract, which also guaranteed her a fixed yearly stipend.[13]

The first of Lili's compositions to be published was the cantata with which she had won the Prix de Rome, *Faust et Hélène*. After signing the contract, of course, there were proofs to be corrected before publication. For this tedious part of the work Lili also had the help of two friends, then Nadia's students—Renée de Marquein and Marcelle Soulage.[14]

The task was not at all unpleasant, however. Lili was very witty and cheerful during these sessions, so much so that those present remembered only the pleasant aspects rather than the drudgery of the task.[15]

This was a relatively untroubled time for Lili. While in Paris, she could take time to go out walking with her friends. Frequently she went shopping with Renée de Marquein.[16] During the months of October and November 1913, when she was not preparing for or participating in concerts of her own works, she spent her time with Miki Piré in Nice.[17]

Beginning early in November, however, Lili began a round of feverish activity. On Saturday, November 8, at the annual public meeting of the Académie des Beaux-Arts, all the prizes awarded by the Academy for that year were officially presented to their recipients. The program closed with the performance of Lili's *Faust et Hélène*,[18] under the direction of an old friend of the Boulanger family who had known Ernest Boulanger even before the births of Nadia and Lili—Henri Büsser.[19]

Figure 28. Lili Boulanger in a quiet moment with Fachoun in her room at 36 rue Ballu (1913).

A little over a week later, the formal public premiere of *Faust et Hélène* was given at the Concerts Colonne, under the direction of Gabriel Pierné. Paul Martineau, who reported this event for *Le Monde Musical,* wrote:

Mlle Lili Boulanger already shows a happy penchant for limpid melodies, an almost astonishing sense of the theater, an admirable ease in expressing passionate sentiments and a healthy continuity of line, never marred by the pettiness or affectations that would quickly have revealed the work of a woman. Age (alas! . . . must one speak of age? . . .) and work will bring to fruition the qualities of an already undeniable talent; of a talent that in no way excludes grace. These things may have been attested to by the enthusiastic audience that obliged Mlle Lili Boulanger, deeply moved, to appear on stage, surrounded by her three admirable interpreters, Mme Croiza, and MM. Devriès and Ghasne.[20]

This was by no means an isolated good review. Claude Debussy also was very favorably impressed, even though he deplored the idea of the Prix de Rome competition itself.

Mademoiselle Lili Boulanger, who has just carried off the

ACADÉMIE DES BEAUX-ARTS

SÉANCE PUBLIQUE ANNUELLE
Du Samedi 8 novembre 1913
PRÉSIDÉE PAR

M. LOUIS BERNIER
PRÉSIDENT DE L'ACADÉMIE

PROGRAMME DE LA SÉANCE

1° Exécution de la scène lyrique qui a remporté le deuxième premier grand prix de composition musicale et dont l'auteur est M. Delvincourt, élève de M. Widor.

2° Discours de M. le Président.

3° Proclamation des GRANDS PRIX de Peinture, Sculpture, d'Architecture, de Composition musicale et des prix décernés en vertu des diverses fondations.

4° Notice sur la vie et les travaux de M. Edouard Detaille, membre de l'Académie, par M. Henry Roujon, secrétaire perpétuel.

5° Exécution de la scène lyrique qui a remporté le premier grand prix de composition musicale et dont l'auteur est Mlle Boulanger (Marie-Juliette), élève de M. Paul Vidal.

PRIX DÉCERNÉS

GRANDS PRIX DÉCERNÉS PAR L'ACADÉMIE DES BEAUX-ARTS. — Peinture. — Sujet du concours : *Le Rhapsode*. — Le 1er grand prix n'a pas été décerné. — 1er second grand prix : M. Domergue (Charles-Louis-Jean-Gabriel), né le 4 mars 1889, à Bordeaux, élève de MM. Humbert et Fr. Flameng. — 2e second grand prix : M. Cazes (Clovis-Alfred), né le 28 octobre 1883, à Lannepax (Gers), élève de M. Cormon. — Une mention honorable à M. Hillemacher (Jean-Marie-Maurice), né le 13 juin 1881, à Verneuil (Eure), élève de MM. Schommer, Baschet et Gervais. — Sculpture. — Sujet du concours : *Chanteurs bucoliques* — 1er grand prix : M. Martial (Armand), né le 2 novembre 1884, à Paris, élève de M. Coutan. — 1er second grand prix : M. Lehuédé (Marcel-Pierre), né le 21 janvier 1886, au Pouliguen (Loire-Inférieure), élève de MM. Coutan et Peynot. — 2e second grand prix : M. Ambrosio-Donnet (Antoine-Marius-Blaise), né le 11 juin 1887, à Vallauris (Alpes-Maritimes), élève de MM. Mercié et Carlès. — Architecture. — Programme : *Un Palais de la Présidence dans la capitale d'une grande République*. — 1er grand prix : M. Séassal (Roger-Pierre-Honoré), né le 14 novembre 1885, à Nice, élève de M. Héraud. — 2e premier grand prix (disponible par suite du décès de M. Janin) : M. Grégoire (Marc-Louis), né le 11 août 1883, à Arcueil-Cachan (Seine), élève de M. Paulin. — 1er second grand prix : M. Castel (Gaston-Désiré), né le 1er avril 1886, à Pertuis (Vaucluse), élève de M. Louis Bernier. — 2e second grand prix : M. Delaitre (Raymond-Honoré-Victor), né le 23 février 1887, à Paris, élève de M. Deglane. — Composition musicale. — Sujet du concours : *Faust et Hélène*, par M. Eugène Adenis. — 1er grand prix : Mlle Boulanger (Marie-Juliette), née le 21 août 1893, à Paris, élève de M. Paul Vidal. — 2e premier grand prix (disponible de 1912) : M. Delvincourt (Claude-Etienne-Edmond-Marie), né le 12 janvier 1888, à Paris, élève de M. Widor. — 1er second grand prix : M. Delmas (Marc-Jean-Baptiste), né le 28 mars 1885, à Saint-Quentin (Aisne), élève de M. Paul Vidal et précédemment de M. Ch. Lenepveu.

PRIX DESCHAUMES (1500 fr.). — Le prix a été partagé de la façon suivante : 1000 fr. à M. Andriku et 500 francs à M. Marius Boyer. — Une médaille de cinq cents francs a été attribuée sur les arrérages de la fondation à M. Eugène Adenis, auteur du livret de la cantate du Prix de Rome en composition musicale.

PRIX MAILLÉ-LATOUR-LANDRY (1200 fr.). — Prix partagé en trois parts égales de 400 fr., entre MM. Didier Tourné, artiste peintre, Gabriel Roby, artiste peintre et Abel La Fleur, graveur en médailles.

PRIX BORDIN (3000 fr.). — *L'Histoire des bâtiments du Louvre et des Tuileries, depuis leur origine jusqu'à nos jours*. — L'Académie a partagé le prix de la façon suivante : 1800 fr. à M. Marius Vachon; 1200 fr. à M. Ch. Harlay, architecte.

PRIX TRÉMONT (2000 fr.). — L'Académie a partagé ce prix, entre MM. Tranchant, peintre et Grange, sculpteur, d'une part, et M. Edmond Malherbe, compositeur de musique, d'autre part.

PRIX ACHILLE LECLÈRE (1000 fr.). — Architecture. — Sujet du concours : *Une Sepulture royale*. — L'Académie a décerné le prix à M. Astruc. — Deux mentions honorables ont été accordées *ex æquo* à MM. Koemptgen et Robida (Henri).

PRIX CHARTIER (500 fr.). — Musique de Chambre. — Le prix a été décerné à M. Emmanuel, compositeur de musique.

PRIX TROYON (1100 fr.). — Paysage. — Sujet : *Betail conduit le matin à l'abreuvoir*. — Le prix a été décerné à M. Laurent (Maurice-Sébastien), élève de MM. F. Humbert, R. Collin et E. Friant.

PRIX JEAN LECLAIRE (2 prix de 500 fr.). — Architecture. — Le premier prix a été attribué à M. Galli (Marcel-Joseph), élève de M. Héraud; le second a été décerné à titre étranger à M. King (William), américain, et à titre français à M. Barthe (Maurice-Marie-Pierre), élève de M. Redon.

PRIX CHAUDESAIGUES (2 annuités de 2000 fr. chacune). — Architecture. — Prix : M. Astruc, élève de M. Redon. — Deux mentions honorables : la première à M. Chaligne; la seconde à M. Petit (Pierre).

PRIX ROSSINI (3000 fr.). — Composition musicale. — Prix : M. André Laporte.

Figure 29. Program for the annual public meeting of the Académie des Beaux-Arts for 1913.

Grand Prix de Rome with *Faust et Hélène,* a lyric episode adapted from the second Faust by Goethe, poem by E. Adenis, is only nineteen. . . . Her experience in the different ways of writing music seems much older! Here and there are many little threads with which one knits together the ends of phrases in this type of work, only Mademoiselle L. Boulanger puts more subtle sleights of hand there. The arrival of Helen on the aerial flutterings of the divisi violins undulates with grace. But hardly has Helen arrived through the voice of Madame Croiza than she takes on the accent proper to a daughter of Zeus overwhelmed by all of her contrary destinies. Meanwhile, Faust murmurs through the beautiful voice of David Devriès.

If the character of Mephistopheles, and the inevitable trio are a little conventional, one must not forget the conditions under which a cantata is written! They are clearly unfavorable.

Actually, it is necessary to have the ideas, the talent at a precise moment of the year—if you aren't in form that particular month, too bad for you![21] It is arbitrary and has no meaning for the future. Useless to complain, all competitions take place in the same way. The judges of these competitions having suffered from the same procedures are not upset by seeing you go through it in your turn. About once a year, someone says that the conditions of the Prix de Rome competition must be changed, and that suffices.

Let the villa [sic] Medici be carefully kept as the most charming of rewards, but let the Prix de Rome competition, which does not respond to any need of our era, be suppressed.[22]

The next day, Nadia and Lili Boulanger came together for a gala performance at the Théâtre Léon Poirier. The results were spectacular. According to Edouard Moullé:

The Nadia and Lili Boulanger Gala, uniting the two sisters the day after the triumph of one of them,[23] had to pique the public's curiosity. A large and paying audience (I was witness to it) flocked to the Théâtre Léon Poirier to hear works by these two muses of music. The concert opened with a lecture by M. Landormy, who knew how to say a number of exquisite things that kept the public under the spell of his improvisation . . . . Nadia's works, of a beautiful musicality, a certain and subtle taste, modern, without exaggeration, do the greatest honor to their author.

Mme Lucienne Bréval was willing to lend the use of her prestigious talent to this solemn occasion, and made us appreciate a song entitled *Reflets* (by Mlle Lili Boulanger), projecting with intensity the melancholy of moonbeams and fugitive illusions.

90

Then a large section of the cantata *Faust et Hélène* was heard, interpreted to perfection by Mme Croiza, MM. David Devriès and Ghasne, accompanied by Mlle Lili Boulanger. . . .

At the end of the concert, the two sisters, united in the same triumph, received the warm approval of a touched and enraptured public, aware of having been able, for an instant, to commune with absolute beauty.[24]

The following evening, at a private soirée at the Palais D'Orsay, three of Lili's works—*Hymne au Soleil, Le Retour* and *Renouveau*—were performed on the same program with works by Nadia Boulanger and Claude Delvincourt. This event included a formal dinner for the recipients of the Prix de Rome and the Prix d'Athènes, both of which had been conferred earlier in the year by the Institut de France.[25]

After a short stay in Nice, Lili returned to Paris[26] for another round of appearances and performances. On December 1 she accompanied the duet from *Faust et Hélène* at an event presided over by the Count d'Haussonville. Yet another performance of *Faust et Hélène* took place on December 5. In the Salle Pleyel at nine o'clock the following evening Lili accompanied David Devriès for part of a program that included the "Air" from *Faust et Hélène* as well as her *Reflets*. Five days later, Lili Boulanger and Armand Martial (the 1913 Grand Prix de Rome in sculpture) were the guests of honor at a formal banquet and musical soirée given for them at the Société La Seine. The "Duo" and "Air" from *Faust et Hélène,* and *Renouveau* were performed.

Every year, M. and Mme Salles, the daughter and son-in-law of Gustave Eiffel, gave an elaborate party to celebrate his birthday. Since M. Eiffel had expressed an interest in meeting Lili Boulanger after she won the Prix de Rome, they had arranged for her to come to the party on December 15, 1913. She not only attended the party, but also accompanied—with her friend Marcel Dupré—a performance of *Faust et Hélène* for the assembled guests. One of Lili's cherished mementos of this occasion was a gold brocaded box with a medallion of her on the cover given to her by the Salles.[27] Laurent Ceillier, writing on the first page of the December 15 issue of *Le Monde Musical*, congratulates Lili on yet another achievement: her *Faust et Hélène* had just been published by Ricordi.[28]

Lili's hectic schedule during the preceding two months would have been likely to tire someone in perfect health. Having successfully completed all of these social and professional obligations, Lili was now totally exhausted. Because of her lack of resistance,

Figure 30. Lili Boulanger in the living room of 36 rue Ballu (1913).

she also became ill during December. Nadia had gone to Russia to give joint recitals with Raoul Pugno, and on Saturday, January 3, 1914, emotional pain was added to Lili's physical suffering: a telegram reached Mme Boulanger and Lili telling them that Raoul Pugno had died in Moscow. Nadia returned to France, and the body of Raoul Pugno was brought back on January 13. The funeral and interment were set for the following day. Lili was quite ill. She could not accompany the mourners to Gargenville for the interment, but she did attend the service in the nearby Église de la Trinité. Nevertheless, it upset her still more that she was unable to be present at the interment of her dear friend, a fact she recorded in her journal that day.[29]

Although no one was aware of it, Nadia had contracted a mild case of measles. For her, this was not serious. But it nearly proved fatal for Lili, who caught the disease from her and almost died of the severe complications she suffered as a result.[30] By early January, Lili's medical problems included a reactivation of her gastrointestinal difficulties and severe liver congestion. These were treated

Figure 31. Cover of the first edition of *Faust et Hélène*. The letters are in gold leaf and red against a black background. The composer's logo (see chapter 6) is centered at the bottom.

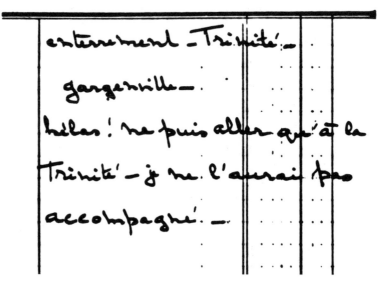

Figure 32. Page from Lili Boulanger's daybook, showing the entry for the day of Raoul Pugno's interment.

by Dr. Paul Chiron, a friend and former student of Dr. Parenteau.[31]

The statutes of the French Academy in Rome (i.e., the Villa Medici, where Lili would be staying during her period as a *pensionnaire* of the French government), required her to arrive in Rome by the end of January at the latest.[32] On January 20, however, a certificate from Dr. Chiron was sent to the Institut. It attested to the fact that he had been treating Lili Boulanger since mid-December, and, although her condition had improved, she was still suffering from a very severe case of anemia and would be too weak to travel for at least twenty days.[33]

At its next meeting, the Académie des Beaux-Arts considered the case of Lili Boulanger. She had asked the Under-Secretary of State to grant her a delay until the twentieth of February. There was no objection to this by the members of the Academy. It was clearly a matter of health, and an exception was made in her case.[34]

Rumors about Lili Boulanger were already beginning to circulate. As reported by a French writer in Rome early in 1914, there was considerable speculation.

It really seemed that she might be frightened away in advance. At least so the rumor about it ran here early in the year when the "stars" [the new winners] were seen to arrive from Paris without her, though the regulation demands that they make the trip together, and by prearranged stages. One month, two months went by. Mlle Lili Boulanger did not arrive. It was said that she was ill. A real illness, or . . . [sic] diplomatic?

To believe all this gossip, the young *pensionnaire* tried to obtain from the Institut, sovereign guardian of the French Academy in Rome, authorization either not to stay in the Villa —and, in this case, she would have taken an apartment in the city with her mother—or to share with her mother the bedroom that was meant for her. Both the one solution and the other being forbidden by the regulations, the Institut had to refuse this authorization. There was talk then of the possible resignation of Mlle Lili Boulanger.[35]

Those who had seen the records would have known the truth of the matter, but, of course, the majority of those who had heard the rumors had no access to anything more official than their neighbor's opinion. The longer Lili Boulanger delayed her arrival in Rome, the more such rumors were going to increase and spread. It is very probable that some of the unpleasantness Lili later suffered in Rome was at least indirectly due to the residual psychological effect of such unfounded gossip.

Proof that Lili was both weak and sick during this period can be found, again, in two letters to Miki Piré. The first, postmarked December 6, 1913, is a very short note, thanking Miki. With it, Lili enclosed two pressed Parma violets, her favorite flower. The reason for a thank-you note at this point is unclear, but the signs are absolutely unmistakable. Lili was already exhausted when she wrote it. There is less control in the handwriting, which lacks its usual uniform size and precision. The letter is written in very faint pencil, as if even holding a pencil were a great effort for her. Not only are there no amenities in this letter—no date, no place— but the envelope has, again, been addressed by someone else, in this instance Lili's former teacher and close friend Georges Caussade.[36]

Despite her weakness, Lili continued her strenuous round of activities for more than a week beyond this. During her attack of measles, when complications had begun to develop, she had been unable to write Miki. Later, a hasty note to her friend revealed a second bout of fever. Since the letter mentions the fact that she had been forbidden to read or write—probably out of fear of weakening her eyes while they were already weak from the measles —this note may even have been sent to Miki surreptitiously. Fortunately for Lili, this second attack of fever was not so serious as the first. This is evident in her handwriting, which, although in pencil, is much stronger and more certain than in the first note. But, again, some of Lili's customary care is lacking: there is no date or place indicated, and the letter itself is written on the back of a scrap of paper that had been used to advertise the December 10 banquet and soirée.[37]

After all that Lili had been through during December and January, even February did not yet find her fully recovered. She had asked the Academy only for a delay until February 20. In December that had seemed a reasonable length of time to her doctor. But Lili's strength did not return soon enough to enable her to leave Paris in time to arrive in Rome by the twentieth of February. A notation in Nadia's handwriting on the cover of a program given by the Société Chorale d'Amateurs indicates that Lili and Mme Boulanger were leaving at eight o'clock that same day for Rome.[38]

Even at this point Lili was not well enough to make the long trip to Rome without stopovers. Consequently, she and Mme Boulanger had arranged to stay with Miki Piré in Nice until Lili was strong enough to continue her journey. This took more time than might otherwise have been expected. Lili, weak and uncomfortable, was not able to leave Nice until early March.[39]

Before Lili and Mme Boulanger left on the next leg of their journey, Nadia had time to join them in Nice for a few days' visit.[40]

It was during her stay in Nice that Lili began to work on a new project—one that had interested her for some time. Miki Piré had brought a copy of *Tristesses,* a collection of poetry by Francis Jammes,[41] to Lili when she had last visited her in Paris. As soon as she had read it, Lili decided she wanted to set these poems to music as a song cycle.[42] She not only appreciated the poems themselves, but also felt a sense of identification with the heroine. For Lili Boulanger this grew into a feeling of "fusion between the young girl evoked by Francis Jammes . . . and herself."[43]

However, Lili felt that the title *Tristesses* was too somber. She contacted Francis Jammes for permission to use the title of another collection of his poems that had appeared in the same volume, and from which the whole volume had taken its name, *Clairières dans le Ciel.* The poet had consented, and Lili was already at work on the song cycle.[44]

Figure 33. Lili Boulanger with Miki Piré in the garden of the latter's home in Nice (winter 1914).

From Nice, Lili and Mme Boulanger continued on to Florence. All Prix de Rome winners were required, by order of the Academy, to present themselves to the authorities in Florence before completing the final part of their trip to Rome, and Lili was no exception.[45] After a few days at the Hotel Baglioni in Florence, Lili and her mother left for Rome, but not before Lili had written to Miki describing her delight in the city of Florence and her ardent desire to visit this beautiful place again as soon as possible. The note is written on a postcard of the Pitti Palace, and also contains the statement that Lili and Mme Boulanger were supposed to leave Florence on the milk train the following day. They expected to arrive in Rome about six hours later. There seemed to be some confusion, however, in the train information they were receiving from various sources. What they had been told in Nice did not correspond to what they were told in Florence.[46] Conflicting schedules and their attendant problems may explain why Lili Boulanger did not actually complete her move into the Villa Medici until March 12.

For months, rumors about Lili Boulanger had been circulating within the French colony in Rome. Her extremely late arrival did nothing at all to squelch these whisperings. Some people had even become a bit skeptical about Lili herself. Her adaptability to life at the Villa Medici, her mental attitude toward the rules and regulations of the Academy, and the truth of her declarations about the state of her health had all been called into question through the constant and ever-increasing gossip about her. Besides, it was absolutely unheard-of for a *pensionnaire* to come to the Villa Medici accompanied by a parent. Such a thing had never been done before in the Academy's history!

With this psychological climate, it is no wonder that Albert Besnard, the director of the Villa, found Lili Boulanger not at all to his liking when she first arrived. Public opinion had conditioned him to react in just this way. Nor had any official communications from his superiors in France been explicit enough or explained the situation fully enough to permit him to form any other judgment about Lili Boulanger and her actions. The only extant communication from the Ministry of Public Instruction in the Archives of the Villa Medici that concerns Lili Boulanger is a terse letter, dated January 31, 1914. It merely states that, because of her health, Lili Boulanger had just been granted permission not to leave Paris until February 16. Since the letter does not give any further details, it sheds no light on the state of Lili's health. From this, Besnard could not possibly have known what it was that kept Lili from arriving on time, thus adding still more speculation, and perhaps a bit more credence to the opinion that her illness was feigned rather than real.[47]

Lili Boulanger's arrival in Rome on March 9, 1914, is attested to in the records of the Villa Medici by Paul Girette, the General Secretary of the French Academy in Rome.[48] But she appears not to have completed her transferral to the Villa itself until the twelfth. On March 13, Albert Besnard wrote a scathing letter to the President of the Academy in Paris, detailing what he felt were Lili's transgressions—or, rather, deviations from the rules and regulations laid down by the Academy. This letter very clearly shows that Besnard had accepted certain rumors as fact, and then based most of his objections to the conduct of Lili and of Mme Boulanger on this "fact."

Mme Boulanger was, undoubtedly, trying to do her utmost to protect Lili. But Besnard felt threatened by this presence of a third party in his dealings with Lili. As a team, he felt they could resist his authority, and, in addition, he believed that the Boulangers did not take the rules of the Academy seriously. Besnard assumed as fact the rumor that Mme Boulanger had wanted to stay at the Villa Medici with Lili. Bitterly resenting what he regarded as the special treatment Mme Boulanger requested for Lili, he objected violently to the President of the Academy that it was not fair, and would set a horrible precedent.

Mme Boulanger had contracted for the services of a chambermaid for Lili,[49] and Besnard opposed what he considered this intrusion of outside personnel into his domain, especially when it was also a question of Lili Boulanger's maid's serving her dinner in her room. What bothered him above all was that he believed Lili was quite well; at all events she looked fine to him. He assured the Academy that, if she were really sick, these evidences of special treatment would not concern him unduly, but here it was the desire of Mme Boulanger to have her daughter receive favors from the administration—favors to which he believed Lili was not entitled—that had upset him.[50]

As for Besnard's objections to Lili's eating alone in her room, they were in conformity with the letter of the law as dictated by the Academy. The rule was explicit. "During their stay in Rome, the pensionnaires are obliged to live in the palace of the Academy and to take their meals there at a common dining table."[51] There seems to have been considerable misunderstanding, however, in the matter of the maid. Besnard believed that he should be able to control her comings and goings, but felt almost powerless to act at all without the approval, in advance, of the Academy, for whatever he might choose to do. Even though she would not live at the Villa herself, he felt that an outside maid did not belong there at all hours of the day and night. He reported to the Academy that both Lili and Mme Boulanger had told him that the Academy itself had devoted a meeting to deciding whether to grant special permission for a maid for Lili, and that they did, in fact, decide in her favor.[52]

By March 15 Lili had written her first letter to Miki Piré from the Villa Medici. It was a comparatively short letter, but in

it Lili expressed her regrets at not being able—or so she believed—
to write in so polished a literary style as her friend. Some day, she
was afraid, Miki would grow tired of her and her letters. If a week
went by without a letter from Miki, Lili would know that Miki
no longer wanted to hear from her and would stop writing too.
The rather depressed tone of this note, coupled with the fact that
it is written in pencil, seems to indicate that Lili was not in very
good health and spirits when she wrote it.[53]

This conclusion is supported by other evidence. In a letter to
Besnard dated Friday, March 20, Lili explains why she is unable
to see the Director that day as he had requested. She was still too
ill to get out of bed. According to her letter, she had asked her
mother to speak to M. Besnard the preceding day to ask for a few
things she considered necessary. (Apparently Lili was completely
unaware of Besnard's antipathy to her mother.) Mme Boulanger
had not found M. Besnard at the office or at home, and finally went
to the wife of M. Girette, the General Secretary of the Villa Medici.
After having transmitted Lili's message to Mme Girette, Mme
Boulanger had to leave. Lili closes her letter with thanks for M.
Besnard's offer to call in the doctor for her—the Villa Medici had
its own staff physician—but declines it because, for the moment
at least, she is feeling a bit better. Undoubtedly all of Lili's decisions and her actions with regard to Besnard were entered into
in complete ignorance of any ill will on his part. But everything
she did up to that point could only further provoke someone
already skeptical about her. After all, first she said she was too ill
to see him, then she refused to see the doctor. Not knowing any
real reason behind this refusal, he could only conclude that she
was simulating illness. This letter, too, is written in pencil.[54]

Once again the case of Lili Boulanger was considered by the
Académie des Beaux-Arts. At its meeting on March 21, 1914, the
members discussed the circumstances surrounding her arrival at
the Villa Medici, as reported to them in M. Besnard's letter. Most
members of the Academy were of the opinion that it was really
a question of internal discipline, and, as such, was up to the Director to settle. They did say, however, that because women were
now admitted to the Villa, there was no reason why chambermaids
could not be provided for them.[55] M. Dagnan-Bouveret, the artist
who was then President of the Academy, took it upon himself to
write to M. Besnard, to tell him of the consensus that had been
reached on this matter, and to assure him of the Academy's support
for whatever he might choose to do as a result.[56]

Meanwhile, Lili's health remained extremely precarious. By

Thursday the twenty-sixth she had written again to Miki Piré. After apologizing for not writing for more than a week, she assured her friend that this omission was purely the result of illness, not of deliberate neglect of her promise to write. For the last nine days, Lili said, she had been suffering from a fever. The constant coughing and sneezing it had brought with it had made it impossible for her to do anything more than lie in bed and think unhappily about her present condition, her life in general, and her broken promise to Miki. This letter has a deeply melancholic mood, as if Lili's new health problems had led her close to despair. The mood is very similar to that of her letters from Berck, and the remedy is the same, too—frequent long letters from Miki to ease her boredom in her present state of inactivity. This letter is addressed to Miki in Paris, where she was staying with Nadia at 36 rue Ballu, and is sealed in gold wax with Ernest Boulanger's signet ring with its motto "tout arrive," which Lili had taken with her to the Villa Medici.

Undoubtedly part of Lili's enforced inactivity at this point stemmed from the location of her room in the Villa Medici. Her bedroom and studio, familiarly known as the "Etruscan Tomb" because of the sloping walls, were located on the fourth floor of the Villa. Even for someone who was in good health, this was quite a climb up and down a seemingly interminable, winding, and dimly lit stone staircase. It is not surprising, therefore, that Lili, who tired easily, would be able to leave her suite only when she was feeling relatively well. Even so, she later confided to Miki that if it had not been for the stone benches set in little niches midway between floor levels, she would never have been able to go up or down the stairs at all.[58]

In addition to the climb, simply leaving her rooms might have been risky for Lili unless she was in reasonably good health. The Baroque structure of the Villa Medici, with its high ceilings and stone interior walls and floors, retains both moisture and cold, and its corridors seem damp and a bit drafty even in the summer. Lili had decorated her walls with hangings that minimized the draft, and had even put up a heavy drapery in the doorway between the bedroom and her workroom, but these amenities did not exist in the other rooms of the Villa. Leaving her own rooms before she was strong enough might have proved too much of a shock to her system.

On March 28, M. Dagnan-Bouveret read to the meeting of the Académie des Beaux-Arts a copy of the letter he had sent to M. Besnard at the Villa Medici. After congratulating M. Besnard

Figure 34. Salon of Lili Boulanger's suite in the Villa Medici (spring 1914). *Photo by Nadia Boulanger.*

on the way he had strengthened discipline at the Villa during his tenure in office, the letter reflects the Academy's astonishment at Besnard's reaction to the arrival of Lili Boulanger. Certainly, they felt, the violence of his response was out of keeping with the situation itself. Lili Boulanger had been there such a short time when he wrote that letter that he could not possibly know for himself what the facts were, the President wrote. The Academy had been thunderstruck by his request for support in such circumstances. The letter then went into the matter of the chambermaids. It was certainly reasonable, they had concluded, to have one or two on the staff of the Villa itself so that young lady *pensionnaires* would not have to suffer the impropriety of having male servants in their rooms. In fact, the Academy had seen this idea as a distinct improvement, one that would permit the administration of the Villa to function more effectively.[59] Furthermore, as far as Lili's health was concerned, M. Dagnan-Bouveret told M. Besnard that the Academy knew for a fact that until the age of sixteen Lili had been sick almost constantly, that her health had forced her to write her prizewinning cantata in bed at Compiègne the year before, and that it was also because of illness that she had been unable to arrive at the Villa Medici with the rest of the prizewinners of 1913. They advised M. Besnard that infractions of the rules were entirely warranted in this one case, and said they believed that his own authority would not be undermined by ignoring a few necessary irregularities. At no time, however, M. Dagnan-Bouveret wrote, had the Academy deliberated on the question of granting permission to Lili Boulanger to have a personal maid at the Villa. All they had considered, he reiterated, was granting her the right to remain in Paris until February rather than leaving in December.[60] In most of the matters under discussion, therefore, the Academy supported Lili Boulanger rather than Albert Besnard, its own representative in Rome.

Meanwhile, Lili had remained in her room ever since moving into the Villa Medici. As she wrote to Miki Piré on March 30, she was almost over her cold but had stayed in her bedroom for the last three days anyway, to avoid any problems that might have resulted from going out too soon. Lili was glad that Miki was in Paris staying with Nadia. She was worried about how alone Nadia must have been feeling and, with Miki there, she would undoubtedly feel much less so. Lili actively hated her illness, which she said had kept her from seeing anything of Rome up to that point.[61]

It is probable that Lili continued to work whenever she could throughout the time of her illness in Rome. Her letter of March 26 to Miki Piré had been written on music manuscript paper, indicating that she must have kept some handy at all times.[62]

Two of Lili's compositions that seem to have disappeared or been destroyed by her—one for cello and piano, the other for oboe and piano—may also date from this period.[63] They were written during 1914, but neither sketches for them nor any trace of the completed works themselves appears to have survived. Lili is known to have worked on *Clairières dans le Ciel, Vieille Prière Bouddhique,* and a setting of Psalm 130 while she was in Rome, but there are no sketches for any of them dating from 1914. However, in an unnumbered composition notebook that begins with studies for *Faust et Hélène,* there are also fragments of settings of Psalm 130, a Kyrie, and Psalm 126. This indicates that Lili took the workbook with her to Compiègne for the final round of the Prix de Rome competition, used it for some initial sketches for *Faust et Hélène,* and continued to use it thereafter as a workbook.[64]

The Variations for Piano, written in 1914, may, in fact, have been begun early during her stay at the Villa Medici. The original manuscript entitled *Morceau pour piano. Thème et Variations*

Figure 35. Charcoal sketch of Lili Boulanger by Jean Dupas (1914).
Photo: M. Tamvico, Paris.

ends with the indication, "Finished Friday the 12th, Copied Saturday the 13th."[65] In 1914 the only month during which there was a Friday falling on the twelfth of the month was June. Therefore the piece must have been finished Friday, June 12, 1914.

Two of Lili's other short works for piano solo were written during her stay at the Villa Medici in 1914—*D'un Jardin Clair* and *D'un Vieux Jardin*. No sketches or autograph manuscripts of these works appear to have survived, however.[66] Nor is there any precise indication of exactly when Lili wrote them.[67]

After recovering from a long bout of illness, Lili Boulanger finally began to enjoy many of the advantages made possible by the Prix de Rome. She established warm friendships with a number of her colleagues, two of whom—Pierre Bodard and Jean Dupas—made portraits of her. Pierre Bodard's oil painting of Lili Boulanger is still in the possession of the Villa Medici, and, on the reverse side, there is the following ink inscription: "To my dear little companion Lily [sic] Boulanger, in warm memory of deep admiration and understanding friendship."[68] In accordance with the traditions of the Villa Medici, this portrait was hung in the common dining room, along with the portraits of the others who had been *pensionnaires* of the Academy in Rome since its inception.[69] The charcoal sketch of Lili Boulanger by Jean Dupas was completed in April 1914.[70]

After her health returned somewhat, Lili entered into a period of intense activity during that spring. The Count and Countess de San Martino e Valperga, friends of the Boulanger family from the time they had spent in Paris, were also in Rome at that time. Lili saw them there, as well as Count Joseph Primoli. The Count had a famous salon "where all the artists, from the oldest to the youngest, were received and met all of Roman society."[71]

Among Lili Boulanger's other friends at the Villa Medici were the sculptor Louis Lejeune, the engraver Jules Piel, the architect Roger Séassal, and the composers Claude Delvincourt and Paul Paray. The Boulangers had known the Delvincourt family for many years, but the others were new friends. Roger Séassal became a close friend, as did Louis Lejeune. The other *pensionnaires* also made Lili feel welcome, and her old nickname, "Little Sister," followed her even to the Villa Medici. Her fellow artists acted toward Lili with warmth and genuine concern for her well-being.[72]

Lili had a charismatic personality. Even today those who were colleagues of hers at the Villa still remember her with affection and admiration. Paul Paray, who knew her rather briefly in Rome, says: ". . . I remember her as an exquisite fellow-student, very gifted, with a brilliant career in composition ahead of her."[73] Jules Piel met Lili during the spring of 1914, when Nadia, the Bouwens, and Georges Caussade were in Rome visiting her. He, too, remembers her ingratiating ways, but comments that she was already in pain at that time.[74]

Lili's friends in Rome included two churchmen. One, the aged Swiss Archbishop Monseigneur Jacquet, first met the young composer in Rome. He developed a strong paternal interest in Lili, whose devoutness he admired. The other, Père Arthur, a Dominican priest, had known Lili and her family in Paris before he went to Rome. He continued to be a close friend of Lili even after

Figure 36. Mme Boulanger, Nadia, and Lili with M. and Mme Bouwens and their daughter Hélène in Rome (spring 1914). *Photo by Georges Caussade.*

she returned to France, was her Confessor, and was a frequent visitor both at the Boulanger's apartment in Paris and at their home in Gargenville.[75] When Lili was unable to see them in person, she corresponded with them.

Even months after her arrival in Rome, Lili Boulanger continued to be the object of speculation and gossip. No one had explained—either privately to M. Besnard or publicly—the reasons behind her seemingly peculiar behavior. New rumors and half-truths were circulating, based on both putative events before her arrival and the apparently inexplicable actions and attitudes of both Mme Boulanger and Lili afterwards. Comparisons were made between her conduct and that of Mlle Lucienne Heuvelmans, and some rather snide rumors even intimated that the Director of the Villa had quite simply bowed to the pressure exerted on him by the Boulangers.

Mlle Heuvelmans's induction into the Villa Medici was accomplished in the simplest way possible. . . . The only revolution brought about by her arrival was . . . the adding of a chambermaid to the domestic personnel of the Villa. . . . Since January 1912, Mlle Heuvelmans lived in the Villa Medici. She lived

106

there like a good fellow, if I may say so, on an equal footing and in perfect camaraderie with those young men with whom her talent made her an equal. . . . They called her just "Heuvelmans." . . . And, since tradition called for the familiar "tu" form to be used among the *pensionnaires*, Mlle Heuvelmans found it natural to be addressed that way by her fellows and to address them that way from the first day.[76]

After explaining some of this familiarity by the fact that, after all, Mlle Heuvelmans had known many of these people before, when she herself was a student at the École des Beaux-Arts, the same reporter continues with his comparison:

It happened a bit differently for Mlle Boulanger . . . when she arrived this year at the Villa Medici. Her education, her habits, are more exclusively feminine, less boyish, if you will, than those of Mlle Heuvelmans.

Add to this that Mlle Lili Boulanger is barely twenty. And you will understand that the induction into the Villa Medici really constituted what I would call a transplantation for her . . . . A certain problem of the "private" chambermaid that Mlle Lili Boulanger was very keen on having with her night and day threatened to stay unresolved; worse yet, to degenerate into a quarrel with the administration. . . . Happily, everything worked out. . . . Don't try to find out whether Lili Boulanger's personal chambermaid sleeps at the Villa or in the city. Be content to learn that this indispensable lady's maid is at her mistress's disposition in the morning, very early, as well as late at night, very late—and that, nevertheless, she is not officially lodged in the Villa. In such a case? . . . *combinazione,* sheer coincidence, you are told![77]

This suggestion of weakness on the part of the Director undoubtedly did nothing to reconcile Besnard to the Boulangers. Besides, it was well known all over the French colony in Rome that Mme Boulanger continued to live nearby. More than that, rumor had it that she went to the Villa "regularly, three and even four times a day to visit her daughter."[78] That Madame Boulanger always arrived in a carriage was considered worthy of note by the gossips, too.[79]

Lili's health, also, remained a subject for speculation. With no real information to go on, many continued to question whether her illness was physical or psychosomatic. Lili's strong desire to conceal the nature and extent of her suffering from almost everyone—an attitude she had had even as a child—intensified the mystery surrounding her.

107

Figure 37. Luncheon party in the gardens of the Villa Medici (spring 1914). Diners include Albert Besnard, Paul Girette, Lili, Nadia, and Mme Ernest Boulanger, Claude Delvincourt, Jacques Débat-Ponsan, Lucienne Heuvelmans, Pierre Bodard, Jules Piel, Roger Séassal, Jean Dupas, and Louis Lejeune.

It happens, too, that the gracious musician Lili Boulanger does not make her appearance at the common dining table: it is evident that an unendurable migraine headache keeps her in her room, and so ill, so ill, that you knock in vain at her door to ask her how she is feeling. . . .

Mlle Lili Boulanger, nevertheless, most often shares her meals with her fellows as the rule requires . . . when she and her mother invite all the *pensionnaires* to dinner . . . in a restaurant![80]

Despite these rumors, Lili Boulanger remained at the Villa Medici and continued her work. During the month of June she completed a salon piece for violin and piano entitled *Cortège*. This was dedicated to her friend Yvonne Astruc.

From Lili's point of view, her troubles with M. Besnard stemmed from the fact, or so she thought, that Mme Besnard did not like her.[81] Although this may seem strange, actually it is explicable. Lili Boulanger had no reason to suspect that the director had not been apprised of her illness, or, for that matter, that he believed she was feigning illness to wrest special favors from the Academy. Normally, in such a situation, the wife of this man would have interceded with him on Lili's behalf. Since she did not, Lili concluded that Mme Besnard was cold to her and not interested in helping her in any way.

Meanwhile, the heat of the Roman summer had begun to be oppressive. It became torrid at the Villa. There were problems with the exposed drainage system at the Villa Medici, and, added to the heat, the improper drainage produced some rather unpleasant odors. On June 6 one of Lili's fellow-*pensionnaires*, Lucienne Heuvelmans, begged M. Girette to have something done about this problem. As far as she was concerned, the smell from the open drainage system was an affront to passersby, as was the stench emitted by the cesspool in hot weather. With wit and obvious sincerity, she pleaded the case for a clean cesspool and an underground drainage system.[82] She had written to the General Secretary because M. Besnard had already returned to France for the summer.

Even Lili's detractors recognized the charismatic effect she produced and the attractiveness of her personality to others. One reporter of scandal even went so far as to admit that "her exquisite good grace, her engaging manner proper to a refined Parisienne, and at the same time her perfect education have long ago conquered everyone in the big house."[83]

In a letter to M. Girette, written from Paris on June 25, Besnard says that Lili Boulanger, unable to secure his approval for her plans, had sent a telegram to the Academy in Paris asking to have her case heard by them, and promising to return to Rome as soon thereafter as possible. M. Besnard further states that a telegram was sent by the Academy in reply, saying that "the Director is always right" and he tells Girette that this puts an end to the whole matter. Furthermore, he blames the entire incident on Mme Boulanger and what he considers her desire to force the administration of the Villa Medici to accede to her wishes. A careful search of the records of the Académie reveals no record of either telegram.[84] It can only be inferred, therefore, that M. Besnard was letting his personal antipathy to Mme Boulanger get the better of him, and that he was determined, at any cost, to oppose her in all possible ways.

Only five days later, M. Girette was in the process of writing his fifth report to the Director since M. Besnard's departure from the Villa. A partial rough copy of it states that M. Girette had indeed granted Lili Boulanger permission to leave the Villa

Medici. The reason he gave was a study-trip through the north of Italy, and she was to be there from July 1 to July 30. According to this rough draft, he had carefully explained to Mlle Boulanger that this authorization to travel in Italy did not give her the right to return to France. Girette further reported that Mme and Mlle Boulanger were about to leave. In addition, the General Secretary indicated that a copy of this statement was to be sent to M. Besnard in Paris informing him, also, that Lili Boulanger's permission to leave the Villa had been granted in his name.[85] Whether this is an exact duplicate of the report that actually reached M. Besnard, or whether any modifications were made in it before it was sent to him cannot be determined.

No records have come to light that reveal exactly what happened to change the situation, but after Lili Boulanger left the Villa Medici on the first day of July,[86] she continued on through northern Italy to Nice. A telegram that she sent to M. Girette in Rome requests him to telegraph her her stipend for the month of July. The address she gave was that of Miki Piré in Nice.[87] It was during this stay in Nice that Lili completed her *Clairières dans le Ciel*.[88]

Lili found living in Rome a very exciting experience. She loved the Villa Medici itself. Her fondness for flowers and plants contributed to this feeling—her bedroom overlooked the gardens of Trinità dei Monti, and her workroom had a fine view of the magnificent gardens of the Villa itself. The gentle sound of water splashing in the fountain of the Villa Medici garden was an added attraction.[89] While in Nice, she described as many details as she could to Miki Piré, and finished by showing her the excellent photographs of her rooms at the Villa that Nadia had taken when she was there that spring.[90]

Lili had returned to France to relax, and from Nice she, Mme Boulanger, and Miki Piré went on to Paris, and then to Gargenville. At the end of July, Lili was preparing to rest from the rigors of the preceding months in the security and pleasant rural atmosphere of Hanneucourt, surrounded by her relatives and closest friends.

On August 3, 1914, a full mobilization for war against Germany was ordered by General Joffre. This action came as a complete shock, and was totally unexpected by the general public. Enormous tension and apprehension were generated by this turn of events. Miki Piré left almost immediately to be with her family in Nice, but not before she and Lili had exchanged keepsakes. Miki gave Lili her Russian baptismal cross, with its Russian in-

Figure 38. View of the Villa Medici fountain and gardens from Lili Boulanger's salon (spring 1914). *Photo by Nadia Boulanger.*

scription meaning "save and protect," and Lili gave Miki a small oval jade-and-gold locket with an Arabic inscription. Lili was extremely fond of the locket, although she did not know what the inscription itself meant.[91] Not knowing whether the circumstances of war would ever allow them to meet again, Miki Piré sent Lili a portrait photograph of herself that had been taken in Nice. On it she had written a simple but affecting declaration of her continued warm friendship for Lili in a time when the rest of the world they both knew was in a frightening state of flux.[92]

Shortly after M. Besnard and his family left Rome in June, Mme Boulanger and Lili, as well as most of the other *pensionnaires,* left the Villa Medici. By August 2 all the male *pensionnaires* and M. Girette had been mobilized, leaving the Villa empty except for the servants.[93]

Upon his return to Rome, M. Besnard was furious. Girette had left no written explanation giving reasons for the early departure, *en masse,* of the male *pensionnaires.* Furthermore, since none of them had had the courtesy to pay M. Besnard the prescribed visit before leaving, he came to the conclusion that they had been induced to leave early, and without permission, by the

Boulangers. On October 18, in a letter to Henri Roujon, Permanent Secretary of the Académie des Beaux-Arts in Paris, Besnard deplores these events and the infractions of the rules that they indicate. He sharply informs M. Roujon that, for the reasons he had given, he himself had not the slightest idea where the *pensionnaires* had gone, and requests M. Roujon to tell him whether Mlles Boulanger and Heuvelmans were thinking of returning to the Villa. Besnard was asking the Secretary this question, he said, because he was certain that M. Roujon must have seen the Boulangers socially in Paris (where Besnard was sure the rest of the *pensionnaires* had followed them). M. Roujon would therefore have more reason to know the Boulangers' plans than he, Besnard, would.[94]

The truth of M. Besnard's charges against the Boulangers is impossible to substantiate or refute on the basis of presently available data, but it does seem that his already negative attitude toward the family had been increasing, and that the lack of explicit written records led him to expect the worst of them.

By October 1914 the *pensionnaires* were widely scattered with their various units. They tried to keep in touch with each other by mail. Some of them expressed serious concern over their future status after discharge from the armed forces. The Académie des Beaux-Arts ruled on October 10 that, as a matter of policy, those who were not mobilized could return to the Villa Medici to complete the unexpired period covered by their awards.[95] In January of 1915 the Minister of Finance ruled that the French government would continue to withhold until the end of the war all monetary payments to *pensionnaires,* with the exception of M. Débat-Ponsan who by then was demobilized, and whose *pension* had only four more months to run as of September first, when the stipends had been suspended.[96]

On January 28, 1915, M. Besnard informed the Academy that, in accordance with the authorization he had received from the Institut, he had written to Mlles Heuvelmans and Boulanger, giving them permission to return to the Villa Medici.[97] However, neither Lili Boulanger nor Lucienne Heuvelmans returned to the Villa during 1915.

During 1915 Lili Boulanger devoted herself mainly to the French war effort. Miki Piré had begun to work in Nice at the Hôpital du Grand-Hôtel, nursing the war wounded. Lili visited her there in September.[98]

Knowing that she did not have the stamina for that type of work, Lili decided to offer her services in another capacity. From her correspondence with some of her former colleagues at the Villa Medici, she realized that one of the greatest needs felt by the men in the trenches was the moral support to be maintained through continuing communication with those at home. She therefore began an extensive program of correspondence with her friends who had been mobilized. To some she wrote letters, to others she sent packages, and to still others she offered her assistance in keeping alive their intellectual and artistic interests. Jules Piel, for example, who had been a Prix de Rome winner in engraving but who was intensely interested in music and was an amateur violinist, relates that in 1915 Lili was kind enough to correct by mail the harmony lessons that he had been working on in the trenches.[99]

When she realized the potential scope of this activity, Lili decided to organize a committee so that all former members of the composition classes at the Conservatoire could enjoy this same type of communication among themselves. She and Nadia spent months bringing this project to fruition. In the process they sought and obtained the patronage of a famous American architect and member of the Institut de France, Whitney Warren, who agreed to serve as president of this new *Comité Franco-Américain du Conservatoire National*.[100] Blair Fairchild, formerly of the United States legation in Teheran, had been on leave in Europe when the war broke out. In addition to his holding a post in the diplomatic corps, he was a respected composer—in fact, he was later to leave diplomacy in order to devote himself to composition.[101] He acted as treasurer of the new group. Both Blair Fairchild and his wife became, in the course of the war, close friends of the Boulangers.[102]

This preliminary organizational work was both time-consuming and fatiguing. Nevertheless Lili managed to engage in other activities as well during this hectic period. On March 25 she directed a performance of *Faust et Hélène* as part of a program given by the Association des Grands Concerts.[103]

Lili frequently made lists of things to do, and a few of these are still extant. In addition to attesting to her logical, orderly approach to life in general, they shed some light on the way she worked. One such list survives from the period beginning April 20, 1915. According to the list, Lili's first priority for April 20 through April 23 was the correction of material in the orchestral score of *Faust et Hélène*. After that followed corrections on the proofs of *Pour les Funérailles d'un Soldat*, *Les Sirènes*, and *Hymne au Soleil*.[104] Next on her list came the correction of errors in *Soir sur la Plaine* and *Reflets*.[105] Finally, she undertook to recopy a substantial number of works, beginning with *Le Retour* and continuing with twelve of the *Clairières dans le Ciel, Attente,* the song *La Source,*[106] *Morceau pour piano et flûte,*[107] *Berceuse pour piano et violon,*[108] and *Cinq Morceaux pour piano.*[109] Although Lili Boulanger does not seem to have been spending much time actually composing music during that period, she was certainly busy correcting the proofs of her earlier works and making fair copies of them, undoubtedly for future distribution to her publisher and to performers. Judging by the clarity and regularity of her handwriting on this list, as well as the fact that it is written in ink, Lili was feeling relatively well during this period.

Another reminder sheet of Lili's indicates that she was then working on corrections for *Renouveau*[110] as well as finishing those for *Pour les Funérailles d'un Soldat.*[111] The list also mentions that she was to take her *Hymne au Soleil* to Ricordi. It gives the names of some of the people with whom Lili was keeping in touch, including Roger Ducasse, Boutterin—one of her former colleagues at the Villa Medici—and Paul Paray, then a prisoner at Darmstadt. In addition to several other friends, there are the names of three doctors, Dr. Brocq, Dr. Chiron, and Dr. Blackman. Whether Lili was to see them as doctors or in a purely social capacity cannot be determined from this list.

Throughout the spring and summer of 1915, Lili continued her efforts on behalf of the mobilized students of the Conservatoire, and, in addition to her other activities, even found some time to devote to composition. The only entries dated 1915 in Lili's composition notebooks are for September 3, 4, and 12, when she was at "Les Maisonnettes." At those times she worked on sketches for her setting of Psalm 24.[112] Later in the same volume is an undated entry containing the bass line of *Du Fond de l'Abîme* (Psalm 130), which may also date from approximately the same period. Her only other composition for that year, *Pièce pour trompette et petit orchestre,* seems to have disappeared, and no sketches for it can now be found.[113]

By late September there was enough support for the Conservatoire branch of the Comité Franco-Américain so that Lili and Nadia could write a joint letter to the eminent French musicians and pedagogues Widor, Saint-Saëns, Fauré, Charpentier, Dubois, Paladilhe, and Vidal. In it the Boulanger sisters told them of Whitney Warren's patronage, described the proposed activities of the Committee, and asked them to permit their names to be used as an honorary committee.[114]

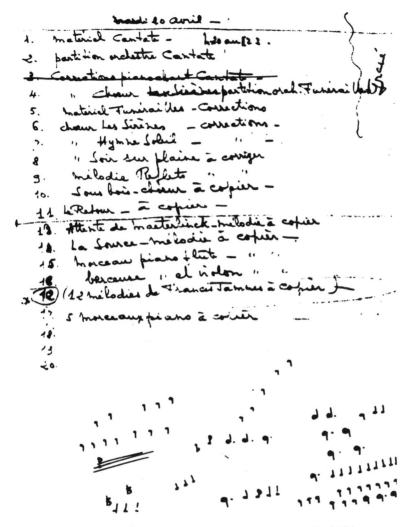

Figure 39. Lili Boulanger's *aide-mémoire* for April 1915.

One of the committee's projects was the establishment of a gazette, so that addresses could be made public and communications addressed to the group could be transmitted to them. Lili and Nadia worked up a circular to be typed and then mimeographed and sent to three hundred former students of the Conservatoire who were then serving in the French armed forces. In it they asked them for news of themselves, their addresses, and news of any of the others about whom they might have heard. The salutation, the date, part of the closing and the signature were to be filled in by hand, as were the envelopes.[115]

On November 7 *Pour les Funérailles d'un Soldat* was given its formal Paris premiere at the Concerts Colonne-Lamoureux under the direction of Gabriel Pierné.[116] Lili conducted the duet from *Faust et Hélène* as part of a benefit program for *L'École des Mutilés de Lyon, Le Vestiaire des Blessés,* on December 20. The honorary presidents of the organization were Pierre Loti and Mrs. William K. Vanderbilt, and the American Honorary Committee included Mr. and Mrs. Whitney Warren.[117]

December 1915 was important to Lili Boulanger for yet another reason. That month the first issue of the *Gazette des Classes de Composition du Conservatoire* was distributed to the mobilized students. Lili and Nadia were co-editors, and, judging from the delighted comments of those who answered their appeal for information, the whole project was a great success. M. Débat-Ponsan, who had already been discharged from service, did all the graphics for the issue. The gazette itself was not pretentious, but it served admirably the purpose for which it had been intended.[118] The famous French musicians with whom Nadia and Lili had communicated had agreed to lend their names to the project, and Charles-Marie Widor and Paul Vidal had even agreed to be active in the organization as Vice-Presidents. The *Gazette* closed with warm wishes for the Christmas season and the coming year, and was signed by Nadia and Lili Boulanger and Jacques Débat-Ponsan.

Lili continued her activities on behalf of the *Comité Franco-Américain.* She sent books and packages to the servicemen, and sometimes material assistance to their families. For the rest of her life she served as co-editor of the *Gazette.* Work of this kind necessitated a great volume of correspondence as well as a clear and well-organized method of procedure.[119]

By mid-February, the Académie des Beaux-Arts was considering the cases of Lili Boulanger and Lucienne Heuvelmans, both of whom had expressed a desire to return to the Villa Medici to work. There was a discussion about whether their stipends would still be suspended even if they did return.[120] On February 18 the Under-Secretary of State had written to the President of the Academy informing him that Mlles Heuvelmans and Boulanger had already been authorized to live at the Villa, but that no stipends would be paid. He had further notified them, he said, "that, even though their *pension* continues to be suspended, they will have to obey the Regulations to the letter."[121] This lack of stipend is understandable because, early in the war, the budget of the Villa

COMITÉ FRANCO-AMÉRICAIN

DU

CONSERVATOIRE NATIONAL DE MUSIQUE ET DE DÉCLAMATION

fondé sous le patronage de

M. WHITNEY WARREN, Membre de l'Institut

Paris le ____ 191__

14, RUE DE MADRID, 14

COMITÉ D'HONNEUR

MM. Camille SAINT-SAENS, Membre de l'Institut.
Gabriel FAURÉ, Membre de l'Institut, Directeur du Conservatoire.
Théodore DUBOIS, Membre de l'Institut, Directeur honoraire du Conservatoire.
Emile PALADILHE, Membre de l'Institut.
Gustave CHARPENTIER, Membre de l'Institut.
Ch.-M. WIDOR, Secrétaire perpétuel de l'Académie des Beaux-Arts, Professeur de Composition au Conservatoire.
Paul VIDAL, Professeur de Composition au Conservatoire.

COMITÉ ACTIF

Président :
M. Whitney WARREN, Membre de l'Institut.

Vice-Présidents :
MM. Ch.-M. WIDOR et Paul VIDAL, Professeurs de Composition au Conservatoire.

Trésorier :
M. Blair FAIRCHILD.

Secrétaires-Fondatrices :
Mlles Nadia et Lili BOULANGER, Grands Prix de Rome.

Les dons en espèces seront adressés à M. Blair FAIRCHILD, Trésorier du Comité Franco-Américain, Banque Lazard, 5, Rue Pillet-Will, Paris.

Pour les dons en nature et pour tous renseignements, prière de s'adresser à Mlles Nadia et Lili BOULANGER, au Conservatoire, 14, Rue de Madrid, Paris.

- - -

Figure 40. Rough draft of a letter written by Lili Boulanger in her capacity as Secretary-Founder of the Comité Franco-Américain, dated February 5, 1916.

had been suspended.[122] Therefore there would have been no money with which to pay the *pensionnaires*.

For several years Lili had wanted to use Maeterlinck's play *La Princesse Maleine* as the basis for an opera libretto. "One might have said that she identified herself with Maeterlinck's poor little heroine just as she had already felt a sense of union between herself and the young girl evoked by Francis Jammes in the 'Clairières.' "[123] Lili had decided that this was the right time to ask for Maeterlinck's permission. Before leaving Paris for her trip to Rome, she wrote to the playwright requesting an appointment

117

with him to discuss her project. On February 16 Maeterlinck had sent Lili the letter she had been waiting for—but it had been addressed to Rome. Only two days later, he sent Lili an edited version of the play containing his suggestions for cutting this extremely long drama to a more manageable size. Finally, having learned that she was going to be in Nice, staying with Miki Piré, Maeterlinck sent Lili another letter on February 20, inviting her to visit him with Tito Ricordi the next day at four o'clock.[124] By March 1 Lili was able to send Nadia a telegram announcing the good news that she and Maeterlinck had reached an agreement in principle.[125]

Even before leaving Paris Lili had not been well. By the time she left Nice for Rome, she still had not completely recovered.[126] Paul Claudel, then the French *Chargé de mission* in Rome, met both sisters at the Villa Medici[127] shortly after their arrival there in 1916. He wrote to his friend Darius Milhaud afterwards, urging him to win the Prix de Rome so that he could enjoy the advantages of life at the Villa Medici. There, he said, was where the Boulanger sisters were then living. "Lili had the Prix de Rome," the poet related. "Naturally she asked me for *La Jeune Fille Violaine*,[128] so that she could put it to music."[129] Later, Claudel denied vigorously to Milhaud that he had granted permission to the Boulangers to use this play, saying, "They asked me for it but, naturally, I refused. It is no more for them than for anyone else."[130]

Months of strenuous activity had taken their toll. By April 2, when she wrote to Miki, Lili had been at the Villa Medici for six weeks, but she had been ill and in bed most of the time. The problem was not so much pain as exhaustion, she told Miki. There was not so much pain as usual, but she was so spent that she could only stay out of bed for about an hour at the most, and even then the furthest she could go was to her window. She apologized to Miki for her long silence, explaining that she had not written out of a desire not to give her own unhappiness to her friend. So that Mme Boulanger would not be too upset, Lili told Miki, they[131] had decided not to tell her everything about Lili's new attack of illness. Above all, Lili was extremely distressed at the realization that she would never be able to complete the things she wanted to do. Recalling to Miki that every time she started a project, she was prevented from finishing it or at least suffered from the interminable delays that constantly impeded her progress, Lili told Miki that she was becoming extremely discouraged. But she hoped that Miki would find peace and happiness. She closed by asking Miki to thank Mme Piré for the letter Lili had received from her. Although she had answered it somewhat later than she thought she should have, Lili told Miki it was simply exhaustion that had kept her from being able to respond sooner.[132]

This time even M. Besnard realized that Lili was not well. After reporting the arrivals of Mlles Heuvelmans and Boulanger as well as that of M. Lejeune, he relates that Lili appeared to have caught a chill while out walking and had been in bed ever since. This illness appeared to him, he said, to be a combination of bronchitis and malaria. He thought that Dr. Marchia Fava might already have ordered Lili to leave Rome as soon as possible, feeling that it would not be good for her health to stay there. He further informed the Academy that Nadia was with Lili, giving her the best of care. Besnard added that he foresaw no immediate danger and that, in any case, his own wife could lend a hand if it became really necessary.[133] Mlle Heuvelmans, he said, had just undertaken a new project—"to make a bust of Mlle Boulanger. She will show this bust as part of her future *envois*,[134] when it will certainly be much admired, as much for its resemblance to its model as for its execution."[135] M. Besnard's rather skeptical attitude toward Lili seems not to have changed too much. Obviously Mme Boulanger was not the only one Lili had tried to keep from knowing the full details of her condition. And in Besnard's case, Lili had been completely successful—he had no real idea of the seriousness of her condition.

Years before, when Nadia was working with Raoul Pugno and Gabriele d'Annunzio on a musical setting for *La Ville Morte*, she had met Eleanora Duse. "This great tragedienne, having learned that L[ili] B[oulanger] was ill—even though she herself was already old and ill—went several times to see L. B., climbing up the four floors of the Villa and bringing her roses."[136] But Lili also had other visitors during this difficult period. Alfredo Casella, whom the Boulangers had known in Paris, had returned to his native Italy during the war. He often went to see Lili and told her "extraordinary and very amusing stories with a completely straight face."[137] Another visitor whom Lili had known from Paris—this time from a dinner party at the Bouwens' home—was the Russian war hero Peschkoff, the son of Maxim Gorky. He, too, went to see Lili when he was in Rome.[138]

Despite her poor health, Lili continued to work on a number of her compositions. During her stay in Rome she completed two major works, settings of Psalms 24 (*La Terre appartient à l'Éternel*) and 129 (*Ils m'ont assez opprimé*).[139] In them she poured out her anguish and torment. Even the opening words of Psalm 129 seem to mirror the tone of some of her letters to Miki. She had,

Figure 41. Terra cotta bust of Lili Boulanger by Lucienne Heuvelmans. *Photo: M. Tamvico, Paris.*

indeed, felt "sorely oppressed" since she was a child. Lili may also have continued to work on two other compositions, which were not completed until the following year—*Vieille Prière boud-dhique* and Psalm 130 (*Du Fond de l'Abîme*).

After she had recovered somewhat, Lili was able to go out a little in Rome with her mother and sister. They accompanied her one day that spring to an audience at the Vatican.[140]

Lili had been feeling for some time that her strength was leaving her. She insisted that Dr. Fava tell her how long she was

Figure 42. Lili Boulanger coming from an audience with the Pope in 1916. In the background are Mme Boulanger and Nadia Boulanger.

going to live and if there was any way she might survive long enough to finish *La Princesse Maleine*. Finally the doctor admitted to her that, in his opinion, she had no more than two years to live, that her condition had progressed too far to expect anything more. Lili did not tell either her mother or Nadia about the results of this consultation, in an attempt to keep the news from them as long as possible.[141] For the second time Lili had to leave the Villa Medici. Once again she stopped in Nice on the way home to visit Miki Piré, who was still working in the hospital, nursing the wounded. Miki sensed that Lili was troubled, and Lili finally confided the whole story to her friend.[142]

While in Nice, Lili again saw Maurice Maeterlinck. The letter he sent her, dated Wednesday, June 21, invites her to meet him that Friday to discuss further the work necessary on the *Princesse Maleine* libretto. A second letter, also addressed to Lili at the home of Mme Piré, tells of Maeterlinck's agreement with what Lili had done with his original play, and suggests that perhaps a few more cuts could be made. In these letters he is very solicitous about Lili's health. It may have been at this time that Maeterlinck gave Lili an autographed photograph of himself dedicated "To my dear little collaborator Lili Boulanger who, by order of the gods of music and destiny, is to give to the Princess Maleine the soul for which she has been waiting."[143]

By the twenty-sixth of June, Lili was back in Paris—this time staying with the Bouwens family at 2, rue de Lota. On Friday, June 30, she wrote to Miki explaining that she had been unable to write her before. Lili had been touched by the warm welcome that Miki and Mme Piré had given her in Nice, and she asked Miki to give Mme Piré her thanks for what she had done, because Lili was too exhausted to write two letters that day. She gave Miki a description of her trip to Paris, as Miki had asked her to do. Lili traveled from Nice to Paris lying down on the seat to minimize the effects of the trip, but even so, she said, those hours in the train had resulted in her being unable to eat any solid food since. The preceding Monday she had gone to see Dr. Marfin, who was, she reported, deeply disturbed about the state of her health. Finding her in very serious condition, he demanded that she exercise the greatest care. For the time being she was to make no trips to the country. He wanted to have Lili try a course of injections which, although it was still experimental, had proved beneficial in some cases. Dr. Marfin wanted to be in constant contact with the doctor who actually administered the treatment. In the meantime, Lili had either to stay in bed or to lie down. She was permitted only three quarters of an hour's ride in a carriage a day, and was forbidden to be on her feet for more than three minutes at a time. She was terribly unhappy about not being able to walk, but what upset her even more was that she had also been forbidden to work or to do anything that might tire her.[144] She even needed help getting dressed. That Wednesday she had seen another specialist, who decided to have her X-rayed before making any final decisions. The radiography was set for that Saturday afternoon, but the same morning the specialist was also going to conduct some tests of her nervous system. Lili did not enjoy these thoughts of what was to come, and asked Miki not to leave her without news. She was more and more in need of moral support from those dearest to her, Lili said. She closed asking to be remembered to Mme Piré and to Miki's younger sister Madeleine. This letter shows that Lili was far from well. Both the letter itself and the envelope are written in the faintest of pencil. The size of the handwriting is very inconsistent, as are the pressure and, consequently, the legibility of the letter.[145]

Meanwhile Lili had heard an unusual story. Through M.

Bouwens she had learned that the wife of one of his friends, M. Galéron, was blind, deaf, and mute. The couple had been married over thirty years, were very happy, had grown children, and Mme Galéron de Calone had also published a volume of poetry. Lili had been so impressed with the accomplishments of this extraordinary person, with all she had done in spite of her handicaps, that she determined to meet Mme Galéron de Calone. As soon as Lili was well enough to go out, she and Nadia went to see the Galéron family, and Lili asked Mme Galéron for permission to set one of her poems to music.[146] It was this work—first called "La Sombre tristesse" and later "Dans l'immense Tristesse"—that Lili completed in Gargenville on August 24, 1916.[147]

Lili worked on several other compositions during 1916, but none of them seems to have survived. One, the Sonata for Violin and Piano, was never completed. The *Sicilienne, Marche Gaie,* and *Marche Funèbre* appear to have been lost or destroyed.[148]

By September 6, when Lili wrote from Gargenville to Miki, she was feeling much better. Her enthusiasm for life had returned with her strength, and she was delighted to let Miki know that she felt as if she was beginning to live again. The mood is entirely different from that which her letters projected during her months of illness. The tone is very optimistic. Lili was able to work again. She felt it both a solemn duty and the expression of an inner need to work, and the months during which she could not had robbed her of this form of release and self-expression. But, this time her concerns were with others almost exclusively, especially Miki, whom she had visited the preceding year in Nice during the month of September. Having seen her friend work in the hospital, Lili was amazed at Miki's stamina, but, even so, she was afraid that if Miki did not take some rest she would lose her health. Although Lili admired Miki's zeal and her nobility of purpose, she said she wanted to let her friend know her feelings in this matter. Even so, she told Miki she realized that her advice would be unlikely to lure Miki away from the inner satisfaction she must be deriving from her work. Lili assured Miki that she was well remembered by all in her circle, and that Miki's letters and her confidence and trust delighted her. She closed asking Miki to write her as soon and as often as possible. The letter has a postscript by Marthe Bouwens, who sent Miki her best and said she was hoping to see her again soon. The regularity and definitiveness of Lili's handwriting and the fact that both the letter and the envelope are in ink are further evidence that Lili's health had greatly improved since June.[149]

On November 30, 1916, Lili Boulanger signed a contract which ceded to the publisher Ricordi all rights to her *Reflets* and *Clairières dans le Ciel*. This contract permits the company to arrange all printing, publication, translation, sale, rental, and performing rights both in the compositions' original forms and in whatever arrangements might be made from them, even for mechanical instruments. These rights were to last for the full duration of authors' rights, as well as those of their families and assignees.[150]

Even having written encouragingly to Miki about her health earlier in the year, Lili found that she had perhaps been too optimistic. At the end of December she had to admit that her strength was not returning so fast as she had hoped. In fact, she felt exhausted again—everything fatigued her. But Miki's continuing moral support and confidence moved her deeply and led her to write these lines from Gargenville to her friend in Nice. Once again, there are signs that all was not really well with Lili. The handwriting has become very minute, almost cramped and quite spidery, and, even though the letter is in ink, the stroke is not so sure as it had been only four months earlier.[151]

During this period, Lili was still forcing herself to do as much as she possibly could. A reminder sheet shows that she was still expecting herself to write to a goodly number of people, including Maeterlinck, Charpentier, Père Arthur, Monseigneur Jacquet, Germaine de Manziarly, and Mme Vidal, as well as to visit various people such as Dr. Brocq, Mme Jumel, Mlle Marcelle Soulage, and her dear friend and former teacher Mlle Nègre. In addition to these activities, she was also waiting to receive proofs from Ricordi.[152]

The state of Lili's health did not improve at all. In fact, it continued to deteriorate. Mme Boulanger and Lili went to Arcachon to stay, in the hope that the sea air would help Lili. On February 14, 1917, in a letter to Miki Piré, the signs of Lili's lack of improvement are unmistakable. The miniscule handwriting on lined paper, the fact that the letter itself is written in pencil and that the envelope is addressed in Mme Boulanger's elegant handwriting—these things alone would show that Lili Boulanger was ill. In addition, Lili mentions in her letter that she had been suffering from a continuing fever, and, though she had wanted to write to Miki before, she had been unable to do so. Despite her own problems, however, Lili was concerned that all might not be well with Miki. She wanted Miki to know that she was willing to share whatever problems her friend might have.[153]

In February, Lili was given autographed photographs of two

people. On the ninth, Théodore Dubois, who had known her all her life, dedicated his "to my dear Lili, very affectionately, with my best wishes," and signed it "An old and faithful friend, Th. Dubois."[154] Claude Debussy, on the other hand, had known only Lili's work. His photograph is dedicated "to Mademoiselle Lili Boulanger in sincere admiration."[155] Debussy's photograph is dated simply "February, 1917." Probably testimonials like that of Debussy and declarations of warm friendship like that of Dubois helped to lift Lili's spirit as much as possible under such depressing circumstances.

Even during this period Lili continued to work at composition whenever she could. Dated entries in one of her composition notebooks carry only one date in February—February 15, when she was at the Hôtel des Pins. After that there are no further notations until March.[156] The only sketches of Lili's that survive from her time in Arcachon in 1917 are studies for the *Princesse Maleine,* but she also worked on other compositions and finished *Du Fond de l'Abîme* and *Vieille Prière bouddhique* while she was there.[157]

By March 23, Lili was feeling well enough to write Miki a short postcard. Lili was worried. She had not heard from Miki in some time and wanted her friend to know that her thoughts were with her. She apologized for not being able to write to Mme Piré, but explained that she was still too ill. This time the message is written in ink, but in the same tiny handwriting as before, and the address has obviously been written by the same hand that wrote the envelope for the previous letter.[158]

Through March and April, Lili continued to work on sketches for the *Princesse Maleine,* but she was unable to apply herself consistently. The dated entries in her workbook read only March 5, 6, 17, and 27, and April 12, 17, and 18.[159] By March 5, she and Mme Boulanger had moved from the Hôtel des Pins to the Grand Hôtel Régina-Forêt et d'Angleterre, which was situated high on a hill overlooking the town. It was here that Nadia, on her visits from Paris, sometimes took pictures of Lili. One such photograph shows Lili lying in bed, looking stoically at the camera, while Mme Boulanger, seated nearby, looks on. Lili's bed had been moved next to an enormous window.[160]

While Lili was in Arcachon, two concerts that included some of her works were given—one in Paris and one in Boston. On March 19 the Concerts Gaulois presented Lili's *Faust et Hélène* as part of a benefit program for French musicians. This performance took place in Steinert Hall at Harvard University and also included lantern slides of Compiègne in addition to the music. The second concert was given on Sunday, March 25, at the *Salle des Fêtes de la Mairie du 6e Arrondissement* in Paris. It, too, was a benefit performance—this time for the *Association des Infirmières visiteuses de France*. On the program was one of Lili's *Clairières*, "Deux Ancolies," performed by Germaine Sanderson and Nadia Boulanger.[161]

Lili continued to work on *La Princesse Maleine*. In April she was able to use only April 12, 17, and 18 for this purpose. She was still very weak. In May she was strong enough to work only on the eleventh, eighteenth, and nineteenth.[162] Fever continued to plague her during May. When she wrote to Miki on May 10, Lili promised to write her friend at greater length in a day or so, because her fever was so high at that time that she was having difficulty concentrating. She just wanted Miki to know that she was thinking of her and was worried about Miki's health. Lili insisted that her friend tell her everything. The writing is still in pencil in this letter, and, once again, the envelope had been addressed by another hand.[163]

Miki went to spend several weeks with her friend in Arcachon. There, for the first time, Lili sang the *Clairières dans le Ciel* in a weak voice for Miki, with Nadia to accompany her. At the foot of the bed there was a piano, and it was this instrument that Nadia used. This scene moved Miki to tears. Later, Lili asked Miki when they were alone if she really thought—all friendship aside—that Lili's compositions were musically worthwhile. It was not until that point that even Miki realized how serious Lili was about her music. Later, Miki went out into Arcachon and bought Lili a little dog made of lead. When she saw it Lili cried. Since dogs were a symbol of fidelity, she said, this present was proof to her that Miki would not forget her.[164]

Lili did not recover. During June she was too ill to work. She was taken back to Paris. By July she was seriously ill. The eminent surgeon Thierry de Martel thought that an appendectomy might alleviate Lili's suffering. On Sunday, July 29, a very weak Lili managed to write a short note to Miki Piré. It was a brief, touching letter—just the news that Lili was to be operated on the next day. She wanted her friend to know that the certain knowledge of Miki's moral support made her feel better.[165] It must have cost Lili an enormous amount of effort just to write these few words. The penciled writing on this small sheet of lined paper is almost too faint to read. The envelope has apparently been addressed by Nadia.

The following day, Dr. Martel performed an appendectomy

on Lili.[166] In addition to the letter written to Miki the day before the operation, Lili had sent her a telegram saying that she was ill. As early as 1914 Lili had felt the threat of death as a real possibility for her at almost any time. She had asked Miki to promise that if she ever received a telegram saying Lili was ill, she would come immediately to join her.[167] It is a measure of how sick Lili felt that at this point she sent her friend such a telegram for the first time. Miki left for Paris as soon as she got this news, and stayed with Lili during the summer of 1917, while she was recuperating from the operation.[168]

Although the operation did alleviate the pain somewhat on a temporary basis, Lili still suffered considerable pain—so much, in fact, that she was given laudanum[169] in an attempt to relieve it.[170] Dr. Martel had told Nadia after the operation that there was no longer any hope that Lili could be cured. Lili's chronic illness had caused considerable damage to her intestines: that she had survived that long was a tribute to her extremely strong will to live. Nadia shared this sad news with Miki Piré.[171]

Lili could no longer keep her knowledge of her own impending death from her family. She was so ill after the operation when she was trying to recuperate in Gargenville that Renée de Marquein had to bring her a container of oxygen from Paris.[172] Even the laudanum was ineffective in combating Lili's intractable pain, and was discontinued.[173] Her worsening condition came as no surprise to Lili, and she accepted it stoically. She admitted to Nadia that she was beginning to suffer again.[174] As Renée de Marquein puts it, "When she became ill, her gaiety disappeared, to return, however, from time to time, but she survived her illness with a great deal of courage and lucidity . . , she was a devout believer and I think that was a help to her."[175]

One of Lili's goddaughters, Madeleine Delaquys, was a gifted pianist. By the time she was five years old the little girl was accomplished enough to audition for the great piano teacher Mme Giraud in her family's home on the rue de Clichy.[176] But Madeleine, too, was ill. She died in Gargenville shortly afterwards, on September 3, 1917. Despite the fact that she was extremely ill herself, Lili insisted on attending Madeleine's funeral. No one could dissuade her from what was, for her, a great effort.[177]

Since May, Lili had been too ill to compose and, after May 19, her composition notebooks contain only one entry before October 17.[178] This inability to work may have been at least partly a reaction to the medication she had been taking. She was not even able to write until September 27, almost two full months after the opera-

127

tion. In a letter to Miki written that same day, Lili told her friend that she had wanted her first written words to be for her. She missed Miki, who had left Gargenville shortly before, but thanked her for a present she had sent the Boulangers just afterwards. Lili thanked Miki also for the confidences she had shared with her, and assured Miki that, although life looked grim to Miki then, she was sure that Miki would find happiness if she waited. Despite Miki's present sadness and discouragement, Lili begged her friend to fight it, and, if it was necessary, not to hesitate to ask for support and encouragement from those closest to her. Lili was still very weak. The handwriting is small, somewhat erratic, and in varying pressures on the lined paper. As for the envelope, it has again been addressed by someone else.

Sometimes Lili was able to go out into the garden in Gargenville. One photograph of her taken there during the summer of 1917 shows her knitting. Another shows her in the company of Père Arthur, who was a frequent visitor to "Les Maisonnettes" that summer.[180] Perhaps the saddest one, however, shows Lili and Mme Boulanger together. Lili is seated facing the camera, in an open doorway, and Mme Boulanger is behind her, bending toward her daughter and looking at her. On closer inspection it can be seen that Lili is strapped to the chair, and that Mme Boulanger is not only leaning toward Lili—she also appears to be physically supporting her. Lili herself looks somewhat grim and determined. Her hands and face both seem to be swollen. But she is still elegantly dressed and carefully groomed. The Lalique pin she is wearing in this picture was a gift from Miki Piré.[181] There are other photographs, too, dating from this period.

Lili remained in Gargenville even after the summer season ended. She wrote to Miki on October 10 that cold and rainy weather had taken the place of the beautiful September days she had enjoyed. Nadia had begun her exhausting work schedule again, and was then in Paris. She was commuting several times a week between Paris and Gargenville, but Lili felt very much alone.[182] Lili was preparing herself, she told Miki, to leave Gargenville. The prospect made Lili very unhappy. She knew that Miki was unhappy too and felt alone, and Lili told her, first, that everyone's thoughts and good wishes were with her, and then that Lili felt that her own sense of isolation had made her more understanding of Miki's. The letter is written in faint pencil: the handwriting is small, uneven in pressure, but regular. Nadia appears to have addressed the envelope for her sister.[183]

On October 15, Lili sent Miki a short note, written on a post-

Figure 43. Lili Boulanger with Père Arthur in the garden of "Les Maisonnettes" (summer 1917).

Figure 44. Lili and Mme Ernest Boulanger in the garden of "Les Maisonnettes" (summer 1917).

card. She wanted Miki to know that her thoughts were with her friend. She apologized for not being able to write at greater length, but two things prevented her. First, Lili was unable to leave her bed because she was suffering from a flare-up of enteritis. Second, her little dog Kitchill[184] was ill, too. He was staying on Lili's bed. Kitchill was also in need of constant care. The card and envelope are both in Lili's handwriting. The pressure is extremely variable, as is the size of the writing, which becomes progressively tinier and tinier. It is obvious that Lili was extremely weak at the time she wrote this note to Miki.[185]

Lili was anxious to try to finish her opera. Even during this period of severe debility she continued to work when she could on scenes of the *Princesse Maleine*. In addition to one entry in her workbook dated simply "October, 1917," there are two others for that month—the seventeenth and the twenty-seventh. By that time, Lili had finished the second scene of the opera. A fair copy of it is dated at the end "Copied Saturday the 27th to Monday the 29th of October 1917/Gargenville."[186] Other entries show that Lili worked again on sketches for the opera in her workbook on November 16 and November 19, but no record of any other activity for that month survives.

By December, Lili had been brought back to Paris and was staying once more in the Boulanger family's apartment at 36 rue Ballu. Before returning she had seen Père Arthur for the last time. Late in the fall he had come to "Les Maisonnettes" to tell the Boulangers that he was entering a cloistered order. They never saw or heard from him again.[187]

On December first, Nadia played Lili's *Nocturne* and *Cortège* at the Salle Gaveau, but Lili was too ill to attend.[188] That month, Lili spent the sixteenth, nineteenth, and twenty-first working on *La Princesse Maleine*,[189] and began to compose *D'un Soir triste*. No sketches for the latter are extant.

During the months of December and January, Lili continued to weaken, but "she still continued to work, having herself carried to the piano from time to time. . . ."[190] There is one final entry in her composition notebook. Dated January 18, 1918, it is yet another sketch for the *Princesse Maleine*. Lili was able to finish *D'un Soir triste* in a version for string trio as well as for cello and piano before her strength deserted her. The orchestration of this work she managed to complete, but the nuances were filled in by Nadia,[191] following the indications in Lili's trio score.

By mid-January, Lili was too weak to write any music at all. "When she was no longer able to write, she dictated, note by note, line by line . . . the work that had been conceived inwardly."[192] Lili was then working on her last composition, the *Pie Jesu*.[193] She managed to sign one document at the end of January; on the twenty-ninth she signed another contract, similar to the one she had signed in 1916, ceding to Ricordi the rights to her compositions *Soir sur la Plaine, Nocturne, D'un vieux Jardin, D'un Jardin clair, Attente, Le Retour,* and *Cortège*.[194]

Société Anonyme des Éditions Ricordi

au Capital de 100.000 francs entièrement versée

Paris - 18, Rue de la Pépinière - Paris

Le soussigné ● **Mlle Lili BOULANGER, demeurant à PARIS, 36, rue Ballu**

déclare par le présent céder à LA SOCIÉTÉ ANONYME DES ÉDITIONS RICORDI à Paris, 18, Rue de la Pépinière, avec garantie de tous troubles, revendications et évictions quelconques, la propriété absolue, pleine et entière, tant pour la France et ses colonies que pour tous les pays étrangers

de ● ouvrage ● ci-après dénommé ● dont **elle est l'**auteur

Savoir :

"Soir sur la Plaine" (paroles d'Albert SAMAIN) chœur (mixte.
"Nocturne" pour piano et violon ou flûte.
"D'un Vieux Jardin", pour piano seul,
"D'un Jardin clair",
"Attente" (paroles de Maurice Maeterlinck) piano & chant
"Le Retour" (paroles de G.Delaquys), piano & chant,
"Cortège", pour violon et piano,
"Cortège", réduction pour piano seul.

En conséquence, LA SOCIÉTÉ ANONYME DES ÉDITIONS RICORDI est subrogée dans tous les droits, moyens et actions de l'auteur soussignée , et pourra, à l'exclusion de tous autres, graver, imprimer, publier, traduire, vendre, louer et faire exécuter le ● dit ● ouvrage ●, tant sous leur forme primitive, que dans les arrangements, transcriptions ou fantaisies quelconques pour tous instruments même mécaniques actuellement existants ou pouvant être inventés pendant toute la durée du privilège accordé ou à accorder aux auteurs, à leurs familles ou à leurs ayants-droit par les lois et conventions présentes et futures de tous pays. L'auteur et les éditeurs reconnaissent et se réservent leurs droits respectifs dans la Société des auteurs, compositeurs et éditeurs de musique.

La présente cession est faite **suivant contrat en date du premier août 1913**

Lili Boulanger

Fait à **PARIS** le **29 Janvier** 1918.

Figure 45. Cession of rights to Ricordi, possibly the last document signed by Lili Boulanger.

Paris was under heavy German bombardment from the north and east. "With the shellings coming closer and closer, Madame Boulanger decided to leave Paris with her daughters, and Lili Boulanger was taken to Mézy. . . ."[195] Mézy was west of Paris, and at that time was out of the immediate line of fire. It was also close enough for Lili to reach in her seriously weakened condition. Just before she left for Mézy, Lili managed to summon enough strength to send a packet to her former teacher Mlle Nègre, whose home had been destroyed by the shelling.[196] This time it was Nadia, not Lili, who sent the telegram to Miki Piré.

Miki arrived in Mézy just after Lili had finished dictating to Nadia the last of the *Pie Jesu*. Before going to see Lili, Miki went to the room Nadia had rented for her in a house next to the one in which the Boulangers were staying. There she took off the nurse's uniform she had traveled in and put on a taffeta dress. Miki was aware when she saw her friend that Lili had changed a great deal. She was swollen, and the tuberculosis had spread to her lungs. Lili had a high fever and was in intense pain. Even the sound of rustling taffeta was enough to upset her. Hoping that she would not offend Miki with her request, Lili asked her if she would change into something quieter.[197]

On the night of March 8, when Lili seemed to be resting relatively comfortably, Miki went in to Paris to hear the premiere of Lili's *Clairières dans le Ciel* and brought back some of her favorite Parma violets. These Lili kept by her bed on a little table, along with the mineral water that was the only nourishment she was able to take orally during the last three weeks of her illness. Several times a lung tap was taken. Each time this was done, a frightened Miki Piré left Gargenville early in the morning in her nurse's uniform to take the train for Paris. In her uniform she would be permitted to travel without difficulty. After arriving at the Gare St. Lazare with the specimen obtained by the lung tap, she crossed Paris (which was then still under heavy bombardment) to take it to the Institut Pasteur on the rue de Vaugirard. She waited at the Institut all day for Dr. Froin to analyze the specimen, then took the results and left. By the time she was ready to cross Paris again, it was after dark.[198]

Suffering from fever and distention, Lili was in constant need of ice. Knowing this, Nadia's friends and students, and Lili's friends, took turns bringing it to her from Paris. Frequently it was Suzanne Vidal or Mina Vaurabourg who braved the Paris bombardments to perform this service for her; sometimes, Annette Dieudonné or a group of Nadia's other pupils delivered this precious substance.[199]

For the last two days of her life, Lili was given periodic injections in an effort to revive her, but these attempts were futile.[200] Miki and Lili had never really discussed religion together. On March 15, when the priest finally came to administer the last rites, Lili looked at him with such faith that Miki was relieved for her friend, knowing that Lili had the consolation of a firm belief in an afterlife.[201]

Lili died quietly later that same day, after receiving the sacrament. They dressed her in the velvet dress Suzanne Vidal had brought to Mézy for this purpose,[202] the same one that Miki had given Lili to wear at the Institut de France when her *Faust et Hélène* was conducted there in November 1913.[203] Then Nadia, Miki, and Roger Ducasse (who had arrived at the house just after Lili died)[204] lifted Lili's body from the bed and placed it on her bier.[205]

The funeral announcement read:

> Your presence is requested at the funeral cortège, service, and interment of Mademoiselle Lili Boulanger, *Premier Grand Prix de Rome*, deceased, fortified with the rites of the Church, the fifteenth of March, 1918, at the age of twenty-four, in Mézy-par-Meulan, after a long and painful illness; which will take place this coming Tuesday, the nineteenth, at twelve noon precisely, at the Église de la Trinité, her parish church. We will gather in Paris, at 36, Rue Ballu."

As the surviving published and unpublished sources show, Lili Boulanger had an extremely eventful life after winning the Prix de Rome. Previously she had enjoyed a reputation within France itself; now, she was an international celebrity. Within a month after winning the coveted prize, she signed an exclusive contract with the major music publishing house of Ricordi. Lili could finally find a few months in which to relax after years of concentrated work, and she spent time with her friends enjoying the luxury of leisure and preparing *Faust et Hélène* for publication. Her sudden fame brought with it an increasing demand for both performances of her works and public appearances by the composer, which met with great success. Lili overextended herself and became ill after months of frenetic social and artistic activity. Illness led to her inability to reach Rome by the deadline specified by the Institut de France, and, subsequently, to false rumors and later misunderstandings between Lili Boulanger and the Director

133

Vous êtes prié d'assister aux Convoi, Service & Enterrement de

Mademoiselle Lili BOULANGER

Premier Grand Prix de Rome

décédée, mnnie des Sacrements de l'Eglise, le 15 Mars 1918, à l'âge de 24 ans, à Mézy, par Meulan, après une longue et cruelle maladie;

Qui se feront le Mardi 19 courant, à MIDI TRÈS PRÉCIS. en l'Eglise de la Trinité, sa Paroisse.

On se réunira à Paris, 36, Rue Ballu.

J'offre à Dieu toutes mes souffrances
pour qu'elles retombent en joies sur toi.

De la part de :

Madame Ernest BOULANGER, sa Mère;
Mademoiselle Nadia BOULANGER, sa Sœur;
Ses Amis et ses Camarades.

Adm. Spéciale de Funerailles DESCLERS, 16, Avenue Rachel. Tél. : Marendet 04-18

Figure 46. Invitation to the funeral of Lili Boulanger.

of the Académie de France à Rome, who persisted in believing that Lili was only feigning illness as part of a plea for sympathy and a demand for special consideration that he believed were unwarranted. With the intercession of the Académie des Beaux-Arts in Paris, he was forced to modify his position somewhat, but he still resented Lili and her mother.

To escape from the rigors of the Roman summer, Lili Boulanger went to stay with Miki Piré in Nice, and later returned to

Figure 47. Lili Boulanger's tomb in Montmartre Cemetery.

Gargenville. After the outbreak of World War I, Lili and Nadia edited a gazette that was distributed to former composition students of the Conservatoire, which provided a medium for the exchange of news. This work, along with Lili's other activities on behalf of the French war effort, greatly curtailed the time available to her for musical composition during 1915.

Lili, along with Lucienne Heuvelmans and Jacques Débat-Ponsan, had been granted permission to return to the Villa Medici. After a short stay in Nice, during which Lili obtained Maeterlinck's permission to set his play *La Princesse Maleine* as an opera, she continued on to Rome, arriving there in early March of 1916. Lili was already in very delicate health and, although her stay at the Villa Medici in 1916 marked a period of great artistic activity, the composer was in a state of extreme physical exhaustion when she was not actively ill. Finally, under the orders of her doctor, she left the Villa Medici for the second and last time, knowing that she probably had no more than two years to live.

In her continuing attempts to regain her health, Lili even consented to experimental medical therapy. Despite her ill health, she continued to compose, and even to perform occasionally, whenever her physical condition permitted. Once again Lili tried in vain to improve the state of her health, through a change of climate. After several months' stay in Arcachon, her condition had deteriorated to such an extent that surgery was performed in an effort to relieve her suffering. The improvement was short-lived, however, and was followed by a constant worsening of her condition. With her health failing, and too weak to write, Lili dictated her last composition, the *Pie Jesu,* to her sister, Nadia. It was completed about three weeks before her death at Mézy in March 1918. Her premature death was a shock to the musical and artistic world, and her funeral on March 19, 1918, was attended by many notables.

5

The Works of Lili Boulanger:
Before the Prix de Rome

A number of problems must be dealt with in any consideration
of the works of Lili Boulanger. There are no opus numbers to
place the compositions chronologically in relation to each other.
Lili almost invariably indicated at the end of each of her original
manuscripts its date of composition and copying and, in her earliest
works, the names of the people to whom she had shown it as well.
Although her own dating must be regarded as the final authority,
it can only be used for those compositions for which her original
autograph manuscript can be found. Unfortunately some of these
now seem to be missing, and the data are frequently not contained
in subsequent copies—particularly in performance scores—of her
works. Under these circumstances, the best evidence for dating
the works is a combination of her own testimony as it is to be
discovered in letters, original sketchbooks, memory lists, and other
documents; the statements of her sister, Nadia; and any stylistic
evidence that may be gleaned from the compositions themselves.
Dates that appear at the end of the published scores of Lili's works
seem to be based on those contained in her autograph manuscripts,
but, in at least one instance,[1] the published date does not agree
with the one in the composer's own workbooks. Whenever possible, works will be discussed in chronological order, but, for the
reasons cited above, a rigorously chronological treatment of Lili

Boulanger's compositions is not yet feasible. Because Lili frequently conceived of her works simultaneously for two or more performing media, a grouping of her works by genre alone is inadvisable.

Lili Boulanger's first extant completed composition[2] is one she wrote in preparation for the *concours d'essai* of the Prix de Rome competition. It was her second composition in her concerted attempt to ready herself for the elimination round of the Prix de Rome. This orchestrally accompanied chorus is frankly a student effort. The work, *Sous-Bois,* has never been published.[3]

Between September 17 and October 3, 1911, Lili completed a cantata, *Frédégonde.* It, too, is a student work, undertaken this time in preparation for the *concours définitif* of the Prix de Rome competition. Apparently, as each part of the work was completed, Lili showed it to those best equipped to help her further her efforts. In this case Raoul Pugno and Georges Caussade were the first to see the first scene as soon as Lili was able to show it to them.[4] Here all that remains is a piano-vocal score, which comprises only the first scene. The separate manuscript containing it was copied from the composition workbook entitled *Cantata II.*[5] The writing again is scholarly and correct, as befits a composition written under such circumstances.[6]

Lili took time out from her concentrated preparation for the Prix de Rome competition to write a short salon piece. Apparently she finished it in two days—October 24 and October 25, 1911. No sketches for this work are to be found, so it is impossible to know when the idea first began to interest Lili or how she developed the concept before it reached its final form. The only autograph manuscript of this composition indicates that the composer originally conceived of it as a piece for flute and piano, although it was later published under the title, *Nocturne, Piano et Violon.*[7] The solo part sounds equally well on either violin or flute. There were no alterations made in the solo part—in other instances, Lili did make alterations when she adapted a piece for use in a different performing medium[8]—and since none of the correspondence between Lili Boulanger and her publisher, Ricordi, is available for study, there is no way to know for certain whose decision it was to issue the piece as one for flute or violin and piano.

There is another version of *Nocturne.* The instrumentation calls for B♭ clarinets, harp, solo violin or flute, along with the traditional string complement. No autograph manuscript of the score appears to be extant.[9] This orchestral transcription was never published, which seems a shame. Even in this short composition, influenced as it very obviously was by impressionistic techniques and practices, the composer shows a real feeling for orchestral sonorities and balances, and a subtlety in their use. If this transcription was indeed made at about the same time as the piece was originally composed, then Lili Boulanger was perhaps even more at home in the free forms of composition where her own imagination determined her artistic decisions than she was in more "scholastic" works.

The textural contrasts in the *Nocturne* are easily visible in the orchestral score. The soloist enters and adds a third texture to the pedal points of the clarinets and violins and the ostinato arpeggios of the harp.[10] The accompaniment figures provide a comfortable feeling of stasis against which the solo line stands out in relief (Example 1). There are also traces in the *Nocturne* of

Example 1

the fact that Lili was influenced somewhat by Wagner's *Tristan* and Debussy's *Prélude à l'après-midi d'un faune*. Short allusions to *Tristan* find their way into several measures (Example 2), and the reentry of the solo part makes a definite allusion to the first phrase of the Debussy work (Example 3). It is certainly possible that these musical paraphrases were perfectly conscious on the part of the composer, since her works do, in some other cases, have extramusical connotations and even definite meanings for those

Example 2

Example 3

closest to Lili.[11] However, no external evidence has yet come to light to prove such a hypothesis true in this instance.

Again Lili Boulanger turned her attention to the Prix de Rome competition. Considering once more the requirements of the *concours d'essai,* she composed two accompanied vocal works. *Renouveau* and *Les Sirènes* were completed in piano-vocal versions on November 8, 1911, and on December 8, 1911, respectively. In both of these works there is the emphasis on the use of broken chords (already familiar from the *Nocturne*) that is characteristic of Lili Boulanger's compositions, especially during this period, and that, in fact, never entirely disappeared from her repertoire of favorite musical devices.

In *Renouveau* there is a freshness that is somehow greater than the sum total of the elements that create it—the abundance of thirds and sixths, the warmth of E major, or even the prevalence of lilting triple meter. The initial entries of the voices are carefully imitative, as befits a piece written with particular compositional "rules" in mind (Example 4), but still the euphony of the music is well suited to the Parnassian verses of Armand Silvestre. It is an interesting coincidence that this poem about growth, youth, and freshness should have been one of those with which Lili won her first major prize as a composer. *Renouveau* exploits the various permutations of solo and choral combinations, and, in line with already-established French tradition, makes use of the voices as instruments—in this case through the effect of a solo vocal line complemented by a combination of instrumental accompaniment and vocalizations in the other voices. All in all it is a well-thought-out piece.[12]

Example 4

Charles Grandmougin's Parnassian poetry requires a totally different kind of treatment, however. His dramatic verses deal with the man-devouring sirens, and Lili's music attempts to depict the melodramatic potential of the situation as vividly as possible. Perhaps in an effort to express the hypnotic effect of the sirens themselves, the composer has chosen to introduce a tonic pedal on F♯ combined with a rolling ostinato of C♯ octaves in the bass, using an open fifth to give the pitching, open effect of the sea. The numbing effect of twenty-eight measures of this type of pattern is mitigated somewhat by the actions of the voices (Example 5), although a properly "scholastic" tone is set in this composition, too, by the imitative entries of the three voices (Example 6).

In one more attempt to mirror the rocking motion of water, the composer adds upper and lower neighbors to the vocal line (Example 7). Finally, the pedal point gives way to pentatonic arpeggios (Example 8), which form a short bridge between the end of the chorus and the beginning of the first solo. These arpeggios also act as the accompaniment to this obligatory solo section, which presents an ornamented version of the first lines (Example 9). The other voices then join in—again, the entries are imitative (Example 10). After a connecting passage in which the voices vocalize on the syllable *Ah!,* there is no break before the recapitulation, accompanied, this time, by the same pentatonic arpeggios—over an F♯ pedal—that had characterized the solo (Example 11). An off-stage chorus vocalizing on the syllable *Ah!* brings with it the reintroduction of a modification of the original accompaniment pattern (Example 12). As the second chorus fades away, pentatonic arpeggios reappear, and the first chorus assumes the vocalization. This arrangement, lasting a full seven measures, brings us to the end of the piece.[13]

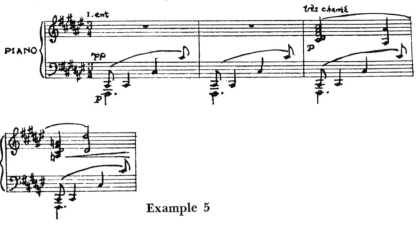

Example 5

142

Example 6

Example 7

Example 8

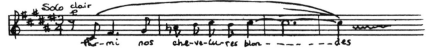

Example 9

Example 10

Example 11

Lili's setting of *Reflets*—an early Symbolist work taken from Maeterlinck's 1890 collection, *Serres Chaudes*[14]—consists of three short, musically interrelated sections, corresponding to the poetic strophes. The Maeterlinck poem is a mood piece, descriptive of a state of deep loneliness and melancholy. The song contains timbral contrasts between the sections, as, for example, when the harp arpeggios of the first stanza are divided between the *ripieno* cellos and second violins during the bridge passage between the first and second verses, and continue to underlie the second stanza,

Example 12

finally being rejoined by the harp at the end of the second poetic line. In this way, the composer has already begun to show a desire to obscure the divisions between one section and the next when the mood of the text remains the same between poetic stanzas. But it also contains the hallmarks of Lili Boulanger's early works,[15] a layered orchestral effect derived from the combination of harp arpeggios and sustained tones in the clarinets and single stand of muted cellos (Example 13), and a mood similar to that of *Nocturne,* but even more reflective and subdued. The dynamic range in *Reflets* never exceeds mezzo forte. Paralleling *Nocturne, Reflets* also fades away into silence at the end.

Early in December 1911, Lili started to work on *Soleils de Septembre,* probably another attempt to prepare for the Prix de Rome Competition. This music can no longer be found.[16]

During the early months of 1912, Lili Boulanger orchestrated *Les Sirènes*[17] and made corrections in the scores of *Renouveau* and *Frédégonde.* Since sketches and first copies of these works are lacking, and the surviving autograph manuscript of *Frédégonde* is incomplete, it is impossible to know exactly what changes were made. By early March of 1912, Lili Boulanger had begun to work

145

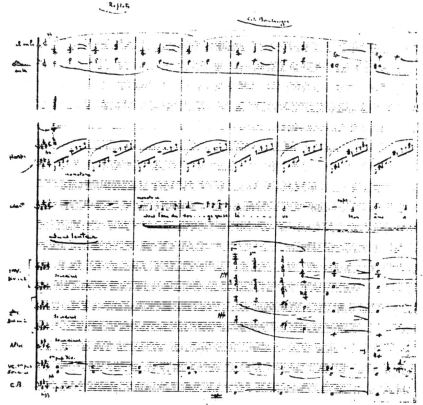

Example 13

on setting Maeterlinck's *La Princesse Maleine* as an opera. In fact, her first sketch is dated March 9.[18] A composition she worked on during mid-April, *Pendant la Tempête,* has apparently been lost or destroyed.

The poem of Lili Boulanger's song *Attente* is, once more, by Maeterlinck—three octameter quatrains taken from his *Serres Chaudes,* just as *Reflets* had been. Contrary to previously accepted dating, she was in the process of composing this piece in April of 1912—April 18, to be exact. Here, too, there is an emphasis on stasis in the accompaniment, which again is made up of two layers. But the composer was also becoming the master of a palette of coloristic chromatic harmonies that reinforced the interplay of overtones above the parallel minor sevenths of the bass after its initial suggestion of traditional triadic harmony (Example 14). There is still a close adherence to the meaning of the text, but it is not so literal an interpretation as before. Sometimes it even

146

Example 14

Example 15

negates the meaning of the words, as in the blossoming that accompanies a statement about lilies that do not bloom (Example 15). The harmonic vocabulary of *Attente* recalls that of early Debussy, especially in the *Cinq Poèmes de Baudelaire*.[19]

After one more attempt to prepare for the Prix de Rome preliminary round,[20] Lili went into seclusion at Compiègne with the rest of the Prix de Rome aspirants in May 1912. At that time she had been studying music theory formally for less than two-and-a-half years,[21] had studied fugal techniques only since June 1911,[22] and had been intensively preparing for the chorus and cantata portions of the competition only since September 1911.[23]

As previously noted, the chorus for the elimination round of the 1912 Prix de Rome competition was *La Source,* a poem of reflective and bucolic mood not too unlike *Renouveau.* The orchestration Lili Boulanger chose to employ calls for not one but two harps, in addition to impressionistic effects from the triangle and cymbals. There is quite specific word-painting, as, for instance, when the harps both indulge in repeated glissandi to introduce the idea of sparkling water (Example 16). Just as in all the works

Example 16

Lili wrote in preparation for this competition, the voices enter imitatively (Example 17), and, as with her other works concerned in some way with depicting water, the piece is in triple meter. The fact that the instrumental accompaniment flows along in 9/8 while the chorus is consistently in 3/4 allows for a sense of free rhythmic interplay, which, in a sense, is a further means of overall word-painting (Example 18). This work is scored for a full orchestra, but, in keeping with the spirit of the text, the music is of almost gossamer consistency, and, with the exception of a few stray measures of mezzo forte during instrumental solos, the most usual dynamic level is pianissimo.

The fugue for this *concours d'essai* is nothing more than a scholastic exercise, written according to the proper formal plan: Exposition: subject, answer, counter-subject (Example 19); Epi-

Example 17

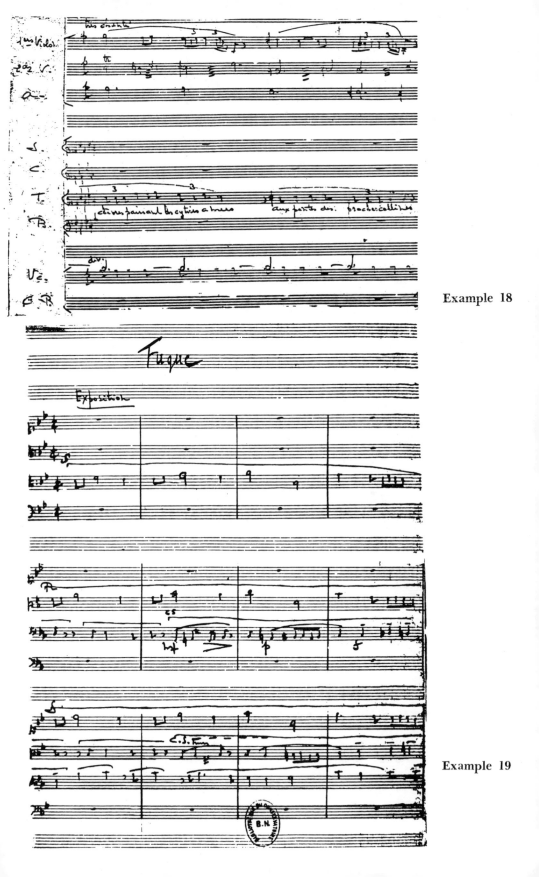

Example 18

Example 19

sode derived from the subject, another exposition, this time in the relative minor (i.e., G minor), another episode based on material from the counter-subject, a restatement of the theme in the sub-dominant, six short strettos, culminating in yet one last stretto over a tonic pedal point that closes the piece.[24]

After her first unsuccessful try for the Prix de Rome, Lili began again to compose pieces to prepare herself for the next year's competition. Her first effort in this regard was *Hymne au Soleil.*[25] Her setting of Casimir Delavigne's moderately romantic dramatic chorus follows the words closely in mood. This means that the four stanzas set by the composer (the fourth, which acts as a poetic *envoi,* also serves as a musical coda) are carefully differentiated from one another in mood and style. The play from which these verses are taken is an example of the French nineteenth-century preoccupation with exoticism.[26] Set in India, this excerpt depicts a Hindu religious rite (Example 20). As in Lili's other pieces in the same genre, there is considerable word-painting. On the words *he leaps,* for example, the soprano part calls for an ascending

Example 20

150

skip of a diminished fifth (Example 21). The first entrance of the chorus had been homophonic, but, in a piece like this, chosen as preparation for the *concours d'essai* of the Prix de Rome competition, it would be necessary for a candidate to show command of fugal writing within a choral context. Lili had not yet done so in this particular composition, but somehow she would have to find a place in the course of the work where such a demonstration would seem natural. The text itself solved the problem neatly for the composer. Since the third couplet deals with the sun god's fiery steeds, which he can barely control, the music now has a reason to employ fugal entries. These carefully worked-out and evenly spaced entries show that both the sun god and the composer are going to keep their resources under control (Example 22).

This section is followed by another homophonic choral pas-

Example 21

Example 22

sage, but now it is only a short invocation. The third stanza consists of a soloist's couplet followed by a passage for soloist and chorus. The contralto soloist enters after an introduction comprised of triplet arpeggios against a background of tremolos in the bass. Again the continuing figurations serve to enhance the intended word-painting. Against this, the soloist sings of fields of flowers and thick woods (Example 23). There is no break between the end of the solo and the reentry of the chorus with a recapitulation of the first verse: the solo continues, above the other voices

Example 23

of the chorus, which are now heard from off-stage (Example 24).

The original figuration that had accompanied the contralto solo continues into this section, which ends with only the soloist's voice remaining. There follows a coda, a real recapitulation of the initial introduction and chorus, then a short section with imitative entries. The composer here leads the listener to expect another fugal section which, however, is not forthcoming, and gives the texture added richness through the use of divisi lower voices (Example 25). Finally the piece reaches its blazing fortissimo climax and ends with surging, insistent power on open fifths that again recall the striking features of the opening measures.[27] Lili followed *Hymne au Soleil* with *La Nef légère,* which was probably a chorus too.[28]

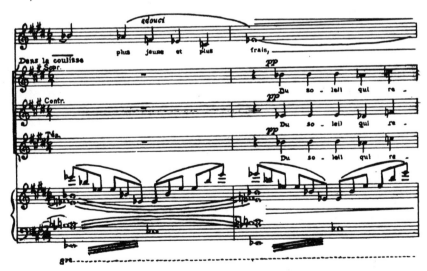

Example 24

153

Example 25

During the summer of 1912, Lili took time out once again from her preparation for the Prix de Rome competition to write a solo song.[29] The text of *Le Retour,* by Lili's old friend Georges Delaquys, a minor Parnassian poet, describes Ulysses' departure for his home in Ithaca at the end of his years of wandering and adventure. It is written in combinations of rhymed octameter and alexandrine verse with a two-line *envoi.* Lili's musical setting is clearly guided by the schematic nature of the poetry. Each time the *envoi* appears, the composer permits herself only minor liberties with the original music. As in Lili's other compositions that attempt to describe or give the feeling of water, this one, too, is in triple meter. The basic mood is reflective, and even such musical directions as "as if through a fog"[30] add still further to the slightly foreboding atmosphere. This song is dedicated to Hector Dufranne, who created the role of Golaud in Debussy's *Pelléas et Mélisande.* Given the Boulanger circle's enjoyment of puns and semi-humorous quotations, the fact that Lili chose to allude to another piece by Debussy, *Prélude à l'après-midi d'un faune,* in the introduction to *Le Retour* (Example 26) was probably meant

Example 26

154

quite consciously as a veiled compliment to the singer. The rolling motions of the accompaniment figurations in the bass are almost constant throughout the work (Example 27). They are discon-

Example 27

tinued only momentarily for dramatic effect, as happens, for example, at the end of the poetic text and in the introduction to the da capo statement of the text (Example 28).

Le Retour shows a transitional stage in Lili Boulanger's evolution as a composer. The style, although it still relies heavily on formulas, has become more personal, and there is a much greater range of expressive possibilities even though the poetic qualities of the text do tend to inhibit the composer somewhat.

Example 28

On the morning of October 13, 1912, Lili Boulanger completed the chorus with baritone solo on which she had been working since the middle of August. *Pour les Funérailles d'un Soldat*, set to verses taken from Alfred de Musset's dramatic poem *La Coupe et les Lèvres*,[31] gave Lili a wider dramatic scope for her setting as well as better poetic quality in the text than she had ever had before. The composer rose to the challenge set her by Georges Caussade—this composition, too, was a homework assignment,[32] although it has none of the attributes of a piece composed out of a sense of duty alone—and the result is a little gem. The predominating funereal aspect of the text is mirrored in Lili's choice of a slow march rhythm in setting it (Example 29).

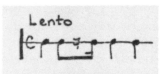

Example 29

The text has been treated as if it were, indeed, a funeral cantata in the grand tradition, played out-of-doors, because wind instruments play a prominent part in the orchestration[33] and a paraphrase of the *Dies Irae* plays an integral part in this work. After the march rhythm has been established in the first two measures by the tympani and snare drums, the winds and brasses enter with sustained chords in piano and pianissimo, after which the winds drop out and the brasses pick up the march rhythm of the percussion section (Example 30).

As the bass voices enter, the woodwinds and first harp sustain pedal points while the cellos and contrabasses take over the rhyth-

Example 30

mic articulation from the percussion instruments, which drop out of the texture at this point (Example 31). This particular change in instrumentation is, actually, suggested by the text itself. The composer has taken the words "Let the drums be muffled" as a signal to silence them altogether. In its ascetic style, the text declamation has a ritualistic flavor, which is further reinforced after

Example 31

157

the end of the first verse. Again the composer has decided to mirror the words "Let the prayer for the dead be said before us" by using a musical device immediately accessible to most of her audience—a literal quotation from the *Dies Irae* of the Requiem Mass (Example 32). There follows an interlude devoted to paraphrases of the

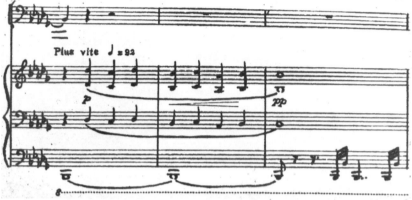

Example 32

opening phrase of the *Dies Irae* against the gradual adding of other instruments—the reentry of the tympani, cymbals, and snare drums, along, finally, with the woodwinds and muted horns.

By the end of this instrumental bridge section between the first and second verses, all instruments except the cornets, trombones, and tuba have reentered. But the horns and trumpets are muted, and the first harp plays delicate pianissimo harmonics, so the scoring is still rather transparent.

There is more strength and urgency in the tenor declamation of the first two lines of the second verse, accompanied at first only by the cornets, trombones, and tuba, which sustain a variant of the initial march rhythm (Example 33). Then the entire chorus joins in for the line "The soul belongs to God." At this point the strings and harps alone accompany the chorus. The strings had been silent throughout the previous tenor solo. Their reentry and the pianissimo arpeggiated chords of the harps create a striking effect (Example 34).

In the ensuing Allegro, Lili Boulanger has again chosen to render the text through word-painting. She uses a return to march rhythms to emphasize that the army has the right to the body of the fallen soldier, and here, too, the orchestration follows the meaning of the words. The strings drop out of the texture for the first statement, which is accompanied by the "traditional" military instruments—the brass section.

158

Example 33

Example 34

159

Before the combined statement is over, divisi basses and the tenors join once more with the strings in a somber, homophonic declamation of the lines, "We want to carry the Captain to his tomb,/ He died as a soldier on Christian soil."[34] At the end of the declamation, the tam-tam and tolling bell add another representative note of finality to the situation. As the tenors and basses continue to chant the text, the pianissimo woodwinds are added to the line, reflecting the soul and God, and the bassoons, sarrusophone, and muted horns represent the army. The parallel motion of the vocal line in this section creates the strong impression of parallel organum, thus enhancing the drama (Example 35).

Example 35

An agitated instrumental interlude heralds the entrance of the baritone soloist, who then describes a vision of the captain being borne into heaven on purple draperies. The vocal line, too, soars with the text (Example 36), against an accompaniment of

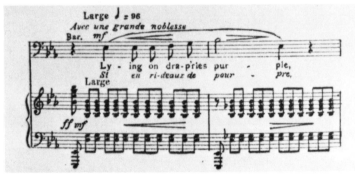

Example 36

triplets in the strings, sustained tones in the woodwinds and brasses, and a pianissimo drum roll.

As the orchestra and the soloist reach the emotional climax of the work, the mood changes once more to that of the opening measures. The tympani and snare drums return to the original march rhythm, and, when the muted strings do enter a measure later, the violins, viola, and cello reiterate the *Dies Irae* motive while the double basses join the percussion section's rhythmic enunciation. The whole chorus, in a deliberately emotionless voice, begins again the cry of the first measures. When the word *silence* is reached, the upper voices drop out of the chorus, leaving only the tenors and basses to request, once more, the prayer for the dead. As the text dies away, only the basses remain repeating the words *the prayer for the dead.* Against a background of rhythmic insistence, pedal points in the winds, and arpeggiated harp figurations, the chorus reenters for the final measures, singing only the syllable *Ah!*—first the sopranos and altos, then the full chorus, and, finally, as the work trails off into nothingness, only the tenors and basses.[35]

Lili Boulanger continued to work on the techniques of setting required cantata texts to music. Her notebooks indicate that on April 13, 1913, she was to show at her lesson *Alyssa,* a cantata she had written. Unfortunately, neither sketches nor manuscripts for this work are to be found. If Lili's mastery of the techniques involved was as complete at this point as it already was for the chorus, it is indeed a shame that this work has been lost.

In May 1913, Lili Boulanger joined the other contestants again at Compiègne for the preliminary round of the Prix de Rome competition. For the 1913 *concours d'essai* the chorus text, *Soir sur la Plaine,* by Albert Samain, was a set of elegiac verses, celebrating the golden sun setting in the west over a lush country scene. As in *Pour les Funérailles d'un Soldat,* the opening is quiet, in this case pianissimo. The scoring is transparent as the soprano soloist enters in the second measure (Example 37). Here, too,

Example 37

the composer uses word-painting to some extent. On "spreads out into the air," the solo dies away, against a background of ascending arpeggios in the first harp, a counter melody in the cellos and flutes, and tremolo figurations in the upper strings (Example 38).

161

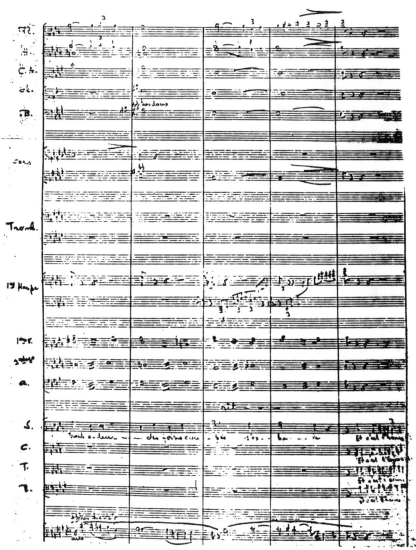

Example 38

The a cappella chorus then enters in a block, declaiming syl-
labically and euphoniously on the sleeping earth (Example 39).
After a short instrumental interlude, the chorus returns, piano,
this time accompanied by pianissimo instrumental pedal points.
The instrumentation is very carefully managed, allowing the voices
to be heard at all times. Considerable textual repetition breaks into
what had begun to seem a piece written completely according to
formula, introducing a welcome note of variety. Another short

162

Example 39

instrumental bridge section precedes the tenor solo, which is accompanied by a flute counter melody. Otherwise the orchestral scoring in this passage is practically nonexistent. As in the preceding year's *La Source,* this is an exceedingly quiet work whose dynamics rarely go above piano. After one measure of transition, the sopranos, contraltos, and the rest of the tenors enter to describe the final fall of night. Before they have finished, the contralto soloist enters, in one of Lili Boulanger's favorite techniques—the dovetailing of sections, this time, too, against a flute solo accompanied by clarinets, strings, and harps. Toward the end of the solo, the clarinet takes over the flute solo, but, although the timbre has changed slightly, the overall effect remains the same. Following another short instrumental section, the full chorus reenters, pianissimo, describing the dark. To depict more vividly the feeling of the sun's actually becoming part of the plain, Lili Boulanger chose to use another of her favorite devices, the syllable *Ah!,* this time with the mouths of the singers closed. In doing so, she creates two choruses, in effect, for the group singing *Ah!* continues to vocalize on that syllable even after the soprano soloist has reentered, singing of the remaining glow after the sun itself has set, and

163

going on to sing alone once more. After another short instrumental interlude, the full chorus sings in pianissimo homophony. Lili creates the illusion of immensity by using the entire chorus divisi against a five-octave range in the accompaniment $(F_2$ to $f''')$, with harp arpeggios and pp pedal points. More *Ah!*'s are used to introduce the idea of a distant sigh, which the soprano soloist describes against still more vocalizing on the syllable *Ah!* This is a very ambitious work. The soprano soloist continues after the *Ah!* has stopped, introducing yet other short solos by the tenor and baritone. This in turn leads to the use of the lower voices imitatively against the upper voices. The composer has saved until the last an obligatory attempt to show her mastery of this technique. Both the sopranos and the tenors are divisi, thus providing a lusher six-part texture for the gentle pianissimo ending. Although this is in some ways a weaker piece than *Pour les Funérailles d'un Soldat,* it does show a technical mastery of the available resources and an inventiveness in handling problems.[36]

The cantata with which Lili Boulanger won the Prix de Rome in 1913 was widely acclaimed as the most musical exercise of this type to have been heard in years. Because this was a competition piece, the composer was still bound to a great extent by the rules and expectations of the Academy's musical hierarchy. She was anxious to be as inventive as she could, while being careful not to offend the sensibilities of the judges.[37] Although these constraints did make the result less of a personal statement than it might have been, the inherent drama of the situation still shines through. As had also been the case with *Pour les Funérailles d'un Soldat,* the libretto Lili had to work with was poetically far superior to the usual texts contestants in the Prix de Rome competition were given to set. The text by Eugène Adenis, after the second *Faust* of Goethe, contains all the elements of true musical drama—desire, love, fear, death, and revulsion.

Lili Boulanger's *Faust et Hélène* is certainly a work with Wagnerian elements. Two leitmotivs are stated in the instrumental introduction and are important to the early development of the composition. The first, a somber theme that appears at the very beginning in the basses, seems to be an expression of Faust's torment, of the state of his soul, as it were (Example 40). The second

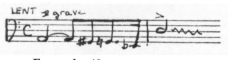

Example 40

appears to reflect the insatiable nature of his longing, a desire that nothing in life can satisfy (Example 41).

Example 41

Mephistopheles enters, his song "like a calm and mysterious psalmody" against a background of gentle harp arpeggios. The mood is one of enchanted sleep. When Faust awakens, his vocal line soars over a B-F♯ pedal (Example 42). Mephistopheles dis-

Example 42

perses the spirits that had troubled Faust's sleep, and they disappear in a cascade of harp arpeggios.

Faust begins to think about Hélène's beauty, and Mephistopheles reproaches him for forgetting so quickly about Marguérite. But he insists that Mephistopheles make no further appeals to his conscience, and this command is accompanied by a variant of Theme II, which further underlines his resolve. In addition, the vocal line itself follows an almost identical melodic sequence (Example 43). In his evocation of Helen of Troy, Faust makes allusion to Theme I (Example 44).

As the frenzy of Faust's desire increases, the key—which had remained in B major until that point—changes abruptly to E major. While part of the orchestra adopts triplet figurations against the generally eighth-note pulsation of the soloist, which further mirrors Faust's state of agitation, the insistent repetition of A♯ D♯ C♯ B leads to an even wilder state of excitement. In his madness, Faust decides to tempt God, and, as the sun sets, Mephistopheles begins the magic rituals that will raise Helen from the land of shades. This interlude ends, after insistent yet graceful arpeggios and tremolos, with the arrival of Hélène herself. Faust is overcome with her beauty and can only murmur her name softly with the support of pianissimo arpeggios in the accompaniment.

The following duet is conventional—probably because the composer knew that such a section would be expected of her by

Example 43

Example 44

the Academy—and it follows traditional models. Lili's mastery of the techniques involved, that is, alternation, unison, and canon is shown here, obviously to the satisfaction of the Prix de Rome jury. The style is impassioned, operatic, Italianate, and not at all the type of writing her earlier compositions would lead the listener to expect. But after the shattering climax, the composer does exhibit one of her most characteristic traits. The triple forte gives way to a delicate pianissimo after the passion has spent itself (Example 45).

Example 45

There follows Faust's short apostrophe to night, a sweet, gentle set piece broken into rudely at the end by Mephistopheles. The music mirrors his warning that there is a rude awakening to follow by taking on an agitated character with tremolos and long chromatic descending passages intended to describe the flight of storm clouds.

For the arrival of the shades of the victims of the Trojan War, Lili chose a march with a somber basso ostinato that repeats an alternating E♭-B♭ figure for thirteen consecutive measures, which conveys very well the sense of obsession that has created the whole situation (Example 46). They menace Faust and Hélène, and

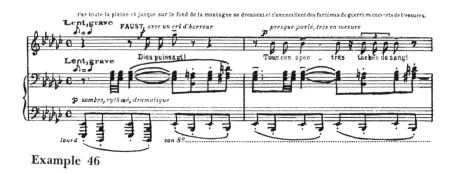

Example 46

Mephistopheles finally succeeds in separating the lovers before Faust is overcome by the shades.

The trio which follows expresses the feelings of all three characters admirably. While Faust and Hélène declare that their love is stronger than death, Mephistopheles intones solemnly on the dire consequences of Faust's folly. Finally Hélène is seized by the specter of Paris and carried back to the land of the dead. Scale passages in parallel octaves announce the final pronouncements of Mephistopheles as, accompanied by agitated tremolos, he declares that misfortune will be upon them for having tempted Providence. After an impassioned declamation of these sentiments, there is a short instrumental interlude and then, finally, the voice of Mephistopheles is heard from afar to declare twice more, now pianissimo, that a sad fate awaits them. As his voice dies away for the last time, the orchestra, too, fades away and seems to evaporate into the air in a triple piano.

As a whole, this work shows hallmarks of Lili Boulanger's style. The pianissimo ending has by now become almost a signature with her. Because of the academic standards of judgment that she knew would be applied to this composition, it is certainly not so personal a statement as her later works—the *Clairières dans le Ciel*, for example—but even so, she has managed to surmount the obstacle presented by having to compose a set piece in a particular place during a set period of time during a given year, and has even made of her effort a living piece of music.

Faust et Hélène was Lili Boulanger's last scholastic work. Once having won the Prix de Rome, she was no longer considered a student. From that point on, she would be on her own artistically, and without the fear of offending a jury with her music. It was perfectly logical that Lili should have dedicated this work— the only one published during her own lifetime—to her sister, Nadia.

6

The Works of Lili Boulanger: After the Prix de Rome

After winning the Prix de Rome in July 1913, Lili appears not to have finished any other compositions that year. No dated sketches are extant for the remainder of the year either.

During her stay at the Villa Medici in 1914, Lili Boulanger was in the process of composing a number of works, some of which were not completed until several years later. One of the pieces she worked on at the Villa was the *Morceau pour piano: Thème et Variations*. Until now it has been believed that the composer never finished this piece.[1] The work has never been published. Only by examining with extreme care her notebooks and sketchbooks did I discover the completed holograph manuscript, folded in half and inserted between the cover and flyleaf of one of her sketchbooks, where it had lain unnoticed until then. It is, as its title indicates, a theme and a set of variations for piano solo, written in a style consistent with her other works from this period.[2] It was finished on June 12, 1914. Mlle Nadia Boulanger was extremely surprised to learn that this work had, indeed, been finished, since she had never before seen it in its completed form.

Cortège, which exists in two versions—one for piano solo, the other for violin and piano—was also written while Lili was at the Villa Medici. In fact, it, too, was completed in June 1914. Since it is dedicated to the violinist Yvonne Astruc, it is most likely that the piece was originally conceived as a work for violin and piano, rather than for piano solo. Idiomatically written for the violin, it is a tasteful little salon piece, bubbling over with high spirits (Example 47). The piano transcription, although it is very well

Example 47

made, misses some of the ebullience of the original version. No autograph manuscripts for this work can now be found, so the only available sources for it are both versions as published by Ricordi in 1919. Still a third arrangement of this piece for flute and piano was also supposed to have been published by Ricordi that same year.[3]

Lili completed two other works during her stay at the Villa Medici in 1914. *D'un Jardin Clair* and *D'un Vieux Jardin* are short genre pieces for piano for which neither sketches nor autograph manuscripts appear to be extant. *D'un Jardin Clair* shares the same *joie de vivre* as *Cortège*. They even share the key signature of B major. Dedicated to Ninette Salles, this work, like all the others from the same period, shows impressionistic influences (Example 48). Ostinato figurations are not used here. The piece

Example 48

is monothematic, with a harmonic structure based on superposed fourths and fifths, while the treble throughout contains melodic fragments and variants of the first four measures. Nevertheless, it creates the aural effect of improvisation. *D'un Vieux Jardin* is also a descendant of the impressionistic school of writing. But it is a more personal statement, involving the use of an almost chant-like melody accompanied at times by convoluted harmonic configurations (Example 49).[4]

Example 49

Lili Boulanger wrote two other works for solo instrument and piano during the year 1914. Both *Pièce pour violoncelle et piano* and *Pièce pour hautbois et piano* seem to have disappeared, as have all traces of any sketches Lili may have made for them. It cannot now be determined whether she worked on these pieces during or after her stay at the Villa Medici.[5]

Clairières dans le Ciel—the most important work Lili Boulanger completed during 1914—is a cycle of thirteen songs chosen from among the twenty-four poems originally included by Francis Jammes in his poetic cycle entitled "Tristesses." In it the poet expresses, in accordance with the Symbolist aesthetic,[6] his feelings toward his lost love, evoking in the process the interplay of fleeting and complex emotions which are aroused in him, for example, by a Madonna at the foot of his bed, two columbines on a hillside, the sight of a country landscape, a keepsake medal given him by his love, a memory of last year's lilacs, and a sudden rainstorm. The poems that Lili selected for her song cycle form a dramatic whole. The poetic cycle and the composer's arrangement of it are compared in the chart.

"Tristesses" and "Clairières dans le Ciel"

Incipit of Poem	Position in "Tristesses" (Jammes)	Position in "Clairières . . ." (Boulanger)
Je la désire	1	
Elle était descendue	2	1
Dans le chemin	3	
Elle est gravement gaie	4	2
Parfois, je suis triste	5	3
Un poète disait	6	4
Son souvenir emplit l'air	7	
Au pied de mon lit	8	5
Elle avait emporté	9	
Si tout ceci n'est qu'un pauvre rêve	10	6
Je ne désire point	11	
O mon coeur! ce sera	12	
Nous nous aimerons tant	13	7
Faisait-il beau	14	
Je garde une médaille	15	12
J'ai quelqu'un dans le coeur	16	
Vous m'avez regardé	17	8
Je songe à ce jour-là	18	
Les lilas qui avaient fleuri	19	9
Deux ancolies se balançaient	20	10
Par ce que j'ai souffert	21	11
Venez sous la tonnelle	22	
Venez, ma bien aimée	23	
Demain fera un an	24	13

Lili identified strongly with the heroine of these poems, a tall, somewhat mysterious young girl who suddenly disappeared from the poet's life. Lili wondered what had become of this girl, and she and Miki Piré speculated together on what had happened to her.[7]

Perhaps one more reason for the fact that there were thirteen songs in *Clairières dans le Ciel* stems from Lili's half-humorous fondness for the number thirteen. Because there were exactly thirteen letters in the form of her name that she habitually used,[8] Lili sometimes amused her friends by letting the number thirteen stand as a symbol for her. Thus, the thirteen songs in the *Clairières dans le Ciel* are a personal and private way, one known only to the composer and those closest to her, of showing how deeply involved she was in what she was doing. It was another way of making the cycle her own. In addition, Lili had chosen a monogram from among several offered to her by the Ricordi company for use on the title pages of her published works. The one she picked, quite deliberately, is one that resembles the number thirteen. Therefore, when *Clairières dans le Ciel* first appeared in printed form, it contained three means of identifying the composer: the composer's name, her monogram, and the fact that the song cycle itself contained precisely thirteen compositions.[9]

"Elle était descendue," the first poem Lili set, describes the heroine in a meadow. It has a mood of gentle melancholy. Ostinato figuration is here used with flexibility and is not permitted to dominate the texture. It obscures neither the words nor their sense. As in all the songs in this collection, the syllabic declamation is carefully conceived and correct. The tenderness of the poet's reverie is reflected both in the lilting accompaniment and in the fact that the song never attains a dynamic level above piano. The poet's changing moods are mirrored in sudden skips in the vocal line and a corresponding increase in chromatically altered notes in the accompaniment (Example 50).

Example 50

The first two songs are meant to be treated as a performance
unit. Written in E major, the quatrain "Elle est gravement gaie"
also carries the same time signature as "Elle était descendue."
The accompaniment pattern of "Elle est gravement gaie" pre-
sages that of Fauré's last songs, especially the "Diane" of the
Horizon chimérique, which he composed shortly after Lili Boulanger's death. The piano counterbalances the brightness of the
vocal line in "Elle est gravement gaie," beginning with resonant,
measured quarter-note chords against the supple grace of the voice
(Example 51), and ending with the impression of distant caril-
lons, as if signaling the end of a dream (Example 52).

Example 51

Example 52

"Parfois, je suis triste," the third song, is a highly segmented
composition, each portion of which deals with a single emotion,
as the poet first describes his unhappy loneliness, then his joy

175

when the thought of his beloved returns to him. Finally he is sad-
dened by the knowledge of an irrevocable separation between
him and his love. Here the composer has woven the vocal line
into the general texture so that its declamatory character is har-
monically fused to the accompaniment. Each reinforces the other
(Example 53). There is an ambiguity in the poem, too, since
the fate of the heroine is never made clear. This uncertainty is
mirrored even in the introduction, where the composer's use of
superposed, sideslipping fifths creates a corresponding aura of tonal
ambiguity (Example 54).

The fourth song of this collection returns to the E major of
the first two. "Un poète disait . . ." is joyous in its evocation of
the elation which the poet and his lady had once shared. The
accompaniment adopts a pattern of running triplet figures, bab-
bling on like the fountain in the poet's heart (Example 55), until
the end, where his desire to give his sweetheart an indefinable
gift leads the composer to add a vocal pedal point of quiet intensity to the final measures (Example 56).

Example 53

Example 54

Example 55

Example 56

"Au pied de mon lit" reintroduces the note of doubt that had characterized the first three poems. It describes the holy image that sustains the poet in times of trouble and distress. This song had a deeply personal meaning for Lili Boulanger, beginning, as it does, with the description of a black Virgin put at the foot of the poet's bed by his mother. Lili kept one of her mother's Russian icons at the foot of her own bed. The identification of the image in the poem with the icon at the foot of the composer's bed is further reinforced by the fact that this particular song is

Figure 48. Lili Boulanger's icon. *Photo: M. Tamvico, Paris.*

dedicated to Mme Boulanger. Beginning simply, almost like one of Mussorgsky's nursery songs (Example 57), it becomes more and more agitated, mirroring the poet's dissatisfaction with himself and his own feelings of unworthiness to be loved by the object of his affections.

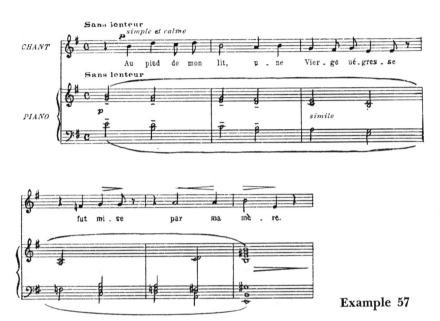

Example 57

In the sixth, "Si tout ceci n'est qu'un pauvre rêve," Lili has elaborated on the restless, troubled aspects of the preceding song. Treating as it does the idea that all the poet's happiness may be only a dream, one more of life's disillusions, the music focuses intently on this mood of melancholy. Perhaps in a sort of double allusion, the composer has chosen to invoke once more the prelude to *Tristan* (Example 58), which literally forms a sort of leitmotiv throughout this song. This particular poem also lends itself to other interpretations. The *Tristan* motive may refer not only to the love theme that runs through this collection of poems, but may also be a somewhat belated way of thanking Miki Piré, who took Lili to a concert when she was in Nice working on this cycle. Lili had been very much impressed by the performance of the *Tristan* prelude she had heard there. Preoccupied as the composer already was with ideas of her own impending death, there can be little doubt that it is not only the poet who wistfully wonders whether he will ever recover from his pain (Example 59).

Example 58

Example 59

Tenderness is the pervading emotion of "Nous nous aimerons tant" (no. 7), describing the poet's dream of love in which there will be no further need of words. A sort of languor is created by the pianissimo opening, by the key of B-flat major, and by the slow tempo and soft dynamics that run throughout this piece. Short sequences of descending eleventh chords add new elements of harmonic interest which, however, are not used for their own sake. Rather, they underline important textual points, in a sense almost depicting in one case the reaching out of a hand (Example 60).

In "Vous m'avez regardé avec toute votre âme" (no. 8), the cycle returns to the mood of the first two songs, gently wistful and characterized by a vague melancholy. The brightness of E major that shines through momentarily is negated by the closing measures, which prolong the final cadence through the use of pedal points in the bass (Example 61).

Example 60

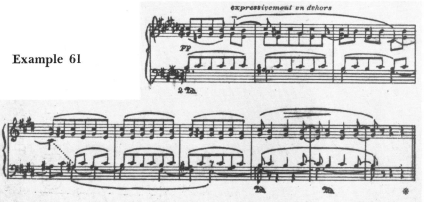

Example 61

The ninth song, "Les lilas qui avaient fleuri," is once again in E major, and the piano accompaniment glides like a harp over the gentle arpeggios of the first four lines of text (Example 62), stopping only when it becomes necessary for the composer to mirror the anguish of the poet with the dissonance of the tritone C to F♯ and a rhythmic layering of the accompaniment (Example 63). This emotional suffering then continues to the end of the song.

Example 62

Example 63

The piano accompaniment for "Deux ancolies," the next in the cycle (no. 10), opens with gentle triplets in the treble. The effect is sheer gossamer, creating the impression of beating wings or splashing water to complement the story of two sister columbines on a hillside, trembling in the wind (Example 64).

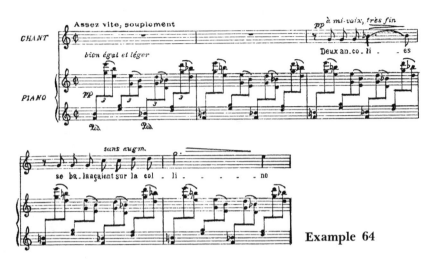

Example 64

There is an overriding sadness in "Par ce que j'ai souffert" (no. 11), which seems once more to be an expression of personal feeling on the part of both the poet and the composer. The general mood is in sharp contrast to that of the preceding poem. The C major of "Deux ancolies" has given way to D minor in "Par ce que j'ai souffert." In this poem, Jammes describes the fact that his own suffering has helped him to understand that of others. Those knowing the circumstances of Lili Boulanger's life and having read some of her letters must see a direct parallel between the words of the poet and the ideas of Lili Boulanger herself. There is almost a feeling of psalmody in the opening measures (Example 65). This is one of the most openly passionate

Example 65

of all the songs in the collection, depicting the hero's sleepless nights and personal agony, knowing that what has happened is irrevocable. As the agitation of the text increases, the harmony, too, becomes increasingly chromatic, while the idea of the permanence of the poet's pain is reinforced with a pedal point in the bass (Example 66). This is the only song of the thirteen that ends forte, as though the composer were here, for the one and only time, daring to bewail her fate openly, in one final outpouring of anguish (Example 67).

Example 66

Example 67

The mood of melancholy continues to deepen into one of almost infinite sadness in "Je garde une médaille d'elle" (No. 12). The somber, measured, opening chords lend a note of finality (Example 68). Later the inner conflicts of the hero are mirrored

Example 68

in the deliberate dissonances between the vocal line and the accompaniment, which appear as the poet, thinking of the keepsake his love has given him, is suddenly reminded of the time it spent hanging around her neck. This makes the medal not only dark, in the sense that it has tarnished from wear, but also sad in the poet's perception because of its melancholy associations. It is this inner tension that the composer has chosen to express chromatically (Example 69). The song trails off with a gentle repetition

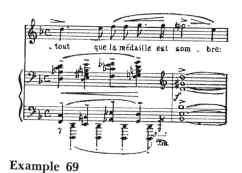

Example 69

of the opening measures, stated pianissimo in the accompaniment. This is one of the most beautiful songs in the cycle as well as the shortest.

"Demain fera un an" (no. 13) is a distillation of the ideas presented in the rest of the cycle. As Schubert did in his *Winterreise*, Lili Boulanger creates a psychological whole out of the disparate elements of the twelve preceding songs by interweaving in this last song elements of the others. This is not all the composer's doing alone. The poem itself is also full of allusions to those in the cycle which preceded it. Just as this poem is the longest and most complicated of Jammes's collection, so, too, the thirteenth and last song is the most complicated. "Demain fera un an" may well be the most poignant song of all, recalling as it does, from the perspective of a later day, an earlier happiness in full knowledge that this state of bliss has been irrevocably lost. It was just a year before, the poet tells us, that the joy went out of his life, and he wonders why he, too, did not die then.

Beginning with a quasi-recitative declamation of the first three lines of the text, the composer begins to build tension through the judicious use of gradually faster note values in the accompaniment, and the eventual fragmentation of her originally long, arching accompaniment patterns as well as by an accelerando and louder dynamics. The vocal line adds a breathless quality in its use of short phrases, punctuated by rests, as the hero describes how he has plunged into the country and across its woods and meadows (Example 70). The poet is torturing himself with his

Example 70

memories, having forced himself to return to the place where he has suffered so greatly. The music, too, begins to remember the dream of happiness by recalling the rhythmic accompaniment pattern of the fourth song (Example 71). A rush of images follows in

Example 71

which the composer does not attempt to keep pace with the actual words of the poet, but rather continues the basic accompaniment pattern, which recalls past joy and juxtaposes present sorrow. The opposition of reality and illusion leads to a fortissimo climax, followed by the reintroduction of the *Tristan* motive from "Si tout ceci n'est qu'un pauvre rêve" (Example 72).

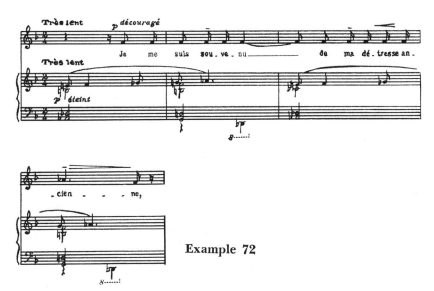

Example 72

Another climax, followed this time by total silence—one of the most effective and affecting moments in the entire cycle—presaging the reentry of the voice, which floats as if suspended in limbo (Example 73). The bass returns to the pattern of the first measures for the next of the poet's tortured questions (Example 74). Then the piano forges ahead alone to the song's climax—and, incidentally, to that of the cycle itself. Once more silence precedes

Example 73

Example 74

the gentle reentry of both piano and voice, and the vocal line
proceeds above rippling triplets. The poet's anguish reappears
suddenly, with chromatically altered notes forming augmented
perfect intervals whose dissonance reflects his mental state (Example 75).

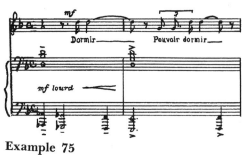

Example 75

Somehow the hero would like to find a way to forget the past that torments him, and here the music, too, rises in crescendo at his frustration. This last emotional outpouring, followed, once more, by silence, leads to utter desolation. Finally the dark foreboding of the bass drops out, and the D minor of the piece gives way to the E major of the first song. Here, as the poet recalls for the last time how his beloved went down to the meadow, both the words and the music of the first couplet of "Elle était descendue" are repeated. The composer had added a repetition of earlier lines to the end of the poem, restating the idea that nothing now sustains the poet. For these last measures, Lili has combined an almost literal quotation of the vocal line from its earlier appearance on these words, a return to the key of D minor, and a reprise of the accompaniment pattern of the opening measures of this song. But that is not all. In the last seven measures, the composer has managed a subtle reference to the second accompaniment pattern of "Par ce que j'ai souffert," thus introducing a final means of summing up the meaning of the cycle from her point of view.[10]

The entire cycle was inspired by the voice of David Devriès, the great tenor who had sung in the first performance of *Faust et Hélène,* and by his qualities as a musician.[11] But, as noted before, individual songs were also dedicated to others. Perhaps, if more documents and other pertinent information become available, it will be possible to trace more of the composer's reasons for dedicating certain songs to specific people, as well as, in some cases, for adopting a particular compositional style in a given song.[12]

As stated earlier, Lili Boulanger is known to have completed only one composition during 1915. This work, *Pièce pour trompette et petit orchestre,* and all sketches for it, seem to have disappeared.

Lili completed two psalm settings during her second stay at the Villa Medici the following year. Both *Psalm 24 (La Terre appartient à l'Éternel)* and *Psalm 129 (Ils m'ont assez opprimé dès ma jeunesse)* were, therefore, finished in the space of a few months' time during 1916. These scores are large-scale choral and instrumental works, and mark a distinct change in feeling tone from that which produced the intimate *Clairières dans le Ciel.* Because of the fact that these works were in the planning stages for some time, it is probably not justified to consider them as a new step in the compositional evolution of Lili Boulanger.[13]

Psalm 24 returns to the brilliant fanfare introduction that had marked a much earlier work of Lili's—the *Hymne au Soleil.* The composer has chosen to treat this in a consciously archaic, regal style, and for that reason has dispensed with both strings and woodwinds, leaving an orchestra composed of trumpets, trombones, horns, tuba, tympani, harp, and organ. This is an assertive work. Both the instruments and the voices are quite aggressive in declaring God's dominion over the earth (Example 76). The wom-

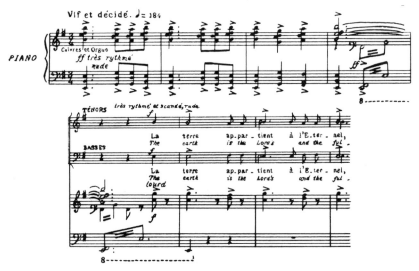

Example 76

en's voices appear to add both greater substance and a degree of word-painting to the composition, entering as they do for the first time on the words "Lift up your heads, O ye gates." The vocal line the sopranos are given to sing reinforces this conclusion (Example 77).

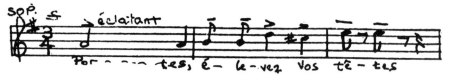

Example 77

After the text has been completed, the composer brings in the chorus one last time, to sing a syllable that had long since become part of her musical vocabulary and is again found in all three of her remaining vocal compositions—the syllable *Ah!*. Reeser has discounted the influence of Mussorgsky and Stravinsky in this work, pointing out that the harmonic language is perhaps the most important aspect of the composition. Lili Boulanger was, at this point, not familiar with Stravinsky's work, but she did know Mussorgsky's.[14] His influence does seem to hang over the piece, just as it does in "Au pied de mon lit."

For *Psalm 129*, Lili has employed full orchestral and choral forces. This is a much more developed statement than *Psalm 24;* perhaps the text itself demands more than just a straight declarative treatment. Here once again is an intensely personal statement on the part of the composer, a fact not at all surprising, considering the text. The parallel ninths of the opening measures foreshadow Honegger's *Le Roi David,* which was not written until after Lili Boulanger's death, and, more specifically, his setting of "Pitié de moi, mon Dieu!" The harshness of the musical setting ably mirrors the ideas of the text (Example 78) and continues until the text permits another type of approach—that is, until the malediction of the enemies of Zion. Here, after an initial fortissimo outburst, the second part of the curse begins piano, perhaps describing the insignificance of the enemies of Zion after the curse has been pronounced upon them. The true aspect of softness finally does enter with the women's voices that accompany the closing benediction, singing *Ah!* (Example 79). Both of these psalms exist in more than one version—*Psalm 24,* for chorus, organ, and orchestra and a transcription for voice and piano; *Psalm 129* in its original orchestral version as well as two piano reductions, one of the orchestral edition, the other a transposition of the first for bass rather than baritone soloist.[15]

Lili's rather depressed state of mind during the summer of 1916 is mirrored in her next work, *Dans l'immense Tristesse.* In it, she has returned to the dark sonorities that had characterized parts of *Pour les Funérailles d'un Soldat.* The vocal line, often dissonant and somewhat convoluted, as befits the text, is accompanied almost entirely by deep, foreboding, bass sonorities (Example 80). Adding to the similarities between this piece and *Pour les Funérailles d'un Soldat* is the use of a bell effect in the piano part of *Dans l'immense Tristesse.* The harmony continues to strike pungent dissonances to convey the anguish of the mother, visiting her child's tomb at night, but finally reaches a sort of resolution after the end of the text, when the piano softly inserts a short quotation from the traditional French lullaby, "Do, do, l'enfant do," and ending with the faintly dissonant sounds of superimposed perfect intervals, followed by two lone reverberating pianissimo B-flats in the bass (Example 81).[16]

Lili Boulanger's setting of *Psalm 130 (Du fond de l'Abîme)* is a monumental work. With the exception of the *Clairières dans*

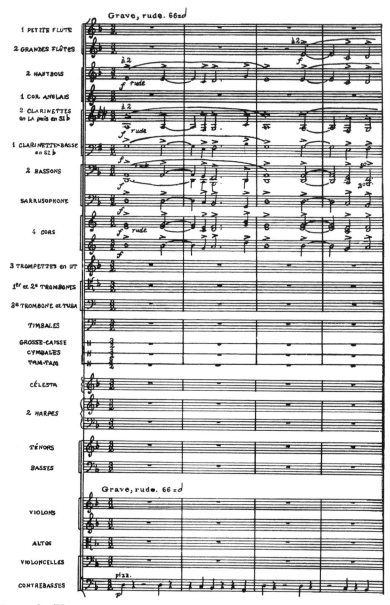

Example 78

192

Example 79

Example 80

Example 81

le Ciel, it is Lili's longest and most complicated extant work completed after her student days. Although Reeser states that the composer was working on this composition as early as 1914, and the published score does, indeed, state that she started it in 1914 and finished it in 1917,[17] the autograph manuscript in the posession of Mlle Nadia Boulanger contains no date of any kind, and the earliest sketches—themselves undated—are to be found in a bound composition notebook with material dating from 1915 and 1916.

Scored for a full complement of woodwinds, brasses and percussion, a full chorus, organ, and strings, with alto solo, *Du fond de l'Abîme* is a synthesis of the homophonic treatment found in *Psalm 24* and the emphasis on counterpoint in Lili's early choruses. Both the voices and the instruments are masterfully treated. The composer shows great sensitivity to the balancing and timbres of voices and instruments.

In some ways, Lili Boulanger has chosen to take the text extremely literally, but this time with considerable ingenuity. Beginning with a solo in the lower parts of the orchestra—in the tuba and cello (Example 82), the composer evokes quite deliber-

Example 82

194

ately the idea of an abyss. The solo itself is almost psalmodic in declamation. The deep introduction may be compared to that in Ravel's *La Valse* and *Concerto for the Left Hand,* both composed after World War I. After the two violins engage in an agitated duet opening with striking ascending fourths and fifths, the lower instruments once more take over, and to their busy figurations is added a new theme, which appears first in the trumpets (Example 83).

Example 83

This theme becomes more and more agitated, reaches a fortissimo, and finally dies away while the first theme is reintroduced. It is here that the full chorus enters, pianissimo at the octave, with "Du fond de l'abîme." The first statement is filled with the traditional minor second denoting fear (Example 84). To this

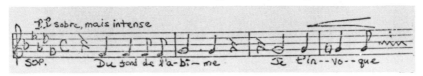

Example 84

homophonic statement are added thematic fragments used for fugáto instrumental sections that weave an intricate web around the voices. After the voices join into the contrapuntal texture, they regroup and end the section in aggressive homophony. A short instrumental introduction precedes the entry of the contraltos and basses in an Allegro section that recalls the brass theme of the introduction. Once more the full chorus enters, to restate the first theme.

The contralto soloist enters in the middle of the second verse, at which time a new theme appears in the clarinets (Example 85). This solo has been heralded by the use, once more, of the syllable *Ah!,* so familiar from the composer's earlier vocal works. There follows a canon between the cello and oboe that echoes the soloist. The rest of the contraltos join the soloist to close the verse.

The two harps introduce the third verse with increasingly

Example 85

agitated arpeggios. The winds begin to echo this theme. Then a viola and cello solo precede the reentry of the contralto, followed by the chorus, which repeats her theme in solemn counterpoint.

For the fourth verse, contralto and tenor solos bring with them a rescoring of earlier figurations, and their melodic lines are prolonged by a new reduced chorus. Against the remaining

196

two contraltos, two tenors, and two basses, the solo contralto continues to sing, doubled by four sopranos. Despite the polyphonic web spun around this section by the composer, the reinforcement given the soloist helps keep her from being submerged in all the musical cross-currents.

After the text proper has ended, the composer adds a coda, echoing the opening themes, and, as in her very early works, dividing the chorus—here to express the contrasting themes of supplication and hope. It is the sorrowful suppliants who end the work, still beseeching God's mercy.[18]

Finished also during the spring of 1917 while Lili was at Arcachon, *Vieille Prière Bouddhique* shares with *Psalm 129* a number of orchestral and choral techniques. Neither sketches nor original dated manuscripts for this work are to be found, but it is probable that the composer actually received this text from her friend Suzanne Karpelès sometime during 1914.[19] It is, indeed, an old Buddhist text, not a Hindu prayer, as has sometimes been claimed.[20] The original is in Pâli, "a sort of Buddhist meditation on 'Universal love.' . . . This text is learnt by heart by the 'SAMANERAS' [*sic*] novices when they receive the first ordination 'PABBAJJA' [*sic*] in the Theravada Buddhist countries like Ceylon, Burma, Thailand, Cambodia and Laos. It is meant for everybody in a general sense."[21] Lili Boulanger's choice of this text is one further expression of her interest in considerations of peace and happiness, and is not simply an attraction to oriental exotica for its own sake.

In the work itself, a sense of stasis is created by the frequent repetitions of a modal formula of very limited range, which gives the piece a pentatonic cast (Example 86). Less than one-third

Example 86

the length of *Psalm 130,* it nevertheless makes use of full orchestra, four-part chorus, and tenor soloist. The composer has chosen to pair the soprano and tenor voices in opposition to the altos and basses, and to use shifting instrumental doubling to vary the timbre. So that the words themselves will not be distorted, she permits only the alto and bass parts to declaim the text homorhythmically, while the sopranos and tenors simply vocalize with their mouths closed. As in Lili's earlier works, she has inserted a bit of word-painting. On the words "Let every creature . . . move freely," she permits more flexibility in the vocal line (Example 87).

Example 87

The second verse brings with it the emancipation of the strings, which, up until now, had simply sustained pedal points. The woodwinds and brasses here fulfill that function, while the strings reiterate the initial formula in unison with the harp, and the altos and basses intone the first lines of text.

A flute solo heralds the entry of the tenor solo around which the instruments intersperse motivic countermelodies and occasional doublings. Throughout this verse, pedal points and slow-moving basses help to reinforce the underlying idea of tranquillity in the text. As the tenor solo comes to an end, sopranos and basses enter, and the technique here is that of canonic vocal entries, harking back to the composer's earliest choruses. As used here, it gives new meaning to the words, emphasizing as it does that everyone should be permitted to follow his own path, according to his own destiny. The whole section has been delicate. As it trails off into silence, the divisi altos enter with a shortened version of the earlier string accompaniment, which is then taken up by the other voices as well. Here, the voices are used as instruments, and simply vocalize with their mouths closed. By the end of the passage, the sopranos are also divisi.

After a long pause, the full chorus enters fortissimo with the melodic outline, while the violins, violas, and cellos once more recall the original modal formula against a background of pedal points in the bass clarinet, horns, sarrusophone, and trombone. There follows a fugato section in which both the voices and instruments participate. Finally, homophony triumphs, only to be followed by a growing vocalization in all parts—sopranos and tenors, as in the opening measures, against altos and basses—on *Ah!*. Both voices and instruments end in a blazing triple-forte climax.[22]

Both *D'un Soir triste* and *D'un Matin de Printemps* were conceived by the composer in three different versions simultaneously.[23] *D'un Soir triste* was written in versions for cello and piano, for piano trio, and for orchestra. *D'un Matin de Printemps* exists in versions for violin (or, alternatively, flute) and piano, for piano trio, and for orchestra.[24] That these are companion pieces has already been remarked.[25] The similarities in their themes are indeed striking (Example 88), but their moods are entirely dif-

Example 88

ferent. One is mournful, almost dirgelike, while the other is, by turns, mordant, animated, agitated, and slightly ironic. These were the last pieces Lili Boulanger wrote with her own hand. Her manuscripts for these works betray the increasing effects of her illness. The notes are minuscule. What reveal most the composer's steadily worsening physical condition are the alternative versions within a single score, the insertion of ideas in the space between staves, and the crossing-out of several measures in what was obviously meant to be the fair copy of the trio version of *D'un Soir triste*. Such alterations are simply not to be found in the extant fair copies of her other works. Throughout the orchestral score of *D'un Soir triste*, too, parts have been deleted or changed after the fair copy was made, and the final nuances are partly in Lili's hand, partly in Nadia's, following Lili's own indications of dynamics and balances in the trio score.

There seems to be no extant autograph orchestral score for *D'un Matin de Printemps*, but the greater precision in the violin (or flute) and piano version makes it appear that Lili finished it slightly earlier than the trio version and *D'un Soir triste*. The two pieces were meant by the composer to complement each other.

On the title page of the autograph trio score, there appears the notation in Lili Boulanger's tiny script that these are "Pieces for trio," and both *D'un Soir triste* and *D'un Matin de Printemps* are listed thereon.[26]

The first of Lili Boulanger's sketches for the *Pie Jesu* are to be found in a composition book she used between 1909 and 1913. These jottings contain the "Amen" and four measures of the bass, which forms an ostinato during the opening measures of the work. It is possible that this was envisioned by the composer as part of a complete Requiem Mass, because a sketch for a Kyrie appears in another of her composition workbooks—one that she used later, between 1913 and 1916. In any event, Lili was never to complete this Mass in its entirety.

The *Pie Jesu* is scored for string quartet, harp, organ, and vocal soloist. The orchestral score and the reduction for organ and voice each exist in two versions—for medium voice and for high voice. Leaving aside other stylistic considerations, Lili has here returned to the techniques of instrumental layering that she used as far back as the *Nocturne* (Example 89). Chromaticism in

Example 89

Example 90

Example 91

the instruments continues, as if expressing inner turmoil in the same way the composer has so frequently mirrored it in the past. Yet here the vocal line does not participate. It carries the text and remains independent throughout the early portion of the work. The voice is supple, graceful, while the accompaniment is earthbound. Knowing the composer's philosophical and religious beliefs, it is entirely possible that the compositional aspects of this piece are deliberately allegorical. After the voice reaches a modal cadence on E (Example 90), the organ and voice engage in a short duet in which the organ accompaniment gains more and more freedom from the ostinato figurations of the earlier measures. This is followed by an instrumental section that reintroduces the voice with a plaintive new statement of "Pie Jesu." As the final section is reached, the original chromaticism dies away to reveal a new sweetness, symbolized too, perhaps, by the entry of the harp, which has remained silent up to this point. The vocal ending is, once again, sweetly modal, but with discreet dissonances in the instruments (Example 91).

The work's serenity is almost certainly as much a comment on the composer's own feelings toward death as it is a proper setting of the text. Although this work is written in the same style—generally speaking—as Fauré's *Requiem,* there is no quotation from the older master here. When properly performed, Lili Boulanger's *Pie Jesu* has a deeply moving eloquence.[27]

7

Lili Boulanger:
Myths and Realities

By the time of Lili Boulanger's death at the age of twenty-four, her name had become well-known among the élite of French society—so much so, in fact, that the normally staid and impersonal newspaper *Le Temps,* which rarely gave even the famous more than a few lines, devoted almost its entire obituary column for March 18, 1918, to news of her and her death. Théodore Lindenlaub, who wrote this article, described Lili's abilities in glowing terms. "Her talent," he wrote, "was of a rare quality, all delicacy and poetry."[1] *Faust et Hélène,* he reminded his readers, was a remarkable work, appreciated by artists and public alike, beyond the confines of the Institut, and it had been given several times with full orchestra during the regular Paris concert season, where it had met with ever-increasing favor. M. Lindenlaub also mentioned the premiere of five of Lili's *Clairières* at a concert given by the Société nationale, which had taken place just a few days earlier. These songs, he said, "moved deeply even those there who did not know that it was a farewell to art and to life."[2]

Considering the fact that France was, at that time, in the midst of a desperate fight for survival, and that Frenchmen were dying every day, it expresses perhaps some measure of the esteem in which Lili Boulanger was held that such notice was taken of her death.

In the months that followed, other glowing testimonials to

Lili Boulanger appeared in widely scattered periodicals. Crussard, writing in the *Journal des Ouvrages de Dames* in June 1918, praised both her gifts and the use to which she had put them. The writer knew that Lili had left works that had not yet been performed, and felt it almost a moral duty that they be heard so that France could give the composer all the recognition to which she was entitled. In closing, Crussard even went as far as to compare her to the virgin martyrs killed in antiquity to bring victory.[3]

Émile Vuillermoz, writing in *France-Aviation* that August, was equally laudatory. After recalling her successes and trials in life, he compared Lili to the poor little Princess Maleine, whose tragic destiny he felt she shared.[4]

Feelings about Lili Boulanger and her untimely death were running high in France. By May, even Albert Besnard had decided to honor her memory in a most singular way—by trying to place Lucienne Heuvelmann's bust of her in the Church of San Luigi Nono, the French church in Rome. But even this gesture (which indicated an astonishing change of heart for Besnard) did not satisfy the anonymous author of the article that appeared in *Excelsior* early in May. The loss of the young composer, he asserted, "has plunged the art world into mourning." Although he found M. Besnard's proposal "touching," he felt that even more of a tribute was in order.

> But why not also perpetuate in the Villa Medici garden itself the memory of this charming Muse who died too soon? . . .
>
> Often, after having lunched in the welcoming refectory adorned with the portraits of all the Prix de Rome winners, she went to seat herself near the marble Minerva, and confided her hopes of glory to the other *pensionnaires*.
>
> It is in this enchanted retreat that one would like to see her image. It is there, above all, that her memory should be honored.[25]

It was during the summer of 1918 that Walter Damrosch met Nadia Boulanger in France and learned about Lili's compositions. He was so impressed that he conducted a concert of Lili's works there[6] and later brought some of the orchestral scores back with him to America, planning to present them during the 1918–19 season in New York. Damrosch had chosen *Pour les Funérailles d'un Soldat* and *Hymne au Soleil* to form part of his opening concert with the New York Oratorio Society on December 3, 1918. Unfortunately, the orchestral parts for *Hymne au Soleil* were lost in transit, and therefore only *Pour les Funérailles d'un Soldat* could be performed. James Gibbons Huneker, the *New York Times* music critic, was extremely snide in his review the next day, complaining mainly about what he felt was a lack of originality in *Pour les Funérailles d'un Soldat*. He did comment, however, on the composer's "effective use of antique ecclesiastical modes" and the "elegiac" atmosphere of the baritone solo which, he felt, was well in keeping with the mood. He strongly believed that the piece itself was ineffective in comparison with Wolf-Ferrari's *La Vita nuova,* which had preceded it on the program.[7] His real objections to Lili Boulanger did not become clearly evident until Walter Damrosch presented her *Faust et Hélène* at Carnegie Hall with the Symphony Society of New York on December 26, 1918. The problem, as Huneker saw it, was that Lili Boulanger was a woman. The review is otherwise strangely contradictory, since he does admit having respect for her ability. "Of the gifts of this girl of 19," he wrote, "there can be no doubt. Indeed, her musical maturity is astonishing. . . ."[8] The conflict between the reviewer's personal prejudices and the evidence of his own senses is nowhere so evident as in the final sentences of his review. "More's the pity," he writes, "that she died so young, as she would surely have achieved a musical personality. But women composers are at best whistling hens."[9] That this was not the last performance of a work of Lili Boulanger in New York was obviously not due to the efforts of this critic.

In 1918 Mme Ernest Boulanger and Mlle Nadia Boulanger, following Lili's wishes, established a prize at the Conservatoire to be awarded each year to a student in the composition classes chosen by examination during January. M. and Mme Richard Bouwens van der Boijen had also given a grant, to be distributed to two young composers in a composition class who were wounded in the war, so that their works could be made known. These gifts to the Conservatoire were not included in the prizes awarded in the spring of 1918, but they were given out during the public ceremony on Sunday, October 10, 1918. The gift of the Bouwens was divided between Georges Migot and Paul Roussel.[10]

On December 3, 1918, a concert in memory of the young composer was given at the Salle Central on the rue Bovy-Lysberg. The program included works of Duparc, Franck, and Chausson, in addition to Lili's complete *Faust et Hélène*. Throughout the following year, works by Lili Boulanger figured in the programs of a number of French musical organizations. On January 17 the Société Musicale Indépendante presented three of her *Clairières*— "Au pied de mon lit," "Je garde une médaille d'elle," and "Par ce que j'ai souffert"—with Paul Koubitzky and Nadia Boulanger. On the twelfth of February, at a concert given by the Élèves de Sinfonia, "Par ce que j'ai souffert," *Nocturne, Cortège,* and the duet from *Faust et Hélène* were performed. There followed a group of five of the *Clairières* on a recital program given by Claire Croiza on March 21, with Nadia Boulanger at the piano. As part of a benefit performance for war widows and orphans, Lili's *Pour les Funérailles d'un Soldat* was given on March 29 at the Théâtre des Champs-Élysées, with Nadia playing an organ transcription of the accompaniment. Still more performances of the *Nocturne, Cortège,* and the *Clairières* followed in April and early May. On May 8 the *Nocturne* and *Cortège* were played in Brussels by Dany Brunschwig (violin) and Geneviève Debelly (piano).[11]

There were other major performances of Lili's music. On the twenty-fourth and twenty-fifth of May, the Concerts Pasdeloup, with Jane Montjovet as soloist, gave "Nous nous aimerons tant," "Deux Ancolies," "Si tout ceci n'est qu'un pauvre rêve," and "Au pied de mon lit" with full orchestra. At the Schola Cantorum on May 25 the featured work was the version for organ of *Pour les Funérailles,* played by Nadia Boulanger. On June 3, 1919, an entire concert was devoted to the works of Lili Boulanger, including the *Hymne au Soleil, Soir sur la Plaine* with Mme Croiza and the Association chorale de Paris under the direction of Désiré-Émile Ingelbrecht, unspecified selections from *Clairières* sung by David Devriès, *Nocturne, D'un matin de Printemps,* and *Cortège* played by Yvonne Astruc, and the complete *Faust et Hélène.* Nadia Boulanger was at the piano. On June 6 the Société Musicale Indépendante once more presented several of Lili's compositions —this time three more of her *Clairières*—"Elle était descendue," "Parfois, je suis triste," and "Demain fera un an"—with David Devriès as soloist and Nadia Boulanger at the piano.[12]

Meanwhile Lili Boulanger's death had also received notice from some of the leading music periodicals in America. *The Musician* for February 1919 gave her a two-column obituary, and printed a picture of her as she had looked just after winning the Prix de Rome. It noted her choral works, mentioned her activities in support of the Franco-American Committee during World War I, and described how Walter Damrosch had first become acquainted with Lili's works. The article credits Walter Damrosch with the opinion that Lili's *Faust et Hélène* was "one of the masterpieces of modern music." "With so little time for experimentation," the obituary concluded, "Lili Boulanger achieved a remarkable success. At the age of 24 she was regarded as one of

Figure 49. Program of the Société Musicale Indépendante for June 6, 1919. *Courtesy of the Département de la Musique, Bibliothèque Nationale, Paris.*

the most talented women composers in France."[13]

Miki Piré had remained devoted to the memory of her friend. Before her death, Lili had asked Miki to write some poems that she could set to music. However, Miki's wartime activities nursing the wounded had made it impossible for her to undertake any such project. It was only after the war that she was able to write a set of poems, which she dedicated to the memory of Lili Boulanger. This collection was important in a number of ways. Not only did it testify to her desire to keep her promise to Lili and provide the poems her friend had wanted. It is remarkable for its lyrical poetic qualities and for the fact that the author did her own illustrations. Some individual poems are actually comple-

Figure 50. Watercolor illustration from *En Recueillement,* showing Lili Boulanger's logo. *Courtesy of M. Arsène Paronian.*

ments to some of the *Clairières*. These poems were also responsible for the meeting of Camille Mauclair and Nadia Boulanger, and therefore for one of the earliest articles about Lili Boulanger. In 1919 Miki was trying to find someone to write a preface for her poems and decided to ask Mauclair, who lived in Grasse, not far from her home in Nice. He agreed enthusiastically, and in 1920 *En Recueillement*, a privately printed collection of poems and watercolors with a preface by Camille Mauclair, was published by Floury in Paris.[14] The poet became so interested in the life of Lili Boulanger that he met Nadia, interviewed her, and later wrote about Lili.[15]

Both Nadia Boulanger and Miki Piré had gone into deep mourning when Lili died. Miki had thought of Lili as a sister, and observed for her an extended period of mourning. She was very much concerned that Lili's works were not receiving so much public attention as she felt they deserved. In 1920 she heard that Albert Spalding would be playing at the Monte Carlo Casino. The violinist describes their subsequent meeting in his memoirs:

> In 1920, I was in Europe with the New York Symphony Orchestra, and one of our concerts took place in Monte Carlo Casino. After the concert I returned to the hotel to pack. I had to hurry to catch my train. In the lobby a young girl, dressed in deep mourning, accosted me. She had with her two pieces for the violin composed by her best friend, who had recently died. When I got to my room I found that they were by Lili Boulanger, a *Nocturne* and *Cortège*, both tone poems. I have played them publicly hundreds of times since.[16]

All during 1920, performances of Lili's compositions written before 1916 continued to find their way onto programs both in France and abroad. On March 18, Lili's *Reflets* was performed in Jordan Hall, Boston. An anonymous member of the audience was moved to write this on his program: "So beautiful, the audience insisted by their applause on hearing it a second time."[17]

On November 10, *Nocturne* and *Cortège* had been given their British premieres in Aeolian Hall (London) by the violinist Olga Rudd.[18]

At the Annual Public Meeting of the Institut de France, held on December 4, 1920, under the chairmanship of François Flameng, two of Lili Boulanger's works for orchestra were performed.[19] Her music often figured in benefit concerts, and was sometimes presented by more or less militant women's groups.

In Paris on January 19, 1921, the Union des Femmes Professeurs et Compositeurs de Musique gave a concert devoted entirely to Lili's works—*Dans l'immense Tristesse,* five of the *Clairières,*[20] *Nocturne, Cortège, D'un Soir Triste,* and *D'un Matin de Printemps.* The Ligue Française Pour le Droit des Femmes presented her *Pour les Funérailles* at the Palais du Trocadéro on March 6, with Nadia at the organ.[21]

Camille Mauclair began to give lectures on Lili Boulanger. The first of these for which there is any record took place at the concert of the Union des Femmes Professeurs et Compositeurs de Musique on January 19, 1921. On June 9 he again gave a speech on Lili Boulanger as part of the concert of her works presented by the Concerts Dandelot at the Salle Pleyel. Here Lili's *Vieille Prière bouddhique* and *Psalm 129* were given their premieres. This was a long concert, including, as it did, all thirteen of the *Clairières,* (sung by Gabriel Paulet, accompanied by Nadia Boulanger), *Pour les Funérailles* (as with *Vieille Prière bouddhique* and *Psalm 129,* under the direction of Henri Büsser). *Pie Jesu* and *Reflets* were also performed. Both the concert and the discourse were well received. The notes for this speech were printed in *La Revue Musicale* in August 1921 as "La vie et l'oeuvre de Lili Boulanger." In the same issue, Georges Migot reviewed the music in the most glowing terms. This first hearing of what he considered Lili's most important works affirmed for him the great loss the world of music had suffered by her early death.[22]

Others, too, were favorably impressed by the compositions performed at this concert. Commenting also on the musical élite who had attended this performance, the illuminating talk by Mauclair and the wonderful performances themselves, Raymond Charpentier, the critic of *L'Avenir,* closed by discussing the composer's astonishing maturity.[23] Paul Le Flem of *Comoedia* and Louis Vuillemin of *La Lanterne* followed suit. M. Le Flem felt with Georges Migot that the concert made Lili's loss even more painful for the music world to bear.[24] Vuillemin's article sums up the quintessence of all the reviews:

In spite of the early age at which a sad fate stole Lili Boulanger from art, this musician has left numerous instrumental and vocal compositions, some of them even very important. Multiple concerts have made them familiar to us. But none of them, nor all together, has yet acted on us with as much eloquence as this one musical recital of selected pages. From this grouping of songs, choruses, miscellaneous pieces, came a true, complete

impression of what Lili Boulanger herself brought to music:
A keen and prodigiously human sensibility, served in its expression by the full range of natural gifts from grace, color, charm and subtlety to winged lyricism, to obvious power, easy and profound. Such virtues, so rarely brought together for the benefit of one single creative temperament, are to be found in her works.[25]

Similar reactions followed the official performance of Lili Boulanger's *Envois de Rome,* presented by the Ministry of Public Instruction and Fine Arts at the Salle des Concerts du Conservatoire National de Musique the following January. Adolphe Julien, critic of the *Journal des Débats,* had this to say:

Usually, the performance session of the Envois de Rome in music, which takes place in the big hall of the Conservatoire around this time of year, is hardly more than a simple scholastic ceremony, a sort of family celebration where the relatives and friends of the laureate whose works sent from the Villa Medici are being played, come to applaud the young composer, whoever he may be, in such a way that all these *envois* produce a similar impression every year, having about equal success, and almost on command. This time, on the contrary, there was something different—exceptional—in this session. . . .
. . . it is incontestable that the pages we heard the other day generally had the mark of a completely feminine grace, perhaps a bit melancholy, and a real sensibility, all qualities that could already be discerned in the cantata that had earned for her the Prix de Rome.
Among these diverse compositions . . . the ones that bore witness without comparison to the most beautiful totality of acquired technique and prolific work were the *Trois Psaumes* for soloists, chorus, organ, and orchestra, whose beautiful character, and I would even say fullness of sound, keenly struck the audience.[26]

Raymond Charpentier of *Comoedia* and Louis Schneider of *Le Gaulois* also remarked that the *Pie Jesu* as interpreted at this concert by Mme Croiza led the public to demand that it be repeated immediately.[27]

The program opened with *D'un Soir triste* and *D'un Matin de Printemps,* continued with the first, fifth, sixth, eleventh, twelfth, and thirteenth of the *Clairières* (with David Devriès as soloist), and went on to all three psalms; then came the *Reflets* and the *Pie Jesu* (with Mme Croiza as soloist), and finally, the *Vieille*

Prière bouddhique (once again with David Devriès as soloist).
The chorus and orchestra of the Paris Opera were under the direction of Henri Büsser. Nadia Boulanger was at the organ.[28]

On November 8, 1923, Lili's *Vieille Prière bouddhique* was performed at the Opéra with a chorus of 250 under the direction of Serge Koussevitzky. Koussevitzky directed the same work again in Nantes at that city's Schola Cantorum on December 21.[29]

Faust et Hélène was scheduled to be premiered by the Monte Carlo Opera during the 1923–24 season, with Léon Jéhin conducting. Jéhin found it an extremely beautiful work. The players were enthusiastic about it, too, and at the end of a rehearsal in mid-March, they rose and applauded as if the composer were there. Jéhin was convinced that the performance would be a complete success.[30] After the dress rehearsal on April 5, he sent Mme Boulanger a telegram stating that it had been extraordinarily well received. It had "fired the public with enthusiasm," and they, in turn had showered their acclaim on Nadia, who had come from Paris for the occasion. He assured Mme Boulanger that the premiere the next day would be a triumph.[31] Jéhin was absolutely right in his estimate of the effects *Faust et Hélène* would produce. Jules Méry described just such a reaction in his review in *Rives d'Azur.* Expressing his own admiration for *Faust et Hélène,* he called it a "pure and radiant masterpiece," saying that it had brought tears to his eyes. He had been moved, he said, both by the beauty of the music and by its unqualified triumph.[32]

Méry had ended his article with a plea that all the works of Lili Boulanger be heard, especially the *Princesse Maleine,* which many knew that she had been setting as an opera when she died. Although Lili had asked Nadia to complete for her both the *Princesse Maleine* and the sonata for violin and piano, Nadia felt that she did not have the outstanding gift for composition that would have enabled her to complete them as Lili had wanted. Even before Lili's death, Nadia had given up composition to devote herself to teaching. Lili's unfinished works, therefore, have remained as the composer left them.[33]

Samuel Dushkin, the violinist who had already played Lili Boulanger's *Nocturne* both in Fontainebleau and in London's Aeolian Hall, gave the piece its American premiere on January 20, 1924, at Aeolian Hall in New York City. Just eleven days later, the Beacon Hill Musical Society (Boston) premiered Lili's *Le Retour.*[34]

On her first tour of the United States, Nadia Boulanger brought along and played some of Lili's works. In her first American performance, an organ recital at the Wanamaker Store in Philadelphia on January 9, 1925, Nadia played an organ transcription of *Cortège,* a work that she later repeated in programs in New York and Cleveland. When Nadia performed in the premiere of Aaron Copland's Symphony for Organ and Orchestra with the New York Symphony Orchestra under Walter Damrosch on January 11, 1925, Lili's *Pour les Funérailles* was also on the program. It received its Boston premiere with the Boston Symphony under the direction of Serge Koussevitzky on February 20.[35]

The Brussels premiere of Lili Boulanger's *Psalm 129* and four of her *Clairières* took place as part of the Concerts du Conservatoire Royal de Musique under the direction of Charles Panzéra on March 9, 1924. *Comoedia* carried news of two subsequent performances of *Psalm 129* in Brussels, the second of which led them to remark, "It is with pleasure that we record the great success achieved by this recently published work."[36]

Scattered performances of Lili's works followed, both in Europe and in the United States. A concert of the works of Lili Boulanger and Gabriel Fauré was given by Nadia Boulanger with Madeleine Greslé the singer, in July 1927. Once more, Théodore Lindenlaub of *Le Temps* had nothing but praise for Lili's music, and for the performances that were given of her *Clairières, Psalms 24* and *129,* and *Pie Jesu.*[37]

In 1939 a group of Bostonians banded together to form what became known as the "Lili Boulanger Memorial Fund," dedicated both to making Lili's works known and to providing financial support for deserving composers. The opening concert, which took place on March 6 of that year, included the American premiere of *Psalm 130,* in addition to performances of Lili's *Pour les Funérailles, Pie Jesu,* and *Psalm 24.* Nadia Boulanger conducted the Harvard Glee Club and Radcliffe Choral Society and members of the Boston Symphony. E. Power Biggs was at the organ.[38] The society held to its purpose of giving grants to gifted and serious composers each year, and, in the course of time, since these grants were first instituted in 1942, has aided such composers as Alexei Haieff (1942), Léo Preger (1945, 1949), Karel Husa (1949), Ned Rorem (1950), Noël Lee (1954), and Charles Wuorinen (1961, 1962). The Board of Judges came to include Nadia Boulanger, Aaron Copland, Walter Piston, Alexei Haieff, and, until his death, Igor Stravinsky. Yehudi Menuhin and Nicolas Nabokov form the Advisory Council. The organization still fulfills its original functions, "to keep alive the memory and the music of the

Lili Boulanger Memorial Fund Concert

NADIA BOULANGER, *Conductor*

THE HARVARD GLEE CLUB

THE RADCLIFFE CHORAL SOCIETY

G. WALLACE WOODWORTH, *Conductor*

AND MEMBERS OF THE

BOSTON SYMPHONY ORCHESTRA

E. Power Biggs, *Organist*

Noémie Perugia, *Soprano*　　　　　　Hugues Cuenod, *Tenor*

Natalie Kédroff, *Contralto*　　　　　　Daniel Harris, *Bass*

Program

Kyrie from the Mass in B Minor	*Johann Sebastian Bach*
Elegischer Gesang, Opus 118	*Ludwig van Beethoven*
San Francesco d'Assisi*	*G. Francesco Malipiero*

(*a*) Il Preludio
(*b*) Finale: La Morte di San Francesco
"Il Cantico del Sole"
Solo: Fred Rogosin

INTERMISSION

It is requested that there be no applause until the close
of the second part of the program.

Pour les Funérailles d'un Soldat	*Lili Boulanger*
Solo:　Daniel Harris	(August 21, 1893–March 15, 1918)

Pie Jesu	*Lili Boulanger*

Daniel Harris

Psaume: Du Fond de l'Abîme*	*Lili Boulanger*

Soli:　Natalie Kédroff, Noémie Perugia
Hugues Cuenod, Daniel Harris
and Special Chorus

Psaume XXIV	*Lili Boulanger*

Solo:　Hugues Cuenod

* First performance in America

Figure 51. Program of the inaugural concert of the Lili Boulanger Memorial Fund of Boston (1939). *Courtesy of the Département de la Musique, Bibliothèque Nationale, Paris, and the Lili Boulanger Memorial Fund of Boston.*

distinguished young French composer, Lili Boulanger (1893–1918), and to aid composers of exceptional talent and integrity by an Annual Award in her name."[39]

It was not until 1960 that Lili Boulanger's works were recorded. The first long-playing record was done for Everest by the Lamoureux Orchestra and Chorale Elisabeth Brasseur under the direction of Igor Markevitch.[40] Recorded at the Salle Pleyel in Paris, the production was personally supervised by Nadia Boulanger. The compositions chosen for this "World premiere recording" of Lili's works were *Psalms 24, 129,* and *130,* the *Vieille Prière bouddhique,* and the *Pie Jesu.* Herbert Kupferberg, writing in the *Herald Tribune,* assessed Lili's work and the composer herself from the evidence presented on this record as "an original and distinctive composer whose music was bold and vibrant. . . . On the basis of these pieces, Mlle Boulanger's loss was a tragedy for French music—and not merely for French music."[41]

Marc Blitzstein's article in the *Saturday Review* was even more laudatory. "When," he asked, "are we to have the important satisfaction of hearing the music of Lili Boulanger regularly in our concert halls?"[42] He regarded this recording as merely an introduction to Lili Boulanger's works and admired the fine performance but was, in some ways, unhappy about the presentation.

> Until we shall have heard the music in many live presentations, until the growing horde of enthusiasts (among which I count myself) has made some dent in the public's musical consciousness, it is doubtful how large a sale such a recording can have. As an example of the producer's own lack of confidence in the project, the back-cover jacket notes give everyone involved the most assiduous attention—everyone, that is, but Lili herself and her works. A woman composer of our own century, almost unknown, no longer alive? How good can her music be?
>
> It is more than good. It is extraordinary. Make no mistake, here was an original talent . . . the music is . . . masculine in its rugged force, utterly feminine in its purity and lyrical outpouring. Honegger, Poulenc, Roussel—to name but three who out-lived her—owe Lili much. . . .
>
> . . . Let us hear more of her. Let us know what we have missed, and what we have been offered.[43]

The recording itself was awarded the Arthur Honegger Prize for religious music by the Académie du Disque Français for the year 1960–61.[44]

When Nadia Boulanger visited the United States in 1962, she

215

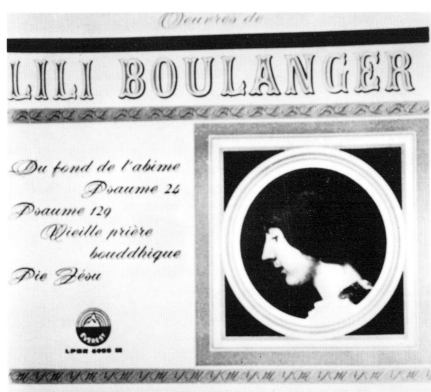

Du fond de l'abime
Psaume 24
Psaume 129
Vieille prière
bouddhique
Pie Jésu

ORCHESTRE DES CONCERTS LAMOUREUX
IGOR MARKEVITCH
CHORALE ELISABETH BRASSEUR

Figure 52. Cover of the first recording of the works of Lili Boulanger (1960). *Photo: M. Tamvico, Paris.*

brought more of Lili's music with her to perform. Under her direction, the New York Philharmonic played Lili's *Psalms 24, 129,* and *130* on February 16, 1962. Nadia herself had been the first woman to be invited to conduct the Philharmonic in 1939, when she was the conductor for half of one concert. No other woman had led the orchestra from the podium in the intervening years, so the 1962 concert was considered as much a tour de force for her as an opportunity to hear the music she was presenting. Some critics reacted to what they considered her rather somber tastes in programming—Fauré's *Requiem Mass* and Virgil Thomson's *A Solemn Music* were the other works on the program. In this instance it was Nadia's personality as well as her reputation that overwhelmed most critics. As Harold Schonberg of the *New York Times* expressed it, "she is the personification of the com-

216

plete musician and of a life dedicated to music . . . the invitation to Mme. Boulanger [sic] to conduct the Philharmonic was not only a gesture to a great lady of music. She proved that she could hold up her end of the baton."[45] This theme of Nadia's proving herself pervaded many of the reviews of the concert, sometimes to the exclusion of meaningful comments about the music itself. Among those critics who did discuss the music, opinion was divided. On the one hand were critics like Schonberg, who felt that Lili's music "simply does not hold up."[46] On the other were those like Irving Kolodin and Paul Henry Lang, who remarked on Lili's musical gifts, and Harriet Johnson, who called Lili "an immensely gifted composer,"[47] and Miles Kastendieck, who found her *Psalm 130* "a stunning work." Kastendieck went on to declare, "the young woman's outpouring in the first work sufficed to make vivid the power of her positive musical thinking."[48]

In 1965, at the suggestion of Mme Dujarric de la Rivière, a second organization, similar to the Lili Boulanger Memorial Fund of Boston, was created in Paris. "Les Amis de Lili Boulanger" had the same aims as its American counterpart: "to promote the works of Lili Boulanger and to give scholarships regularly to young composers."[49] After the death of its first president, Mme Paul Valéry, the presidency of the Administrative Council passed to His Excellency M. Gaston Palewski, a member of the Institut de France and President of the Conseil Constitutionnel. Igor Markevitch was named President of the Comité Actif, whose Vice-Presidents included Mlles Annette Dieudonné, Marcelle de Manziarly, and the Marquise Roussy de Sales, as well as M. Jean Françaix, and, until his death, Pierre Blavet.[50] It was officially recognized by the French government on August 16, 1971. The honorary committee included many luminaries—Her Late Majesty, Queen Elisabeth of Belgium and Her Majesty Queen Marie-José, Their Serene Highnesses the Prince and Princess of Monaco, Georges Auric, the late Robert Casadesus, Madame Robert Casadesus, Marc Chagall, Cesar Chávez, Clifford Curzon, the late Marcel Dupré, Bernard Gavoty, Maurice Gendron, the Dowager Countess of Gramont, Julien Green, Gian Francesco Malipiero, the late Roland Manuel, Yehudi Menuhin, Olivier Messiaen, Darius Milhaud, the Marquise Origo, Jean Papineau-Couture, Paul Paray, Marc Pincherle, the Prince and Princess Guy de Polignac, Svatislav Richter, the late Claude Rostand, Arthur Rubinstein, the late Gustave Samazeuilh, the late Igor Stravinsky, and Sir Michael Tippett, to name just a few.[51]

Three members of the honorary committee banded together

to record more of Lili Boulanger's music. Yehudi Menuhin and Clifford Curzon performed *Nocturne, Cortège,* and *D'un Matin de Printemps,* and the rest of the recording was devoted to the complete *Clairières dans le Ciel,* as interpreted by Eric Tappy (the only performer on this record not a member of the committee) and Jean Françaix.[52]

To coincide with the fiftieth anniversary of Lili Boulanger's death, Les Amis de Lili Boulanger organized an exhibit at the Bibliothèque Nationale in Paris, in addition to arranging for a number of public concerts both in the library itself and in the hall of the O.R.T.F. (Office de Radiodiffusion-Télévision Française). The first of ten concerts in the Music Division of the library—which were to include both the works of Lili Boulanger and those of young composers who had received awards from Les Amis de Lili Boulanger—took place on March 9, 1968. The "Exposition Lili-Boulanger" lasted until March 30. In it were included photographs, portraits, letters, manuscript and published music, documents, and other memorabilia pertaining to Lili Boulanger, many of which were listed in the catalogue issued by the Bibliothèque Nationale.[53] M. Gaston Palewski inaugurated this exhibit on Friday, March 8, 1968, at 5:30 P.M. It had originally been scheduled to remain only until March 22, but was held over an extra week by popular demand.[54]

The O.R.T.F. concert took place on March 26, 1968. Bernard Gavoty, music critic of the *Figaro,* who had attended the dress rehearsal, couched his review in generalities, but remained laudatory of Lili's music in the small space he actually allotted to it. As far as he was concerned, the *Vieille Prière bouddhique* was "a precious jewel," as was the *Pie Jesu.* The strength of *Psalm 24* betrayed none of what he would have expected of a woman's work. He closed by congratulating the conductor, Charles Brück, the soloists, the orchestra, and the chorus.[55] But the critic of *Le Nouveau Journal* was certainly not laudatory. He was incensed that the fiftieth anniversary of Lili Boulanger's death should have been treated with such ceremony, as if she had been another Debussy. The two records of her music that had recently appeared had convinced him that she was unworthy of public attention, and these manifestations of interest in her music galled him. He felt that her memory excited interest mainly because she had had an attractive personality. As it turned out, Jacques Bourgeois had another objection to Lili Boulanger. He was skeptical of her for the simple reason that Nadia Boulanger had been so active and vocal in promoting her sister's works. In this critic's opinion, Lili

Boulanger was nothing more than a sentimental myth. "It must be said," he complains, "that this myth was valliantly kept alive for half a century by her sister, Nadia Boulanger, with an obvious sincerity, a will of iron and the tentacular authority which her position as an eminently cosmopolitan teacher of composition gives her."[56] He was not the only one who felt this way about Nadia's persistent efforts on behalf of Lili's music.

But, despite the detractors, the exhibits and the concerts did re-awaken interest in Lili Boulanger and her music. The mayor of the Ninth Arrondissement, in which the rue Ballu is located, had attended the O.R.T.F. concert at the invitation of Igor Marke-vitch. On discovering that Lili had been a resident of his district, he decided to name part of the rue Ballu after her.[57] A ceremony was subsequently held on October 15, 1970, formally renaming the crossroads of the rue de Vingtimille and the rue Ballu *Place Lili-Boulanger,* as M. Gerville-Réache, the Mayor, had suggested.[58] A commemorative plaque designed by Marion Tournon-Branly of the Fontainebleau Summer School of Fine Arts[59] had previously been placed on the building at 36 rue Ballu on October 17, 1968.[60]

In 1972 M. Samitier, then Mayor of Gargenville, decided to honor the memory of Lili Boulanger by naming after her the street on which "Les Maisonnettes" still stands. This renaming took place amid great festivities: it seemed that the whole town had turned out for the occasion. On June 10, 1972, all the local dignitaries gathered late in the morning, along with representa-tives of Les Amis de Lili Boulanger—Mme Dujarric de la Rivière, the Secretary; Mlle de Manziarly; and M. Doda Conrad, a member of the Honorary Committee—a representative from the Depart-ment of Cultural Affairs (M. Roy) ; and Nadia Boulanger. The local band opened the ceremony, MM. Samitier, Roy, and Conrad spoke, after which the local clarinet ensemble played. Then Nadia Boulanger unveiled the plaque.[61]

The anniversary of Lili Boulanger's death is commemorated each year. During the years immediately after her demise, articles generally appeared in the major newspapers and magazines during the month of March, recounting her achievements in spite of great physical suffering. The writers emphasized her lack of world-liness and her sheltered life. One such article, written by Lili's old friend Georges Delaquys, appeared in *Le Journal* on the eve of the anniversary of her death in 1939.[62] It also announced the special Mass that was to be held the next day, March 15, at the Église de la Trinité. That, too, was held every year.[63] There, those who had been moved by Lili's music, Lili's friends, Nadia's

Vous êtes prié d'assister au SERVICE qui sera célébré
en l'Église de la Sainte-Trinité (Chapelle de la Sainte-Vierge), le
Mercredi 19 Mars 1975, à 11 heures 30 précises, à la mémoire de

LILI BOULANGER

GRAND PRIX DE ROME

21 Août 1893 — 15 Mars 1918

et de

MADAME ERNEST BOULANGER

NÉE PRINCESSE MYCHETSKY

19 Décembre 1858 — 19 Mars 1935

" J'offre à Dieu toutes mes souffrances
pour qu'elles retombent en joie sur toi "

Figure 53. Invitation to the 1975 commemorative mass for Lili and
Mme Ernest Boulanger.

friends, and Nadia's students and former students all gathered.
In 1940 Jeanne Mercier had this to say: "Every year that I was
in Paris in March, I went on the anniversary of Lili's death to the
Requiem Mass at which some of her compositions were played.
The service was always attended by a crowd of Nadia's friends,
among them all the highlights of musical Paris."[64] These commemorative ceremonies have continued up to the present day,
leading sometimes to charges of morbidity leveled against Nadia
for her emphasis on the day of Lili's death. Perhaps her critics
are overlooking the religious significance of this ceremony.

Lili Boulanger had had the good fortune to be born into a
family with a long tradition of artistic accomplishment, which
has been documented as far back as the late eighteenth century.[65]
She was surrounded during her short life by a devoted family,
and friends who did all they could to protect her from harm
and keep her as comfortable and happy as possible under the
circumstances. Under such conditions, she might have become
simply a spoiled, dependent child. That Lili became instead a
creative, productive human being, willing and anxious to help
others, is a tribute both to her own personality and to her up-
bringing. But that she should have chosen to pursue a career as

a composer, and was successful in her work despite all the frustrating obstacles placed in her way by ill health, must be attributed to her own exceptional talent and excellent training, as well as to her extreme dedication and perseverance.

Lili's early style was marked by the frequent use of ostinato figurations for coloristic effect (Examples 1, 5, 27, and 29) although, even in the few years during which her first works were written, the composer showed a growing tendency to soften her use of any unmodified musical formulas. Most of Lili Boulanger's compositions are settings of texts, and as the composer's command of her craft increased, she tended toward an ever-greater rapprochement between the text and the music. She did not force the songs she wrote to conform to any preconceived musical forms, nor fit to them any unrelieved ostinato patterns. This development can be seen very clearly in the *Clairières dans le Ciel,* in which highly segmented forms predominate, reflecting the composer's response to the free-flowing styles and moods of the poet. Jammes's poetic forms are not those of classical verse. They are in what may be described as free alexandrine verse whose rhymes, when they occur at all, result from the internal meanings of the poem rather than being imposed by external considerations of poetic form. Likewise, Lili Boulanger's musical forms are not those of the strophic or the through-composed song. They follow instead the patterns set by the words, turning to repetition for dramatic effect, and breaking away from any strict reliance on tradition.

When setting poetry with a clearly delineated formal structure, however, the composer generally did make use of more traditional musical forms. In *Pour les Funérailles d'un Soldat,* for example, a text originally written by Musset for choral recitation within the setting of a dramatic poem, Lili has broken the verse down into smaller units but, within each of them, has kept a single mood and style, following the Musset text, each line of which has a consistent mood. The composer's changes of mood between sections are quite noticeable. This desire to adapt the musical structure to the nature of the text can be observed in all of Lili Boulanger's vocal works. Other early compositions such as *Les Sirènes, Hymne au Soleil,* and even *Faust et Hélène* exhibit the same tendencies. Lili continued to use this procedure in her mature works—just as she had in her earlier ones—only when it was demanded by the form of the text. This can be seen in her treatment of the three psalms, and in the *Vieille Prière bouddhique,* as contrasted with the variable, sometimes almost amorphous structures she used when setting the *Clairières dans le Ciel,* where the emphasis on fleeting moods in the poetry is reflected in Lili's music.

These aesthetic considerations of hers place her, once again, directly in the mainstream of the French tradition, with its insistence that the form and style of the words set by composers be an important determinant of the final form and even of the style of their compositions. This operating principle is equally evident in a composer such as Debussy, in his *Trois Chansons de France* (1904) and his *Trois Ballades de François Villon* (1910).

Frequently in her early compositions Lili Boulanger made references to the works of other composers. These allusions and direct citations were undoubtedly conscious on her part and were intended either to amuse her friends and acquaintances, or to remind them of a particular personal event. A fondness for allusions to *Tristan,* for example, found for the first time in the *Nocturne* (Example 2), was transmuted in "Si tout ceci n'est qu'un pauvre rêve" into a direct citation with definite textual raisons d'être (Example 53). After the *Clairières dans le Ciel,* none of Lili Boulanger's extant works contain such musical quotations.

Later, in Lili's psalm settings and her *Pie Jesu,* none of the liturgical chants or intonations is used, despite the fact that the composer had earlier employed the *Dies Irae* in a funerary context in *Pour les Funérailles d'un Soldat* (Example 32). It is as though Lili has eschewed any earlier literal-mindedness in favor of evoking a mood rather than explicitly setting a scene. The single exception is her short reference to "Do, do, l'enfant do" (Example 81) in *Dans l'immense Tristesse.* This cessation of learned allusions or citations in Lili's most mature music may, indeed, provide further evidence of her adherence to the Symbolist aesthetic, which emphasizes the evocation of internal states without too much art or erudition being evident to the reader. Given the composer's own artistic tastes, Lili gravitated to this school of poetry above all others, as is shown in her choice of verses by Maeterlinck, Jammes, and, even as a young child, Verhaeren. This fact may help to explain in part her success in the 1913 *concours d'essai,* since the required text was by Albert Samain, a moderate Symbolist.

One feature of Lili Boulanger's music that appears in both her early and late works is the use of parallel perfect intervals and of modality to represent one or more of the following ideas: the Orient, a religious rite (Christian or pagan), or, quite simply, conscious archaism. The "orientalizing" aspect may be traced from the opening of the *Hymne au Soleil* with its superposed fourths (Example 20), and a conscious reference to the parallel organum of the Church is to be found in *Pour les Funérailles d'un Soldat* (Example 35), as is a direct quotation from the Requiem Mass itself—from the modal *Dies Irae* (Example 32). The superposition of perfect intervals, both as archaizing and to create a religious context, recurs later in *Psalm 24* (Example 76). The pentatonic tendencies of *Vieille Prière bouddhique* cannot be ignored (Example 86), nor can its affinities for Phrygian modal patterns in various transpositions. Even in Lili's last work, the *Pie Jesu*, there are suggestions of the transposed plagal Dorian mode (in the version for medium voice) in the vocal part (Examples 90 and 91), undoubtedly referring, once more, to the religious significance of this composition.

From her earliest compositions to her last works, Lili Boulanger was constantly aware of the potentials of both voices and instruments, and made idiomatic use of them. As early as the *Nocturne* (Example 1), she realized the effects that could be created by instrumental layering and by a judicious use of timbre. In line with the French tradition, she often treated voices themselves as instruments in her choral works, making of them yet one more timbre added to the total texture in *Les Sirènes* (Example 12), the last measures of *Pour les Funérailles d'un Soldat, Psalm 129* (Example 79), *Psalm 130,* and the *Vieille Prière bouddhique*. Normally, her vocal lines are declarative, and they follow the text in their stress and length. They are not melismatic except when the overall effect demands it—for example in the "Amen" of the *Pie Jesu* (Example 91). When she uses voices as instruments, however, Lili treats them exactly as if they were instruments, and the result is sometimes a long vocal line, as, for example, in *Psalm 129* (Example 79).

Lili Boulanger had a special fondness for the harp, and a particular feeling for its characteristics and potentials. From her first extant work, the *Nocturne,* to her last, the *Pie Jesu,* harps figure prominently in her orchestrations. The composer used them not only in the traditional impressionistic places to "describe" water—in *La Source,* for example (Example 16)—but also to create a new texture, to add aural depth to her compositions, and to reinforce overtones, as in *Nocturne* (Example 1), *Soir sur la Plaine* (Example 38), and *Pie Jesu* (Example 91). As in her use of other instruments and of voices, Lili Boulanger did not demand any new techniques of the performers, but, as in all of her music, the writing demands complete technical control at all times in order to produce the desired effect. In this sense her music demands virtuosity of all who perform it. Rather than inventing new techniques, Lili excelled in the subtle combination of existing techniques to create new and sometimes startling aural effects.

Perhaps because of her emphasis on subtlety, Lili rarely ended her compositions on crashing fortissimo chords. Definite, assertive, frankly optimistic works like the *Hymne au Soleil, Renouveau, Psalm 24,* and *Vieille Prière bouddhique* are unusual among her artistic output. In most of Lili Boulanger's compositions there is more than a slight suggestion of doubt, uneasiness, regret, or melancholy, and, although sections of the other works may attain loud dynamics, they are used only to mirror fleeting, intense emotion. It may well be for this reason that the composer uses such dynamic levels as forte and fortissimo sparingly, to reserve these resources for the moments of greatest dramatic impact, as she has done in "Demain fera un an" (Example 70), for example. Because of Lili's penchant for quiet endings after compositions filled with inner anguish, her works tend to give the impression of serenity, or at least of resignation.

In her harmonic language, Lili Boulanger remained a descendant of the impressionist school. She used chords and progressions for their coloristic effect, just as she employed old modes and suggestions of the pentatonic scale when it suited her artistic purpose. Sideslipping superposed fifths, forming tonally ambiguous sevenths, were used to suggest emotional emptiness, and to mirror an equally equivocal situation in the text in "Parfois, je suis triste" (Example 54), while a succession of ninths conveyed the idea of harshness in the opening measures of *Psalm 129* (Example 78). During her compositional evolution, Lili Boulanger used each group of instruments or even each individual timbre as an element in its own right. This attitude carries through even to the *Pie Jesu,* where a modified modality is combined with different tonal centers in differing instruments within one and the same work.

Because of her wide musical interests, Lili Boulanger was exposed to and reacted to the influences of composers from the masters of the sixteenth century to Mussorgsky and Debussy. Even if it were not for her harmonies themselves, some of her instrumentations in reaction to particular textual situations would identify her as a composer in the French tradition (*Pour les Funérailles d'un Soldat,* for example).[66] It was not until after her death that Ravel used the same sort of introduction in a low register that opened Lili's *Psalm 130,* or that Honegger used his parallel ninths in *Le Roi David* and otherwise employed choral textures reminiscent of Lili's *Psalm 129.* Throughout her life Lili Boulanger continued to experiment constantly with both form and style, bending traditional forms where she felt it necessary and attempting to create new ones when the existing materials did not lend themselves to such treatment. It is impossible to know what new forms might have emerged from her labors had she survived. Clearly though, Lili Boulanger was not a composer without antecedents, and she was certainly not without effect, albeit on a small, élite circle of musicians to whom her work was known.

Lili Boulanger's music stands on its own merits. The best of her works display firmness, delicacy, strength, and mastery of compositional technique. Sadly, her music has remained in comparative neglect, except for occasional church performances of the *Psalms* and the *Pie Jesu* and for sporadic concert revivals. The glowing tributes to her and her works that have appeared in the press from time to time have not yet sufficed to bring her compositions into the active repertoire. This may be due in part to a strange attitude on the part of people who have come into contact with the legend of Lili Boulanger without ever having known anything about the real person. Some are as skeptical as Besnard, preferring to conclude that a good many of Lili Boulanger's extraordinary accomplishments were really embellishments after the fact. Either unwilling or unable to pursue their investigations any further, they adopt in their writings about the composer a maudlin approach or an ironic one. Both tend to discourage others from entering into research on the subject, thus perpetuating the cycle of half-truth and fantasy that has until now obscured the facts. There is also a reticence on the part of many who have known Lili's sister, Nadia. Some appear to be concerned that in considering Lili's works seriously, they might find something about which they would be critical, and possibly displease Nadia, so that they become too inhibited even to look at the works of Lili Boulanger. There is also an additional problem created by the fact that all of Lili's music is difficult to obtain commercially, and that the manuscripts and other relevant material remain in the personal possession of Mlle Nadia Boulanger. This in itself would not necessarily be an inhibiting factor, were it not that Mlle Boulanger's heavily laden teaching schedule, lectures, and travel severely limit the time when the documents can be examined and she be available for consultation on this subject. Any in-depth work on Lili Boulanger, therefore, must of neecessity be a long-range project. These are the main reasons that no comprehensive work on Lili Boulanger has ever before been completed.

Since 1968 there have been signs of a renascence of interest in the works of Lili Boulanger.

On both sides of the Atlantic her memory continues to be perpetuated, through concerts and through the dissemination of information about her, inaccurate though that sometimes is, in music reference books as well as in more popular publications. The fourth edition of the *Ullstein Lexikon der Musik,* for instance, lists Lili under Nadia's entry, and incorrectly identifies the younger girl as the student only of her older sister.[67] In 1970 Norbert Duforcq compared Lili's religious music to that of Fauré, Franck, Debussy, and other French masters,[68] reminding his readers that she had been the first woman composer to win the Premier Grand Prix de Rome. He did not mention any of her works except the *Psalms,* however.[69] That same year, the entry under Lili Boulanger's name in the *Dictionnaire de la Musique* correctly listed all of her major works, but stated erroneously that she studied with Fauré in addition to her other teachers.[70]

The following year saw the appearance of the fourth edition of Nicholas Slonimsky's monumental *Music Since 1900.* It gave the facts surrounding Lili Boulanger's winning of the Prix de Rome,[71] but incorrectly listed the place of death as Paris[72]—an error that had been held over from previous editions. An article on Lili Boulanger by Christiane Trieu-Colleney was featured in the Christmas 1971 issue of *Jeunesse et Orgue.* It spoke in glowing terms of the composer's gifts, both musical and moral, and of her courage. The author then compared her to such composers as Ravel and Debussy, who had been active at about the same time, noting that Lili's compositions rank with the finest produced in France during that period.[73] Most of the information in this article is accurate, but the author did make it seem that Lili Boulanger finished a sonata for violin and piano, which in fact she did not.[74] Jacques Chailley's article on the Boulanger family for the 1971 supplement to *Musik in Geschichte und Gegenwart,* while substantially correct in most matters, errs occasionally on dates.[75] He described the relative neglect of Lili's works since her death, and ended by saying that, as of 1971, her great compositions were beginning to be recognized as major and perhaps even "prophetic" works.[76]

In 1972 the young Brazilian composer José Almeida Prado, a student of Nadia Boulanger who had never known Lili, was inspired by the works of Lili Boulanger to write an extended composition dedicated to her memory. It was his intent to evoke the moods of her music through his, and all seven movements have evocative titles. Three of them also have subtitles taken from the *Tristesses* of Francis Jammes. The work itself he named *Portrait de Lili Boulanger*.[77]

Early in 1973, two articles appeared in the American music magazine *High Fidelity* that were announced by the editors of the periodical as a debate between a representative feminist (Judith Rosen) and a representative psychologist (Grace Rubin-Rabson) under the headline "Why Haven't Women Become Great Composers?" Perhaps it is unfortunate that Lili Boulanger's name entered into the cross fire on this occasion. Dr. Rubin-Rabson, while conceding Lili's talent, dismissed her work because most of Lili's compositions used voices. In Dr. Rubin-Rabson's opinion, a composition with text demonstrated verbal ability, a typically "feminine" gift, rather than true compositional ability.[78] Ms. Rosen, on the other hand, used two stories to show how Lili Boulanger had been discriminated against because of her sex. The first stated that Lili Boulanger had entered the Prix de Rome competition anonymously in 1913. The second said that Lili Boulanger was denied entrance to the 1918 Prix de Rome competition although she had "submitted an original composition to the committee . . . because that year the donors of the prize had restricted the competition to males under thirty. . . ."[79] Neither of these incidents ever happened, and the fact that this "information" was printed in a widely read music magazine perpetuated inaccuracies regarding Lili Boulanger. Anyone even slightly knowledgeable about the rules of the Prix de Rome competition as it was conducted in the early 1900s would have known that the first incident could never have occurred, and anyone who had seen even one of the contemporary pieces of publicity involving Lili Boulanger's participation in the Prix de Rome competition would have realized that she could not possibly have entered the competition anonymously.[80] The second incident could not have happened, either. First, the Prix de Rome competition had been suspended during World War I because most of the men had gone to war. Second, the war did not end until November 1918, by which time Lili Boulanger had been dead for nearly one year. Third, it would have been naive to have conducted a competition during wartime and then insisted on limiting it to males of draft age, knowing full well that that group would be the one least likely to be present to participate.[81] Finally, and most importantly, surviving records prove that both of these stories are utterly false.[82] A letter to the magazine written at that time and correcting these errors[83] elicited the response that *High Fidelity* had been primarily concerned with generating reader interest and in fostering debate, and in this instance was not primarily concerned about the ultimate accuracy of the data presented.[84] No retraction of these inaccuracies ever appeared in the pages of *High Fidelity.* As a result, these impossible tales have persisted, and they continue to be widely quoted.[85]

On the other hand, Christopher Palmer's book *Impressionism,* published that same year, presented accurate data about Lili Boulanger.[86] By including her in this volume, this respected writer on music placed her exactly where she belongs—in the legitimate continuum of the French Impressionist tradition. The fact that this study appeared on both sides of the Atlantic makes it the first historically oriented English-language volume in almost fifty years[87] to recognize her importance as a composer.

By 1974, due in part to the interest of Nadia Boulanger's former students and colleagues and to the growing feminist movement, ever-greater attention began to be paid to Lili Boulanger's works. In addition to the activities of the Lili Boulanger Associations in Paris and Boston, which continued to promote performances of Lili's music, a concert devoted entirely to compositions by Lili Boulanger was held on March 19, 1974, at the Peabody Conservatory in Baltimore, Maryland. A benefit for the Peabody Scholarship Fund, given under the aegis of His Excellency Monsieur Kosciusko-Morizet, Ambassador of France to the United States, it was organized by Flore Wend, a member of the Conservatory staff who had obtained Nadia's permission to present such a program. The program, conducted by Dr. Flora Contino, who had studied for years with Mlle Nadia Boulanger, included *Nocturne, Cortège, D'un Matin de Printemps,* three of the *Clairières* ("Les lilas qui avaient fleuri," "Vous m'avez regardé avec toute votre âme," and "Un poète disait . . ."), the *Pie Jesu,* and the complete *Faust et Hélène* with full orchestra. In addition to the music, there were introductory remarks by Richard Franko Goldman, at that time President-Director of Peabody, with a narration by Dr. Elliott Galkin, both of whom are former students of Nadia Boulanger.[88] The concert was extremely successful.

Paul Hume's enthusiastic review appeared two days later in the *Washington Post.* He was very much struck by Lili's works. He felt that the *Clairières,* because of the high technical level of the vocal and piano writing, would be "welcome on any song recital," but that it was the composer's projection of the moods of the text that revealed her real gifts. The *Pie Jesu* he found "brief but touching," but reserved his highest praise for *Faust et Hélène*. Commenting on the instrumental writing in the cantata, he noted Lili's "striking sense of color and dynamic levels," then went on to praise the "great expressive heights" reached in the duet between Faust and Hélène. All in all, he considered it a concert that "ended by shedding glory on . . . the composer."[89]

That same year, two feminists interested themselves in the music of Lili Boulanger. In the spring came the release of a recording by pianist Sister Nancy Fierro.[90] It contained a selection of keyboard works by five women composers, including the first recording of the piano version of Lili Boulanger's *Cortège* and the premiere recording of *D'un vieux Jardin*. Sister Nancy had, for a short time, been a pupil of Nadia Boulanger.[91] During the fall an article on women in music was published in a journal whose readers were mainly teachers of music at the primary and secondary school levels. Miriam Green's article in the September–October issue of the *American Music Teacher* mentions both Nadia and Lili Boulanger in the most glowing terms. Ms. Green comments on the "rich heritage" left by Lili Boulanger as well as on the achievements of her older sister. Most of her data are accurate, but she reiterates the story that, after Lili won the Prix de Rome "men must have felt threatened . . . and from then on it was decided to *disqualify* [*sic*] women from the competition."[92]

By the following year, interest in Lili Boulanger's music had increased considerably. Nadia Boulanger herself attended the performance of Lili's *Pie Jesu* and *Psalm 130* at Trinity Chapel, Cambridge on March 1, 1975. Christopher Palmer, the critic on that occasion, reported that the psalm was "an extraordinary piece: even some of the most seasoned academics were visibly shaken by it." He praised the performance of the Sidney Sussex College Musical Society under the direction of James Wood, noting that the climaxes had "brought the audience to the edge of their seats." This composition he considered the composer's masterwork, although he also found the *Pie Jesu* (which had preceded it on the same program) to be endowed with "the hallmark of a true visionary in art."[93] A similar reaction to another of Lili's works was reported to Nadia Boulanger by the Roumanian-born composer Marcel Mihalovici after he heard it broadcast by France Culture later that same month. In the letter he wrote to Nadia describing his impressions, he said that he had been deeply moved by *Faust et Hélène*, which he considered a masterpiece, the work of a major composer. Despite certain infelicities in the libretto, he expressed the hope that this work would become part of the permanent symphonic repertoire.[94]

During the rest of the year, Lili Boulanger was mentioned and her works promoted and performed more frequently, often by feminists who had had no direct connection with Nadia Boulanger. In the spring issue of the *College Music Symposium,* whose readership consists mainly of college music professors, for example, composer-musicologist Edith Borroff cited Lili Boulanger as one example of a French woman composer whose works were not universally accepted or often performed.[95] In conjunction with the New York Philharmonic, the popular American feminist magazine *Ms.* cosponsored a Pension Fund Benefit Concert in November 1975, devoted entirely to the works of five women composers. In preparation for this, the November issue of *Ms.* published biographical sketches of all the composers whose works were to be on the program, including Lili Boulanger. Once again the same false reports that had appeared in *High Fidelity* were repeated. There are several other small errors of fact in the article as well.[96] Early in November the two-record album *Woman's Work,* researched and produced by violinist Marnie Hall, was released. Among the eighteen women composers represented on these records is Lili Boulanger. This time her *Nocturne* and four of the *Clairières* are included. Ms. Hall had never had any contact with Nadia Boulanger, nor had those whom she had chosen to perform these works.[97] The original album notes, based on inaccurate printed sources on Lili Boulanger, erred in a number of particulars. Once again Nadia was credited with being her younger sister's first teacher. It is an exaggeration to say, as Ms. Hall did, that Lili attended "only a few concerts during her lifetime," and that she "lived in the narrow intimacy of her mother, her sister, and some friends." In one case, however, things simply could not have happened as stated. It is claimed that Lili met at the Villa Medici "people who remembered her father" from his student days there. Those who might have known him during his stay there in the 1830s were long since dead when Lili arrived there in 1914. *Clairières* was also misdated, assigned to the period between 1916 and 1918.[98]

The New York Philharmonic Pension Fund Benefit Concert was scheduled for November 10, and the week preceding it was one during which Lili Boulanger's works were played over both of the major classical music stations in New York City. On November 6 feminist-musicians Norma Davidson and Joyce Strong,

a Texas-based violin and piano team, performed Lili's *Nocturne,
Cortège,* and *D'un Matin de Printemps* live on Robert Sherman's
WQXR-FM program "The Listening Room" as a preview of their
November 11 recital at the Mannes College of Music in New York,
where they were to feature works by women composers. The
following evening Donna Handly, then one of the editors of *Ms.*
magazine, was the producer-commentator for a program of music
by women composers on WNCN-FM. On it she included seven
of Lili's *Clairières* (numbers 7–13), playing the Tappy-Françaix
recording. Neither the Davidson-Strong duo nor Donna Handly
had ever had any personal contact with Nadia Boulanger.[99]

On Monday, November 10, 1975, the New York Philharmonic
held its Pension Fund Benefit Concert at Avery Fisher Hall, before a capacity audience. Not only was it the first time an entire
Philharmonic concert had been devoted to works by women composers, but it was also the Philharmonic conducting debut of
Sarah Caldwell, who was to be the first woman to conduct an
entire Philharmonic program from the podium since Nadia Boulanger had pioneered in this endeavor in 1962. Since those involved in selecting the music for this occasion (including the
conductor and Donna Handly, who was then acting as liaison for
Ms.) did not know Nadia Boulanger, they based their programming decisions solely on what they considered to be the merits
of each score.[100] Among the five works on the program was Lili
Boulanger's *Faust et Hélène,* with soloists Gwendolyn Killebrew,
Joseph Evans, and Lenus Carlson.

Unfortunately, the program notes and other articles in *Lincoln Center,* the program booklet for that evening, contributed
to the further perpetuation of inaccurate information about the
composer. While avoiding the fairly common mistake of calling
Lili Boulanger the first woman ever to win the Prix de Rome,
Shirley Fleming, the program annotator, repeated once again the
old story that Lili had been taught at home by Nadia, and added
a new one—that the Prix de Rome jury had awarded the prize
to Lili before hearing more than one-third of her cantata. She
also quoted at length what appears to be a spurious interview
with Lili Boulanger and her mother. This "interview," of which
Nadia Boulanger assures me that she has neither recollection nor
written record among her family papers,[101] was reported in the
Musical Leader as having been conducted with the Boulanger
family the day after Lili won the Prix de Rome.[102] This article
is further suspect, since the original "interview"—the one copied
verbatim in the *Musical Leader*—appeared first in *The Sun* on

231

July 20, 1913, more than two weeks after Lili Boulanger was awarded the prize, but, strangely enough, the dateline on it was July 11, almost a week after her success in the competition.[103] Therefore it is most likely that the "interview" never took place, or at the very least, did not take place under the circumstances that the anonymous reporter for *The Sun* claimed it did. Mrs. Fleming erred again on the date of the New York premiere of *Faust et Hélène,* which she incorrectly listed as December 6, 1918, instead of giving its proper date of December 26, 1918.[104] Speight Jenkins's article, "A Ms-ical Celebration!" appeared in the same issue of *Lincoln Center,* and recapitulated the same stories about Lili Boulanger that had surfaced in the February 1973 issue of *High Fidelity.* "Lili won the Prix de Rome under an anonymous name [sic] in 1913," he wrote. "Submitting a composition under her own name a few years later she was rejected because the affair was supposed to be all-male."[105] Of course the capacity crowd at Avery Fisher Hall took all this misinformation home with them that night.

Because of the pioneering nature of this concert it was widely reviewed, not just in the New York press, as would have been customary with a New York Philharmonic performance, but also in national newsmagazines and in out-of-town newspapers. As with Nadia Boulanger's 1962 appearance as conductor of the New York Philharmonic, some publications chose to treat mainly Sarah Caldwell's considerable personal achievement in becoming the second woman to conduct that orchestra in its long and distinguished history, and said little about the music itself.[106]

Unlike the reaction to the 1918 American premiere of *Faust et Hélène,* even critics who disapproved of the rest of the concert and of the conductor as well, found something to admire in the cantata. Byron Belt is typical of these. "It has," he wrote, "stature and deep emotion, qualities utterly lacking in everything else on the program."[107] Bill Zakariasen of the *Daily News,* while objecting to some of the other musical selections, called *Faust et Hélène* "simply gorgeous, full of intoxicating melody and shimmering late-romantic orchestration. One can't help but think," he continued, "that had she been a man, works such as 'Faust and Helen' would be standard repertory by now."[108] Another critic remarked that the work "stands up well against the works of such contemporary composers as Ravel and Debussy,"[109] while *New York Times* critic Donal Henahan was moved to remark that the revival of this piece alone "could have justified the entire concert."[110]

232

Out-of-town newspapers and magazines with national and international readership also had high praise for the work. The anonymous reviewer for United Press International (U.P.I.) whose critique appeared in the Philadelphia *Evening Bulletin,* stated that this composition "showed that women composers can write great music."[111] Major American newsmagazines such as *Time* and *Newsweek* also praised *Faust et Hélène.*[112] Andrew Porter of the *New Yorker* called it "a substantial and attractive product of *wagnérisme*—at once delicate, sensuous, and intellectual. . . . The romantic appeal of the music and its strong, fine working," he continued, "were evident."[113]

Unfortunately, some of these reviews, laudatory though they were of Lili Boulanger's music, also perpetuated two of the errors about the composer that had appeared in the program booklet. The *Newsweek* and U.P.I. critics, for instance, repeated the story that the composer had entered the Prix de Rome competition anonymously, while those from the *New Yorker* and the *Boston Globe* described Lili as a student of Nadia Boulanger. Thus, these false statements were given a new lease on life by being published once more in otherwise responsible journalistic publications. Critic Byron Belt would, perhaps, also have benefited from further information about Lili Boulanger's acquaintance with other composer's works. He charged in his review that the music for *Faust et Hélène* had been "lifted almost intact from the opening of Arnold Schoenberg's monumental "Guerrelieder,"[114] not knowing that she never heard or studied any of Schoenberg's works.[115]

The early months of 1976 brought with them perhaps the greatest and most widely diversified kind of interest to date in the music of Lili Boulanger on the part of Americans. By January a revised version of the biographical information on Lili Boulanger had been included in the program notes for a new pressing of the *Woman's Work* album, correcting the inaccuracies that had existed in those published the previous November to accompany the two-record set.[116] On January 6 the November 10 New York Philharmonic Pension Fund Benefit Concert, which had been taped live during the performance, was broadcast over radio stations throughout the United States, thus bringing *Faust et Hélène* to a national audience for the first time.

Radio station WQXR-FM dedicated the last week of February to the performance and promotion of the works of women composers. Once more Robert Sherman programmed Lili Boulanger's compositions. On February 23 it was the *Pie Jesu* that was aired;

on February 24, the *Vieille Prière bouddhique*. He also spoke warmly about the composer's gifts and the artistic merit of her music.[117]

Meanwhile, *Ms.* corrected in print some of the inaccuracies that had appeared in its November issue and in the Philharmonic program notes, just as Donna Handly had corrected two of them over the air in her November broadcast.[118] In its March issue, the magazine printed a letter to the effect that Lili Boulanger had entered the Prix de Rome competition openly and under her own name in 1913, and that she never again entered this competition. It further corrected the contention that the composer had simply worked for a humanitarian organization during World War I, stating that she and her older sister had, indeed, helped to found one.[119] The publication of this letter constitutes a major breakthrough in the attitude toward Lili Boulanger taken by most writers and publications, since it is the first time that any periodical has been willing to correct in print misinformation about this composer. Hopefully, it marks the beginning of a trend toward a more responsible attitude where she is concerned.

Interest in Lili Boulanger has been increasing on college campuses also. On March 3 Vassar College held a session of its Women's Studies Symposium devoted to women composers. Among the subjects discussed were the spurious incidents and misinformation relating to Lili Boulanger's life and works, and how these "data" had been disproved through research.[120] As a result of the discussion and the musical examples played that night to illustrate the lecture, the Vassar library ordered the Tappy-Françaix recording.[121]

The record by Sister Nancy Fierro and the Gemini Hall album were reviewed in the May issue of *Stereo Review*. Paul Kresh found the piano works recorded by Sister Nancy "pastel-pale and pretty," but not so "winsomely appealing" as Lili Boulanger's "bitter-sweet" songs.[122]

Lili Boulanger's music was used as a symbol of French art and the French spirit during and immediately after World War I, as well as a symbol of women's artistic liberation. It is now serving again as a rallying point for feminists. The most important thing about Lili's music, however, is not that it is now being championed by any particular group—however helpful this may be in making the composer's achievements known to the general public. What is most important about it is that it is extraordinarily good music, written by a composer of great creative gifts who was also a person of intelligence, warmth, and genuine humanity. It is music that deserves to be heard and judged on its own considerable artistic merits.

Appendix A

La Décade Philosophique

"La Distribution des prix du Conservatoire. . . ."
La Décade philosophique, Oct. 24, 1797, pp. 244–47.

La distribution des prix du Conservatoire de Musique, pour les cours d'Etude de l'an V, s'est faite le 3 Brumaire, dans la belle salle de l'Odéon, en présence du Directoire exécutif, des Ministres, du Corps diplomatique, de l'Institut national des Sciences et Arts, et des Fonctionnaires publics. Toute la salle, illuminée avec profusion et parfaitement ornée, était remplie d'un nombre immense de citoyens et de femmes mises avec élégance. Le coup-d'oeil était magnifique; le Directoire est entré vers sept heures du soir. Il a été accueilli par de vifs applaudissemens [*sic*]. Aussitôt, le concert a commencé. . . .

. . . Le Ministre de l'Intérieur chargé par le Directoire de la distribution des couronnes, a fait en général l'éloge de la musique, sans cependant négliger de rappeler l'influence particulière exercée par ce bel Art dans le cours de notre révolution.

Après son discours, a commencé cette distribution attendue impatiemment par les élèves, et qui a été vue avec le plus grand intérêt par les spectateurs. Chaque élève couronné était appelé à haute voix par le secrétaire du Conservatoire, et conduit par son maître au Ministre de l'Intérieur qui lui offrait une palme.

235

Appendix B
Biographie Universelle

Fétis, François J. *Biographie Universelle des Musiciens et Bibliographie générale de la Musique.* Paris: Firmin Didot, 1866, p. 41.

Au charme de son chant se joignait un jeu naturel et plein de verve comique. Un heureux mélange de gaîté, de sensibilité et de finesse, donnait à son talent dramatique un caractère particulier. Elle jouait surtout fort bien les rôles de soubrette et de servante, et les habitués du Théâtre Feydeau ont gardé longtemps le souvenir de son talent dans les personges [sic] si différents de la soubrette des *Evénements imprévus,* et de la servante des *Rendez-vous bourgeois.*

Appendix C
Conservatoire

Ministère de l'Intérieur. Conservatoire de musique, *Distribution des Prix pour le cours de l'Année 1835.* Paris: n.p., p. 1.

Composition. Premier Grand-Prix de Composition Musicale, remporté à l'Académie royale des Beaux-Arts de l'Institut de France, par M. BOULANGER (Henri-Alexandre-Ernest), de Paris, âgé de 20 ans. (élève de M. *Le Sueur,* pour la Composition, et de M. *Halévy,* pour le Contrepoint.)

Appendix D
Histoire de l'Académie de France à Rome

Lapauze, Henry. *Histoire de l'Académie de France à Rome,* vol. 2 (1802–1910). Paris: Plon, 1922, pp. 244–45.

Quelques mois plus tard, l'architecte Famin fut arrêté à Anagni, sous prétexte qu'il était sans passeport, et traîné en prison avec les menottes serrées de près, entre cinq gendarmes à cheval. M. de La Tour-Maubourg exigea des excuses du Saint-Siège. Sur sa demande, on révoqua le sous-préfet coupable qui fut enfermé pour un mois au fort Saint-Ange, et les collègues du fonctionnaire furent, par circulaire officielle, avisés de sa déchéance. Ce gouverneur avait pourtant un semblant d'excuse: la peur du choléra terrorisait le péninsule, et en chaque étranger apparaissait l'image même du fléau. . . .

. . . Les autres pensionnaires groupés autour d'Ingres, commençaient à regretter leur vaillance quand survint, foudroyante, la mort de Sigalon. Le malheureux revenait de Paris. Le dimanche, il avait dîné chez Ingres, plein de santé, enfin heureux de vivre, après le succès de sa copie du *Jugement dernier* qui lui valait d'autres travaux importants. Pris du choléra le lundi, il mourait le jeudi suivant, 18 août. Dans la nuit du 18 au 19, Simart, affolé, et croyant être en proie au choléra, vint réveiller Bonnassieux qui réussit à le calmer. A son tour pris de terreur, Bonnassieux communiqua le même frayeur à ses camarades. Ce n'était qu'une alarme. Elle suffit pour déterminer les pensionnaires à réclamer leurs passeports.

Appendix E

Dictionnaire des Opéras

Clément, Félix and Larousse, Pierre. *Dictionnaire des Opéras*. Paris: Larousse, 1904, p. 991.

La musique est agréable. La romance chantée par la marquise . . . rappelle assez heureusement le style ancien. L'air: *Vive le veuvage* est vulgaire; mais les couplets de la soubrette: *Aimons qui nous aime,* sont charmants. Nous rappellerons encore l'air de chasse chanté par le baron; il est bien travaillé et ingénieusement imitatif ainsi que le duo scénique du déjeuner. Quand aux couplets de Nicolas, ils ont été applaudis en raison de leur excentricité bouffonne.

Appendix F
Nadia Boulanger
to Léonie Rosenstiel: Letters

November 20, 1971

Le Concours du Prix de Rome se passait en deux épreuves: un concours d'essai et un concours définitif.

Le concours d'essai consistait en une mise en loge des candidats pendant cinq jours, à Compiègne, pour la composition d'une fugue sur un sujet donné, ainsi qu'un choeur avec orchestre sur un texte imposé.

Six candidats étaient alors retenus pour le Concours définitif qui durait un mois et avait lieu à Compiègne également. Il s'agissait cette fois-là de composer une cantate pour soli et orchestre sur un texte imposé. . . . L'oeuvre était jugée d'abord par le jury de la section musicale, puis dans une séance solennelle par toutes les sections composant l'Institut qui décernaient alors officiellement le prix. Ce prix donnait droit à un séjour à la Villa Médicis, ainsi qu'à une pension.

June 8, 1972

A Gargenville, se réunissaient beaucoup d'artistes: Eugène Ysaye, Jacques Thibaud, Joseph Hollmann, Fernand Pollain, Wilhelm Mengelberg, Maurice Léna, Paul Vidal, Gabriele d'Annunzio, Emile Verhaeren, et d'autres encore parmi les innombrables amis qui faisaient partie du cercle de M. et Mme Raoul Pugno et de Madame Ernest Boulanger. Les séances Pugno-Ysaye restèrent fameuses entre toutes, mais c'était surtout une atmosphère incomparable autour de l'être génial qu'était Raoul Pugno, avec un apport incessant de livres, de tableaux, d'objets d'art, un véritable commerce d'êtres extraordinaires et de choses, un échange constant, des transformations perpétuelles dans les lieux mêmes, constructions, aménagements, déménagements, etc., dans l'atmosphère aussi de Madame Boulanger, si spirituelle, d'une énergie incroyable et qui savait créer une ambiance où chacun se sentait à l'aise.

June 8, 1972

Plus d'une fois, Raoul Pugno passant devant la maison et entendant

238

de la musique, crut que Nadia était au piano alors que, à sa grande surprise, c'était Lili qui improvisait. . . . Raoul Pugno prit la petite fille en affection tandis qu'elle se liait avec sa fille Renée.

La séance du 5 Juillet reste mémorable: dès l'exécution des pre-mières pages, une atmosphère étonnante fut créée et chacun se sentit en présence d'une révélation. Les trois chanteurs (Mme Croiza, David Devriès, Henri Albers) et, au piano Nadia Boulanger, étaient dirigés par Lili Boulanger, debout près du piano, mince silhouette en robe blanche, si simple, calme, grave et souriante, telle une image inoubliable.

Appendix G
Le Monde Musical

Mangeot, A. "Soirées et Auditions Diverses." *Le Monde Musical,* March 30, 1912, p. 99.

Que de monde chez Mme Boulanger! Mme Bathori y chantait, ou plutôt y récitait du Debussy et du Ravel. Mlle Nadia Boulanger y pleyélait en compagnie de R. Pugno du Saint-Saëns, du Nicolaieff, et la *Petite Suite* de Debussy, bien petite en effet. L'orgue parla en la personne de Franck, auguste et vénéré. Mais la nouveauté atten-due de la soirée était les débuts, comme compositeur, de la "petite soeur," Lili Boulanger, dont le choeur des *Sirènes* montre déjà une science certaine et un quatuor vocal Renouveau, d'une grande fraî-cheur d'inspiration. On le redemande à Mlles Brothier, Sanderson, MM. Paulet et Tordo.

"Le Prix de Rome." *Le Monde Musical,* no. 9, May 15, 1913, p. 146.

Treize concurrents sont entrés en loge à Compiègne pour l'épreuve éliminatoire du concours de Rome, laquelle consiste, on le sait, en un choeur orchestré et une fugue./ Nous avons revu cette année les seconds prix des précédents concours: Marc Delmas, qui est à son septième essai, Mignan à son sixième Delvincourt à son cin-quième. A défaut d'autre mérite, la persévérance de ces musiciens vaut déjà une récompense. Ils sont d'autant plus en droit de l'espérer que l'Institut pourra disposer cette année de *deux* premiers grands prix./ M. Scotto entre également en loge pour la cinquième fois:

239

MM. Saint-Aulaire et Dupré, pour la quatrième fois: MM. de Petzer, Laporte et Mlle Lili Boulanger (soeur de Nadia Boulanger) pour la seconde fois. Les "bleus" sont MM. de Lapresle, Grandjany, Tournié et Mlle Guillot./ Sont admis au concours final. MM. [sic] Dupré, Mlle Lili Boulanger, MM. Marc Delmas, Mignan et Delvincourt.

"Le Prix de Rome." *Le Monde Musical,* nos. 13 and 14, July 15 and 30, 1913, pp. 208–9.

Mlle Lili Boulanger nous a donné une des plus belles cantates qu'on ait entendues depuis de longues années, (Exception faite pour celle de M. Paul Paray) . Son oeuvre est tout à fait supérieure et s'imposait à/ tous dès la première audition. Le prélude, le prologue de Méphistophélès, les dialogues, l'air de Faust chantant à Hélène un hymne, d'abord héroïquement présente, empreint ensuite d'une poésie et d'une tendresse exquises, les descriptions orchestrales, très réussies, l'air d'Hélène, le duo qui n'est qu'un trop court chef-d'oeuvre d'expression amoureuse, enfin. . . . le trio extrêmmement poignant, la fin particulièrement réussie avec les lamentations de Méphisto qui s'éloigne en emportant le corps de Faust, font de cette cantate une oeuvre tout à fait hors pair.

Il faut féliciter Mlle Lili Boulanger d'avoir à son âge un tel talent, une telle expérience de la scène, une musicalité émouvante tour à tour caressante et désespérée, rude et souple, et la faculté innée de voir juste et de frapper juste. Sa cantate fut la révélation de cette journée.

Martineau, Paul. "Concerts Colonne. Concert de Musique française: Franck, La Cantate de Mlle Lili Boulanger, A. Bruneau, Debussy, Berlioz." *Le Monde Musical,* no. 22, November 30, 1913, p. 323.

Déjà sont évidents chez Mlle Lili Boulanger, un penchant heureux pour les claires mélodies, un sens presque étonnant du théâtre, une admirable aisance pour exprimer les sentiments de passion, et une robuste continuité dans la ligne, jamais entachée de mesquineries ou de mignardises qui viendraient révéler la femme. L'âge (hélàs! . . . faut-il parler d'âge? . . .) et le travail épanouiront les qualités d'un talent déjà indéniable; d'un talent qui n'exclut point la grâce: ce que purent constater les enthousiastes applaudisseurs, qui obligèrent Mlle Lili Boulanger à paraître sur la scène, tout émue, entourée de ses trois admirables interprètes: Mme Croiza, MM. Devriès et Ghasne.

Moullé, Edouard. "Salles Diverses. Gala Nadia et Lili Boulanger." *Le Monde Musical,* December 1, 1913, p. 326.

Le Gala Nadia et Lili Boulanger, réunissant les deux soeurs au lendemain du triomphe de l'une d'elles, devait nécessairement piquer la curiosité du public. Une assistance nombreuse et payante, (J'en ai été le témoin), accourut au théâtre Léon Poirier pour entendre quelques oeuvres de ces deux muses de la musique. La séance s'ouvrit par une conférence de M. Landormy, qui sut dire à ce propos quantité de choses exquises qui tinrent le public sous le charme de son improvisation. . . .

. . . oeuvres d'une belle musicalité d'un goût très sûr et très fin, modernes, sans exagération, font le plus grand honneur à leur auteur.

Mme Lucienne Bréval avait bien voulu prêter le concours de son prestigieux talent à cette solennité, et nous fit apprécier une mélodie intitulée *Reflets* (de Mlle Lili Boulanger), rendant, avec intensité la mélancolie des clairs de lune et des illusions envolées.

Puis ce fut l'audition d'un important fragment de la cantate *Faust et Hélène* de Mlle Lili Boulanger, interprété avec la plus absolue perfection par Mme Croiza, MM. David Devriès et Ghasne accompagnés par Mlle Lili Boulanger. . . .

A la fin de cette séance, les deux soeurs, unies dans un même triomphe, reçurent les chaudes acclamations d'un public ému et enfiévré, reconnaissant d'avoir pu communier un instant avec le beau absolu.

Appendix H
Le Ménéstral

"Nouvelles Diverses: Revus et Départements." *Le Ménéstral,* no. 19, May 11, 1912, p. 150.

C'est mercredi dernier que les aspirants au prix de Rome se sont rendus à Compiègne pour entrer en loge au palais et y subir l'épreuve préparatoire. Rarement cette épreuve aura réuni un tel nombre de concurrents; ils devait être quinze, quatorze seulement se sont présentés, parmi lesquels une jeune fille, Mlle Lily [*sic*] Boulanger, soeur cadette de Mlle Nadia Boulanger, qui elle-même concurrait il y a trois ans et remportait le second prix. . . . C'est de 10 heures à midi qu'a eu lieu au palais, mercredi, la dictée des paroles du choeur et du sujet de fugue. Le jury, composé de la délégation de l'Institut, comprenait MM. Saint-Saëns, Th. Dubois, Paladihle [*sic*], Widor, assistés de M. d'estournelles de Constant, chef du bureau des théâtres au sous-secrétariat des beaux-arts, et M. Arsène Alexandre, conservateur du palais de Compiègne. Par ordre formal de M. Saint-Saëns, le sujet du choeur a été rigoureusement tenu secret. Notons que les logistes, qui trouvent au palais la plus confortable installation, sont d'ailleurs l'objet d'une scrupuleuse surveillance pour éviter toute communication avec le dehors, même avec leur famille. Depuis 1809, c'est le service du palais qui assure cette consigne. Les logistes quitteront le palais le lundi 13. Le 14 mai aura lieu la designation des six concurrents admis au concours définitif, pour lequel ils entreront en loge de nouveau le 23 mai.

"Nouvelles Diverses: Paris et Départements." *Le Ménéstral,* no. 20, May 18, 1912, p. 158.

Les jurés du prix de Rome se sont réunis mardi au Conservatoire pour juger le concours d'essai. Malgré le nombre extraordinaire des aspirants . . . l'épreuve a paru si faible que les examinateurs n'ont pas cru devoir atteindre le maximum des admissibles, qui est de six, et qu'ils n'ont reçu que quatre élèves au concours définitif.

"L'Examen des classes de composition musicale." *Le Ménéstral,"* no. 6, February 8, 1913, p. 48.

signalons le succès de Mlle Lili Boulanger, élève de MM. G. Caussade et P. Vidal, et qui a obtenu, après un examen très brillant, le prix Lepaul [*sic*] et le droit d'être exécutée à la classe d'orchestre. Deux choeurs: *Pour les Funérailles* et le *Printemps,* lui ont valu cette récompense particulièrement flatteuse. Mlle Lili Boulanger est la soeur cadette de Mlle Nadia Boulanger qui fut le second Grand Prix de Rome. Mlle Lili Boulanger concourra à son tour pour ce prix cette année.

Appendix I
La Vie Heureuse

"Rêvant au Grand Prix de Rome, Mlle Lily [*sic*] Boulanger." *La Vie Heureuse,* June 13, 1913, p. 150.

Voici quatre ans, à pareille date, Mlle Nadia Boulanger obtenait un Grand Prix de Rome de musique, pour la première fois décerné à une femme. Pour le même concours, Mlle Lily [*sic*] Boulanger, sa soeur, vient à son tour d'entrer en loge. Toutes les femmes admireront cette continuité de vocation et du talent et souhaiteront qu'il s'y joigne une aussi heureuse continuité du succès.

Appendix J

"War in Laces"

Vuillermoz, Émile. "La Guerre en Dentelles." *Musica,* no. 131, August 1913, p. 153.

Il y a quelques mois, à cette même place, je dénonçais aux musiciens l'imminence du "péril rose": les événements n'ont pas tardé à me donner raison. . . . Mlle Lili Boulanger, vient de triompher, au dernier concours de Rome, de tous ses concurrents masculins et a enlevé, avec une autorité, une rapidité et une aisance propres à inquiéter sérieusement les candidats, qui, depuis de longues années, suent sang et eau pour se rapprocher laborieusement de ce but. Et qu'on ne s'y trompe pas: cet exploit a toute sa valeur. Non seulement la galanterie des juges (?) [*sic*] n'a pas eu à intervenir et à faciliter la victoire mais on peut dire qu'on a été plus sévère pour cette jeune fille de dix-neuf ans que pour ses compétiteurs. Les sentiments misogynes du jury étaient connus. L'entrée d'une Ève dans le paradis terrestre de la Villa Médicis était redoutée par certains patriarches à l'égal d'une catastrophe irréparable. Le précédent établi par les sculpteurs n'apaisait pas leur émoi. C'est donc avec une attention impitoyable que fut écouté la cantate féminine qui prenait, dans ce milieu, la valeur et le danger d'une conférence féministe. Et il a fallu toute l'écrasante et indiscutable supériorité de cet ouvrage de dame pour triompher des devoirs scolaires qui l'encadraient.

La galanterie, d'ailleurs, ne trouve pas dans le concours de musiciens son dernier asile. La frêle grâce de Mlle Lili Boulanger n'a ému que les spectateurs, attendris au spectacle du groupe touchant que formaient la concurrente et sa soeur réunies au piano dans une collaboration attentive et affectueuse. L'ardeur de la lutte rendait insensibles à cette poésie les jeunes mâles rivaux, dévorés d'ambition. . . .

Et c'est là que la supériorité de l'éternel féminin apparut aux observateurs. Auprès de ses camarades exaltés et trop visiblement portés à croire "que c'était arrivé", la jeune fille, qui avait droit à toutes les impatiences et à toutes les nervosités, fit apprécier le plus parfait sang-froid. Son maintien modeste et simple, ses yeux baissés sur la partition, son immobilité pendant l'exécution, son abandon absolu à la volonté de ses excellents interprètes à qui elle ne se permit pas une seule fois de battre la mesure ou d'indiquer une nuance, tout contribua à servir sa cause, d'ailleurs excellemment défendue, et à faire remarquer la puérilité masculine. En vérité, l'heure est grave pour le sexe prétendu fort. Si les sévriennes de la musique se décident à lui disputer les lauriers officiels, il est vaincu d'avance. . . . Jusqu'ici la femme, qui a su apporter dans les autres arts une forme de sensibilité si personnelle et si savoureuse, qui a créé de la grâce, de la souplesse et de la force dans le poème et dans le roman, qui nous a même donné le goût d'une certaine âpreté dans la vérité et d'une sorte de cynisme courageux dans la sincérité, n'a pas trouvé le moyen de s'exprimer en musique. La technique actuelle harmonique et orchestrale ne lui convient-elle pas? Devra-t-elle attendre qu'une géniale créatrice forge un style nouveau à son usage? N'a-t-elle pas encore découvert le filon qu'elle saura seule exploiter? L'avenir nous l'apprendra . . . l'épreuve de la cantate n'est pas une épreuve de composition au sens artistique du mot, c'est un concours, et dans un concours Ève n'a rien à redouter d'Adam. Toutes ses qualités la servent et lui assurent la victoire. Saluons donc aujourd'hui Mlle Lili Boulanger avec l'héroïsme résigné qu'apportaient les "morituri" à saluer César!

Appendix K
Les Hommes du Jour

"Lili Boulanger." *Les Hommes du Jour.* no. 286, July 12, 1913, p. 2.

je le dis et je le proclame avec une assurance indéracinable . . . que Lili Boulanger sera une grande musicienne, ou, plutôt un grand musicien; cela est évident.

Appendix L
Comoedia Illustré

Loisel, Paul. "Le Concours de Rome." *Comoedia Illustré,* July 20, 1913, p. 936.

Le féminisme vient de remporter une grande victoire, impatiemment attendue depuis le jour où les femmes furent admises à concurir pour le prix de Rome de musique . . . c'est l'énergique et mignonne Mlle Boulanger.

Appendix M
La Revue S. I. M.

Debussy, Claude. "La Musique espagnole. Faust et Hélène par Lili Boulanger." *La Revue S.I.M.*, December 1, 1913, pp. 43–44.

Mademoiselle Lili Boulanger qui vient de remporter le grand prix de Rome avec *Faust et Hélène,* d'après le second Faust de Goethe, poème de E. Adenis, n'a que dix-neuf ans. . . . Son expérience des diverses manières d'écrire la musique en a bien davantage! Il y bien, ça et là, les petites ficelles avec lesquelles on noue les fins de phrases dans ce genre d'ouvrage, seulement Mademoiselle L. Boulanger y met plus de fine rouerie. L'arrivée d'Hélène sur des battements aériens de violons divisés, ondule avec grâce. Mais à peine arrivée Hélène, par la voix de Madame Croiza, prend l'accent qui convient à une fille de Zeus, accablée par tout de destins contraires. Cependant que Faust susurre par la jolie voix de David Devriés [*sic*].

Si le personnage de Mephistophélès, l'inévitable trio, sont un peu conventionnels, il ne faut pas oublier les conditions dans lesquelles on écrit une cantate! Elles sont nettement défavorables.

En effet, on demande d'avoir des idées, du talent, à un moment précis de l'année,—si vous n'êtes pas en train ce mois-là, tant pis pour vous! C'est arbitraire et n'a aucune signification pour l'avenir. Inutile de dépleurer, tous les concours se passent de la même manière. Les juges de ces concours ayant souffert des même errements, ne sont pas fâchés de vous y voir à votre tour. Une fois par an, à peu près, on dit qu'il faut changer les conditions du Concours de Rome et cela suffit.

Que l'on garde précieusement la villa [*sic*] Médicis comme la plus charmante des récompenses, mais qu'on supprime le Prix de Rome qui ne répond à aucun besoin de notre époque.

Appendix N
Le Miroir

Boudouresque, Léon. "Deux femmes—Qui l'eût dit?" *Le Miroir,* July 5, 1914, pp. 5–8.

L'installation de Mlle Heuvelmans à la Villa Médicis se fit donc de la façon la plus simple du monde . . . La seule révolution provoquée par cette arrivée fut . . . l'adjonction d'une femme de chambre au personnel domestique de la Villa. . . .

Depuis janvier 1912, Mlle Heuvelmans vit à la Villa Médicis. Elle y vit en bon garçon, si j'ose dire, et sur le pied d'une parfaite camaraderie avec les jeunes gens dont son talent fit la commensale . . . Ils l'appellent Heuvelmans tout court. . . . Et, comme la tradition veut que l'on se tutoie entre les pensionnaires, Mlle Heuvelmans a trouvé naturel d'être tutoyée par ses camarades et de les tutoyer, dès le premier jour.

Il en est allé un peu différemment pour Mlle Boulanger . . . lorsqu'elle arriva, cette année à la Villa Médicis. Son éducation, ses habitudes, sont plus exclusivement féminins, moins garçonnières, si l'on veut, que celles de Mlle Heuvelmans.

Ajoutez que Mlle Lili Boulanger n'a guère plus de vingt ans. Et vous comprendrez que son installation à la Villa Médicis ait constitué pour elle ce que j'appellerai une transplantation. . . .

Il semble bien qu'elle en soit effarouchée, quelque peu, par avance. Du moins le bruit en courut ici, au début de l'année, quand on vit les "clous" (promotion nouvelle) arriver de Paris sans elle, alors que le règlement exige qu'ils fassent ce voyage en corps, et par étapes fixées d'avance. Un mois, deux mois s'écoulèrent. Mlle Lili Boulanger n'arrivait pas. Elle était malade, disait-on. Maladie réelle ou . . . diplomatique?

À en croire les potins, la jeune pensionnaire s'efforçait d'obtenir de l'Institut, souverain tuteur de l'Académie de France, l'autorisation soit de ne pas loger à la Villa—et dans ce cas elle aurait pris en Ville [sic] un appartement avec sa mère,—soit de faire partager à sa mère la chambre qui lui était destinée. L'une et l'autre solution étant également interdites par le règlement, l'institut dut refuser cette autorisation. On parla alors de la démission possible de Mlle Lili Boulanger. . . . Certain problème de la femme de chambre "particulière", que Mlle Lili Boulanger tenait beaucoup à avoir auprès d'elle nuit et jour, menaça de rester insoluble, pis encore; de dénégrer [sic] en conflit avec la direction . . .—Par bonheur tout s'arrangea. . . . Ne cherchez pas à savoir si la femme de chambre personnelle de Mlle Lili Boulanger dort à la Villa, ou bien en ville. Contentez-vous d'apprendre que cette indispensable soubrette est à la disposition de sa maîtresse le matin, dès la première heure, aussi bien que le soir, tard, très tard—et que, cependant, officiellement, elle n'est pas logée à la Villa. Alors? . . . *combinazione,* vous dit-on! . . . Il arrive aussi que la gracieuse musicienne ne paraisse pas à la table commune; c'est évidemment, qu'une migraine insupportable la retient dans sa chambre, et si malade, si malade, que vous frappiez vainement à sa porte pour lui demander des nouvelles de sa santé. . . .

Mlle Lili Boulanger, toutefois, partage le plus souvent les repas de ses camarades, comme le veut le règlement . . . quand elle et sa mère invitèrent tous les pensionnaires à dîner . . . au restaurant!

Appendix O
Funeral Invitation

Invitation to the Funeral of Lili Boulanger, March 19, 1918. From the Nadia Boulanger Collection.

Vous êtes prié d'assister au Convoi, Service & Enterrement de/ Mademoiselle Lili BOULANGER/Premier Grand Prix de Rome/ décédée, munie des Sacrements de l'Église, le 15 Mars 1918,/à l'âge de 24 ans, à Mézy, par Meulan, après une longue et/cruelle maladie;/ Qui se feront le Mardi, 19 courant, à MIDI TRÈS PRÉCIS,/en l'Église de la Trinité, sa Paroisse./On se réunira à Paris, 36, Rue Ballu.

Appendix P
Maitrī Bhāvanāva

(SINHALESE)
(From the Collection of the Venerable Kosgoda Sobhita)

MAITRĪ BHĀVANĀVA

(TRANSLITERATION)

```
Aham avero homi, abyapajjo homi, anigho homi, sukhi attanam
pariharami.  Aham viya mayham ācariyupajjhāyā mātāpitaro
hitasattā majjhattikasattā verīsattā averā hontu abyāpajjā
hontu anighā hontu sukhī attānam pariharantu dukhā muncantu
yathāladdasampattito māvigacchantu.  Kammassakā imasmim
vihare imasmim gocaragāme imasmim nagare imasmim lankādīpe
imasmim jambudīpe imasmim cakkavāle issarajanā sīmaṭṭhaka-
devatā sabbe sattā averā hontu abyāpajjā hontu anīghā hontu
sukhī attānam pariharantu dukkhā muncantu yathāladdhasam-
pattito māvigacchantu.  Kammassakā puratthimāya disāya
dakkhiṇāya disāya pacchimāya disāya uttarāya disāya puratthi-
māya anudisāya dakkhiṇāya anudisāya pacchimāya anudisāya
uttarāya anudisāya haṭṭhimāya disāya uparimāya disāya sabbe
sattā sabbe pānā sabbe bhūtā sabbe puggalā sabbe attabhāva-
pariyāpannā sabbe itthiyo sabbe purisā sabbe ariyā sabbe
anariyā sabbe devā sabbe manussā sabbe amanussā sabbe vini-
patikā averā hontu abyāpajjā hontu anīghā hontu sukhī attānam
pariharantu dukkhā muncantu yathāladdhasampattito māvigacchantu
kammassakā.

        Puratthimasmim disābhāge santi devā mahiddhikā
        tepi mam anurakkhantu ārogyena sukhena ca.

        Dakkhinasmim disābhāge santi devā mahiddhikā
        tepi mam anurakkhantu ārogyena sukhena ca.

        Pacchimasmim disābhāge santi devā mahiddhikā
        tepi mam anurakkhantu ārogyena sukhena ca.

        Uttarasmim disābhāge santi devā mahiddhikā
        tepi mam anurakkhantu ārogyena sukhena ca.

        Puratthimena dhataraṭṭho dakkhiṇena virulhako
        pacchimena virūpakkho kuvero uttaram disam
        tepi mam anurakkhantu ārogyena sukhena ca.
```

මෙත්‍රී භාවනාව

අහං අවෙරෙ හොමි අබ්‍යාපජ්ජො, හොමි අනීඝො හොමි සුඛී අත්තානං පරිහරාමි අතං විය මය්හං ආචරියුපජ්ඣායා මාතාපිතරෝ ඤාතිසාලොහිතා මිත්තාමච්චසත්තා වෙරිසත්තා අවෙරා හොන්තු අබ්‍යාපජ්ජා හොන්තු අනීඝා හොන්තු සුඛී අත්තානංතං පරිහරන්තු දුක්ඛා මුච්චන්තු යථාලද්ධ සම්පත්තිතො මාවිගච්ඡන්තු කම්මස්සකා ඉමස්මිං විහාරෙ ඉමස්මිං ගොචර ගාමෙ ඉමස්මිං කස්සරෙ ඉමස්මිං ලංකාදීපෙ ඉමස්මිං ජම්බුදීපෙ ඉමස්මිං චක්කවාලෙ ඉස්සරජ්ජනා සීමට්ඨකදෙවතා සබ්බෙ සත්තා අවෙරා හොන්තු අබ්‍යාපජ්ජා හොන්තු අනීඝා හොන්තු සුඛී අත්තානංතං පරිහරන්තු දුක්ඛා මුච්චන්තු යථාලද්ධසම්පත්තිතො මාවිගච්ඡන්තු කම්මස්සකා පුරත්ථිමාය දිසාය දක්ඛිණාය දිසාය පච්ඡිමාය දිසාය උත්තරාය දිසාය පුරත්ථිම අනුදිසාය දක්ඛිණාය අනුදිසාය පච්ඡිමාය අනුදිසාය උත්තරාය අනුදිසාය හෙට්ඨිමාය දිසාය උපරිමාය දිසාය සබ්බෙ සත්තා සබ්බෙ පාණා සබ්බෙ භූතා සබ්බෙ පුග්ගලා සබ්බෙ අත්තභාවපරියාපන්නා සබ්බා ඉත්ථියො සබ්බෙ පුරිසා සබ්බෙ අරියා සබ්බෙ අනරියා සබ්බෙ දෙවා සබ්බෙ මනුස්සා සබ්බෙ අමනුස්සා සබ්බෙ විනිපාතිකා අවෙරා හොන්තු අබ්‍යාපජ්ජා හොන්තු අනීඝා හොන්තු සුඛී අත්තානංතං පරිහරන්තු දුක්ඛා මුච්චන්තු යථාලද්ධසම්පත්තිතො මාවිගච්ඡන්තු කම්මස්සකා.

පුරත්ථිමස්මිං දිසාභාගෙ සන්තිදෙවා මහිද්ධිකා
තෙපි තං අනුරක්ඛන්තු ආරෝග්‍යෙන සුඛෙන ච.

දක්ඛිණස්මිං දිසාභාගෙ—පෙ—ආරෝග්‍යෙන සුඛෙන ච,
පච්ඡිමස්මිං දිසාභාගෙ—පෙ—ආරෝග්‍යෙන සුඛෙන ච.

උත්තරස්මිං දිසාභාගෙ සන්ති දෙවා මහිද්ධිකා
තෙපි තං අනුරක්ඛන්තු ආරෝග්‍යෙන සුඛෙන ච

පුරත්ථිමෙන ධතරට්ඨා දක්ඛිණෙන විරුළ්හකො,
පච්ඡිමෙන විරූපක්ඛො කුවෙරො උත්තරං දිසං.
තෙපි තං අනුරක්ඛන්තු ආරෝග්‍යෙන සුඛෙන වාති.

MEDITATION ON UNIVERSAL LOVE
(TRANSLATION)

May each thing that breathes,
Without enemies, without obstacles,
Overcoming pain and attaining happiness,
Be able to move freely,
Each in the way destined for him.

May all creatures everywhere,
All the spirits and all who have been born,

248

Without enemies, without obstacles,
Overcoming pain and attaining happiness,
Be able to move freely,
Each in the way destined for him.

May all women,
May all men,
Aryans and non-Aryans,
All gods and all humans and all who have died,
Without enemies, without obstacles,
Overcoming pain and attaining happiness,
Be able to move freely,
Each in the way destined for him.

In the East and in the West,
In the North and in the South,
May all the beings that exist,
Without enemies, without obstacles,
Overcoming pain and attaining happiness,
Be able to move freely,
Each in the way destined for him.

Appendix Q
Excelsior

"A la Villa Médicis." *Excelsior*, May 3, 1918, p. 3.

La mort toute récente de Mlle Lili Boulanger, la première musicienne qui obtint le prix de Rome, a plongé dans le deuil le monde des arts.

M. Albert Besnard, directeur de l'Académie de France à Rome, a décidé que le buste de la jeune fille, sculpté par son amie, Mlle Heuvelmans, autre prix de Rome, serait placé dans l'église Saint-Louis des Français.

Pensée touchante assurément.

Mais pourquoi ne pas perpétuer aussi dans le jardin même de la Villa Médicis le souvenir de cette charmante Muse trop tôt disparue? . . .

Souvent, après avoir déjeuné dans l'acceuillant réfectoire orné des portraits de tous les prix de Rome, elle alla s'asseoir près de la Minerve de marbre, et confia aux autres pensionnaires ses espérances de gloire.

C'est dans cet asile enchanteur qu'on aimerait à voir son image. C'est là surtout que doit être honorée sa mémoire.

Appendix R
La Lanterne

Vuillemin, Louis. "Musique." *La Lanterne,* June 21, 1921.

Malgré le jeune âge auquel un sort déplorable a ravi Lili Boulanger à son art, cette musicienne a laissé de nombreuses compositions instrumentales et vocales; quelques-unes même fort importantes. De multiples concerts nous les ont rendues familières. Mais aucun d'eux, ni tous ensemble, n'avait autant d'éloquence que cette unique audition de pages choisies. De ce groupement de mélodies, de choeurs, de pièces diverses, est résultée une impression exacte, totale de ce qu'apportait en propre à la Musique [*sic*] Lili Boulanger: Une sensibilité aiguë et prodigieusement humaine, servie dans son expression par la gamme complète des dons naturels depuis la grâce, la couleur, le charme et la subtilité, jusqu'au lyrisme ailé, jusqu'à la force claire, aisée et profonde. De telles vertus si rarement assemblées au bénéfice d'un seul tempérament créateur.

Appendix S
Le Journal des Débats

Julien, Adolphe. "Les Envois de Rome." *Le Journal des Débats,* February 4, 1923, p. 4.

D'ordinaire, la séance d'audition des envois de Rome en musique, qui a lieu dans la grande salle du Conservatoire vers cette époque-ci de l'année, n'est guère qu'une simple cérémonie scolaire, une sorte de fête de famille où les parents et amis du lauréat dont on exécute les oeuvres provenant de la Villa Médicis viennent applaudir le jeune compositeur, quel qu'il soit, de façon que tous ces envois produisent chaque année une impression similaire en remportant un succès à peu près égal et presque de commande. Cette fois-ci, au contraire, il y avait quelque chose de changé, d'exceptionnel dans cette séance . . . . il est incontestable que les pages que nous entendîmes l'autre jour portaient généralement la marque d'une grâce toute féminine, peut-être un peu mélancolique, et d'une réelle sensibilité, toutes qualités qu'on avait pu déjà discerner dans la cantate qui lui avait value de remporter le prix de Rome.

Entre ces diverses compositions . . . celles qui témoignent sans comparaison de la plus belle somme de science acquise et de travail fécond était les *Trois Psaumes* pour soli, choeur, orgue et orchestre, dont le beau caractère, et je dirai [*sic*] même l'ampleur sonore, ont vivement frappé l'auditoire.

Appendix T

The Completed Works of Lili Boulanger

I. *Published*

Completed	Composition	Genre	Publisher	Dedicated to
1911	**Nocturne**	Violin or flute and piano, and orchestral transcription	Ricordi 1918	ma chère Marie-Danielle Parenteau
1911	**Renouveau** (**Armand Silvestre**)	Vocal quartet and piano or orchestra	Ricordi 1918	mon cher Maître et Ami Paul Vidal en respectueuse gratitude et sincère affection.
1911	Les Sirènes (Charles Grandmougin)	Mezzo, Chorus and Piano	Ricordi 1918	Madame Engel Bathori
1911	Reflets (Maurice Maeterlinck)	Voice and piano	Ricordi 1919	M. et Mme Paul Gentien

I. Published (continued)

Completed	Composition	Genre	Publisher	Dedicated to
1912	Attente (Maurice Maeterlinck)	Voice and piano or orchestra	Ricordi 1918	Madame J. Montjovet
1912	Hymne au Soleil (Casimir Delavigne)	Contralto solo, chorus and piano	Ricordi 1918	Comte H. de San Martino e Valperga
1912	Le Retour (Georges Delaquys)	Voice and piano	Ricordi 1919	H. Dufranne
1912	Pour les Funérailles d'un Soldat (Alfred de Musset) English version by Frederick H. Martens: "For a Soldier Burial"	Baritone solo, Chorus and orchestra	Ricordi (Paris) 1919	mon cher Maître et ami Georges Caussade en profonde reconnaissance et sincère attachement.
		Baritone solo, Chorus and piano	Ricordi (N.Y.) 1918	—
1913	Soir sur la Plaine (Albert Samain)	Soprano, Tenor and orchestra	Ricordi 1918	la mémoire de mon grand ami Raoul Pugno
1913	Faust et Hélène (Eugène Adenis)	Tenor, baritone, mezzo, chorus and orchestra. Piano reduction	Ricordi 1918	ma soeur Nadia Boulanger
			Durand 1970	

Completed	Composition	Genre	Publisher	Dedicated to
1914	D'un Jardin Clair	Piano	Ricordi 1919	Ninette Salles
1914	D'un Vieux Jardin	Piano	Ricordi 1918	Lily Jumel
1914	Cortège	Violin and Piano and flute and piano	Ricordi 1919	Yvonne Astruc
1914	Clairières dans le Ciel (Francis Jammes)	Voice and piano	Ricordi 1919;	
			Durand 1970	
	Elle était descendue . . .			Maître Gabriel Fauré
	Elle est gravement gaie			ma petite Miki [Piré]
	Parfois, je suis triste			Fernand Francell
	Un poète disait . . .			Yvonne Brothier
	Au pied de mon lit			ma chère Maman
	Si tout ceci n'est qu'un pauvre rêve			mon grand ami Monsieur Tito Ricordi
	Nous nous aimerons tant			Henri Albers
	Vous m'avez regardé			—
	Les lilas qui avaient fleuri			R. Plamandon
	Deux ancolies			mes chers Marthe et

I. Published (continued)

Completed	Composition	Genre	Publisher	Dedicated to
1914	Clairières dans le Ciel (Continued)			Richard Bouwens van der Boijen David Devriès
	Par ce que j'ai souffert Je garde une médaille d'elle Demain fera un an			— mon cher ami Roger Ducasse
1916	Psaume 24 (La Terre appartient à l'Éternel)	chorus, organ and orchestra; also transcription for voice and piano	Durand 1926	Monsieur Jules Griset
1916	Psaume 129 (Ils m'ont assez opprimé)	Baritone and orchestra	Durand 1924	—
1916	Dans l'immense Tristesse (B. Galeron de Calone)	Voice and piano	Ricordi 1919	ma chère Claire Croiza
1917	Psaume 130 (Du fond de l'Abîme)	Voice, chorus organ and orchestra	Durand 1925	la mémoire de mon cher Papa
1917	Vieille Prière bouddhique	Tenor solo, chorus and orchestra	Durand 1921–1925	—
1918	D'un Matin de Printemps	Violin and piano or flute and piano	Durand 1922	—
1918	Pie Jesu	Voice, string quartet, harp and organ	Durand 1922	—

II. Unpublished

Completed	Composition	Genre	Publisher	Dedicated to
1911	Reflets (Maurice Maeterlinck)	Voice and Orchestra		
1911	Sous Bois (Philippe Gille)	Chorus and Orchestra		
1911	Frédégonde (Charles Morel)	3 soloists and orchestra		
1912	Fugue for the Concours d'Essai	Four voices		
1912	La Source (Anon.)	Chorus and Orchestra		
1913	Fugue for the Concours d'Essai	Four voices		
1914	Morceau pour piano Thème et variations	Piano		
1914	"Elle était descendue" (Clairières—No. 1)	Voice and Orchestra		

II. Unpublished (continued)

Completed	Composition	Genre	Publisher	Dedicated to
1914	"Au pied de mon lit" (*Clairières*—No. 5)	Voice and Orchestra		
1914	"Si tout ceci n'est qu'un pauvre rêve" (*Clairières*—No. 6)	Voice and orchestra		
1914	"Nous nous aimerons tant" (*Clairières*—No. 7)	Voice and orchestra		
1914	"Je garde une médaille d'elle" (*Clairières*—No. 12)	Voice and Orchestra		
1914	"Demain fera un an" (*Clairières*—No. 13)	Voice and Orchestra		
1918	D'un Soir triste	Cello and piano (marked "transcription"); versions also for trio and for orchestra		

Appendix U
Personalia

Adenis, Eugène Colombo (1854–1923), French dramatic writer whose production includes mainly opera librettos. A segment of his adaptation of Goethe's second *Faust* was used as the libretto of Lili Boulanger's *Faust et Hélène*.

Albers, Henri (1866–1926), baritone of the Opéra-Comique and former student of Fauré. He was one of the three soloists in the performance of Lili Boulanger's *Faust et Hélène* at the Institut de France on July 5, 1913, and is the dedicatee of "Nous nous aimerons tant."

Annunzio, Gabriele d' (1863–1938), Italian novelist, playwright, poet, and patriot. Nadia Boulanger and Raoul Pugno set his *La Ville Morte* to music in 1911. He also was a member of the Gargenville circle.

Astruc, Yvonne (1889–   ), French violinist and wife of the pianist Marcel Ciampi, she was a close friend of the Boulanger family. Lili Boulanger dedicated *Cortège* to her.

Auber, Daniel François Esprit (1782–1871), French composer of operas and chamber music, and Cherubini's successor as Director of the Paris Conservatoire in 1842. Julie Hallinger-Boulanger introduced him to her son, Ernest.

Barbier, Jules (1825–1901), French librettist, with Michel Carré wrote the libretto of Gounod's *Faust*. He was a friend of Ernest Boulanger, and the families remained close for three generations.

Barrère, Camille (1851–1940), French Ambassador to Italy (1897–1924). Lili Boulanger met him in Rome, where he and his wife received her at the Embassy.

Bathori, Jane Engel, pseudonym of Jeanne-Marie Berthier (1877–1970), famous French singer and champion of modern French music, she gave premieres of the works of such composers as Debussy, Ravel, and Milhaud, as well as of Lili Boulanger. Lili Boulanger dedicated *Les Sirènes* to her.

Besnard, Albert (1849–1934), French painter, Director of the Villa Medici during Lili Boulanger's term there as a Prix de Rome laureate.

Boieldieu, François-Adrien (1775–1834), French composer of comic operas. Julie Hallinger-Boulanger performed in the premiere of his *La Dame Blanche* (1825), and introduced him to Ernest Boulanger.

Boulanger, Nadia (1887–   ), older sister of Lili and renowned French music pedagogue. She has also been active as a pianist, organist, conductor, and composer. At the Paris Conservatoire, she studied with Paul Vidal, Louis Vierne, Alexandre Guilmant, Gabriel Fauré, and Charles-Marie Widor. After winning the Second Grand Prix de Rome in 1908, she collaborated with Raoul Pugno on a number of works, notably musical settings of Verhaeren's *Les Heures Claires* (1909–1912) and d'Annunzio's *La Ville Morte* (1911), as well as both intrumental and vocal compositions of her own. She abandoned composition for pedagogy, and her students have come to include such musicologists as Jacques Chailley, such composers as Aaron Copland, Jacques Françaix, Walter Piston, Léo Preger, and Virgil Thomson, such conductors as Igor Markevitch, and such pianists as Dinu Lipatti. Since 1921, she has taught at the Conservatoire Américain de Fontainebleau, of which she has been the Director for many years. She is Chapel Master of Prince Rainier of Monaco, and has been made a Fellow of the Royal College of Music in London and of the American Academy of Arts and Sciences. From the French Government Nadia Boulanger has received the Ordre des Arts et Lettres and was made an Officier de la Légion d'honneur. Her foreign distinctions have included the Order of *Polonia restituta*, of *St. Charles de Monaco*, and the *Ordre de la Couronne de Belgique*, as well as numerous honorary degrees from colleges and universities in both Europe and America. In addition to her teaching, conducting, and performing activities, she has also served as a member of the jury for the Tchaikowsky Competition in Russia and the Leeds International Competition in England.

Bourgaud-Ducoudray, Louis-Albert (1840–1910), winner of the Grand Prix de Rome in music in 1862 and later professor of the history of music at the Conservatoire. After 1906 all students there were required to study with him. Lili Boulanger audited his history classes.

Bouwens van der Boijen, William (1834–1907), architiect born in Holland, studied at the École des Beaux-Arts in Paris, and became a naturalized French citizen. He was named architect of the Crédit Lyonnais building in Paris as a result of his outstanding achievements as a residential architect in that city, and also designed the tomb of Alexandre Dumas fils. A close friend of the Boulangers, he was Lili Boulanger's godfather and also her mathematics tutor. His children and grandchildren were also dear friends of the Boulangers. Lili Boulanger dedicated "Deux ancolies" to his son, Richard, and his daughter-in-law, Marthe.

Brothier, Yvonne (1889–   ), French soprano known for her roles in comic opera who won prizes in voice and *opéra-comique* at the Conservatoire in 1913. She became a close friend of the Boulanger family, and Lili Boulanger's "Un poète disait . . . " is dedicated to her.

Büsser, Henri (1872–1973), winner of the Premier Grand Prix de Rome in music in 1891, composer of operas, orchestrator, and conductor of the Paris Opera for over fifty years. A friend of Ernest Boulanger, he remained on good terms with the family after the elder Boulanger's death in 1900. Büsser conducted Lili Boulanger's *Faust et Hélène* at the Institut de France on November 8, 1913, in its first performance with full orchestra. For his hundredth birthday in January 1972, the O.R.T.F. and the Institut de France both scheduled festivities in his honor, and he was given a special luncheon by the late President Pompidou.

Caplet, André (1878–1925), French impressionist composer and conductor who completed the orchestration of Debussy's *Gigues* (1912). Nadia Boulanger first met him in Paul Vidal's accompaniment class in 1900, and he became a good friend of both Boulanger sisters.

Casella, Alfredo (1883–1947), Italian composer, pianist, conductor and pedagogue, educated in France, where he met the Boulanger sisters at the Conservatoire. After his return to Italy during World War I, he frequently visited Lili at the Villa Medici in 1916.

Caussade, Georges (1873–1936), professor of harmony at the Conservatoire, close friend of the Boulanger family, and teacher of Lili Boulanger. *Pour les Funérailles d'un Soldat* was dedicated to him.

Chapuis, Auguste (1859–1933), French composer, teacher of harmony at the Conservatoire, and organist. Lili Boulanger accompanied Nadia to his harmony classes in 1898.

Ciampi, Marcel (1891–   ), pianist, husband of the violinist Yvonne Astruc. Both he and his wife frequently played chamber music with the Boulangers.

Croiza, Claire Conelly (1882–1946), mezzo-soprano and good friend of Nadia Boulanger, performed in the premiere of *Faust et Hélène* on July 5, 1913. Later, she became the dedicatee of *Dans l'immense Tristesse*.

Dallier, Henri (1849–1934), French organist and composer who taught at the Conservatoire. Nadia Boulanger became his assistant in 1908, but he and his family had already been friends of the Boulangers for years before, and members of the Gargenville circle.

Delaquys, Georges (1880–   ), French writer of musical comedies, novels, and dramatic poems. The husband of Renée Pugno, his family was close to the the Boulangers. Lili Boulanger was the godmother of his daughter, Madeleine. All were members of the Gargenville group.

Delavigne, Casimir (1793–1843), French dramatic and lyric poet who may, perhaps, best be classified as a semi-Romantic. He was a minor poet, but adept in the dramatist's craft. It was part of his play *Le Pariah* (1833) that Lili Boulanger set as *Hymne au Soleil*.

Delibes, Léo (1836–1891), French composer of operettas, operas, and ballets. He is most famous for his ballets *Coppélia* (1870) and

Sylvia (1876), and for the opera *Lakmé* (1883). Delibes was a friend of Ernest Boulanger.

Delvincourt, Claude (1888–1954), French composer, conductor, winner of the Second Grand Prix de Rome in music (1913). The Delvincourts and the Boulangers were good friends.

Devriès, David (1881–1936), tenor of the Opéra-Comique, one of the three soloists in the premiere of Lili Boulanger's *Faust et Hélène* on July 5, 1913. The composer wrote *Clairières dans le Ciel* with him in mind, and dedicated "Par ce que j'ai soufert" to him.

Dubois, Théodore (1837–1924), French composer and organist, Director of the Conservatoire (1896–1905), and Saint-Saëns's successor at the organ of the Madeleine in Paris. He was a close friend and adviser to the Boulanger family both before and after the death of Ernest Boulanger.

Ducasse, Roger (1873–1954), Fauré's assistant and protégé, who became like an older brother to the Boulanger sisters. A composer of works for solo piano, voice, and orchestra, he was much influenced by Fauré and Debussy. Lili Boulanger dedicated "Demain fera un an" to Roger Ducasse.

Dupré, Marcel (1886–1971), French organist and composer. He had been Nadia Boulanger's classmate in Guilmant's organ class in 1902, and became a close friend of the Boulanger family.

Duse, Eleonora (1869–1924), great Italian tragedienne. Nadia Boulanger met her while working on d'Annunzio's *La Ville Morte*. Lili Boulanger met her in Rome.

Duvernoy, Alphonse (1842–1907), French piano virtuoso, composer, and teacher at the Conservatoire. He was married to Pauline Viardot's daughter. In 1902 he was Nadia Boulanger's piano teacher.

Emmanuel, Maurice (1862–1938), French music historian and composer who studied under Théodore Dubois, Léo Delibes, and Louis Bourgaud-Ducoudray at the Conservatoire. He was Bourgaud-Ducoudray's successor there, and Lili Boulanger audited his classes.

Enesco, Georges (1881–1955), Rumanian violinist-composer and conductor who frequently audited Fauré's classes at the Conservatoire while Nadia Boulanger was a student there.

Fairchild, Blair (1887–1933), American composer, student of Albert Spalding at Harvard. Fairchild wrote choral and symphonic works and a ballet pantomime. He entered the American diplomatic corps, settled in Paris, and became a student of Widor. During World War I he represented the American Friends of Musicians in France. He and his wife became good friends of the Boulangers.

Fauré, Gabriel Urbain (1845–1924), French composer and teacher of composition at the Conservatoire. He was a friend of the Boulanger family, often attended receptions at their home, and influenced both Lili and Nadia Boulanger after 1902, when they attended his composition classes. Lili dedicated "Elle était descendue au bas de la prairie" to him.

Francell, Fernand (1880–1966), French lyric tenor who studied at the Conservatoire and made his debut at the Opéra-Comique in 1906. He had a long and successful career there. In 1913, he sang Paco in the premiere of de Falla's *La Vida Breve*. He became a friend of the Boulanger family, and Lili Boulanger dedicated "Parfoi, je suis triste" to him.

Galéron de Calone, Bertha (1859– ?), daughter of an archaeologist, she was born deaf, mute, and blind. Her collection of verse, *Dans ma Nuit* (1925), received a prize from the Académie Française. Lili Boulanger set her "Dans la sombre Tristesse" to music as *Dans l'immense Tristesse*.

Gédalge, André (1856–1926), professor of counterpoint and fugue at the Conservatoire, was Nadia Boulanger's teacher in 1901. Lili Boulanger audited some of his classes.

Gobillard, Paule (d. 1946), French Impressionist painter who studied with her aunt, Berthe Morisot, Manet's sister-in-law. Mlle Gobillard was the sister of Mme Paul Valéry, and the whole family was part of the Gargenville group.

Gounod, Charles François (1818–1893), French composer of songs, sacred music, and operas. Winner of the Prix de Rome in 1839, he wrote such operas as *Faust* (1859) and *Roméo et Juliette* (1867). He was a very close friend of Ernest Boulanger.

Grandmougin, Charles-Jean (1850–1930), French Parnassian poet, writer of dramas in verse and opera librettos, as well as prose works. Lili Boulanger set his *Les Sirènes* to music as part of her preparation for the Prix de Rome competition.

Guilmant, Alexandre (1837–1911), French organist and composer, who followed Widor as professor of organ at the Conservatoire (1896). Nadia Boulanger studied organ with him at the Conservatoire in 1902.

Halévy, Jacques Fromental, pseudonym for Lévy (1799–1862), French opera composer, best known for his *La Juive* (1835). He was a friend of Julie Hallinger-Boulanger who introduced him to Ernest.

Hasselmans, Alphonse (1845–1912), famous Belgian harpist and professor of harp at the Paris Conservatoire, one of the founders of the contemporary school of harp playing. He also wrote about fifty pieces for harp. Lili Boulanger took harp lessons from him.

Hollmann, Joseph (1852–1927), French cellist and composer of cello solos and concertos, who was George Bernard Shaw's favorite cellist and a member of the Gargenville group.

Homolle, Théophile (1848–1925), French archaeologist who directed the excavations at Delos and Delphi. He and his family were members of the Gargenville circle.

Jammes, Francis (1868–1938), French poet who belongs to the Symbolist movement by virtue of the liberties he took with versification and syntax, but diverges from that poetic movement in his clarity. Lili Boulanger set his "Tristesses" (1902–6) to music as *Clairières dans le Ciel*.

Karpelès, Suzanne (ca. 1888–1968), French orientalist, founder and first curator of the Royal Library of Pnom Penh (1925), and of the Buddhist Institutes in both Cambodia and Laos (1930). A prolific scholar, she was responsible for the translation into Khmer of the entire Buddhist canon, a work that totaled more than one hundred volumes. After having been introduced to the Boulanger family by Louise Gonet, it was she who supplied Lili Boulanger with the text the composer set to music as *Vieille Prière bouddhique*.

Labiche, Eugène (1815–1888), French writer of comedies such as *Le Chapeau de paille d'Italie*. He created a new type of comedy based on frenzied activity, and was a prolific writer, numbering more than three hundred plays to his credit. Ernest Boulanger and he were good friends.

Laparra, Raoul (1876–1943), at first a student of Massenet, later a classmate of Nadia Boulanger in Fauré's composition classes at the Conservatoire, Laparra won the Prix de Rome in musical composition in 1903. He was greatly influenced by Spanish popular music, which he used in both his zarzuelas and his *opéra-comique, Habanera* (1908). Also, he wrote his own librettos, made scale models of his own scenery, and designed his own costumes.

Legouvé, Ernest (1807–1903), French dramatist who collaborated with Eugène Scribe on *Adrienne Lecouvreur* (1849). He was a friend of Ernest Boulanger.

Lemaître, Frédérick (1800–1876), famous French actor, known for his fiery performances in Romantic drama. He was the brother-in-law of Julie Hallinger-Boulanger.

Léna, Maurice (d. 1923), French playwright and minor poet. He was one of the members of the Gargenville group.

Maeterlinck, Maurice (1862–1949), Belgian Symbolist and mystic poet known for such dramas as *La Princesse Maleine* (1889) and *Pelléas et Mélisande* (1892), as well as for such collections of poetry as *Serres Chaudes* (1889). His works were often set to music—Debussy set *Pelléas et Mélisande* as an opera (1902); Chausson set certain of his *Serres Chaudes* (1893–1896). Lili Boulanger set his "Attente" and "Reflets" and was working on setting *La Princesse Maleine* as an opera when she died.

Mangeot, Auguste (1883–   ), French critic who studied under Lavignac at the Conservatoire. He wrote critical articles on Lili Boulanger for *Le Monde Musical*.

Mengelberg, Wilhelm (1871–1951), Dutch conductor of international renown, member of the Gargenville group.

Musset, Alfred de (1810–1857), French Romantic poet and dramatist, one of the leaders of the literary movement. Lili Boulanger set part of his *La Coupe et les Lèvres* as *Pour les Funérailles d'un Soldat.*

Paray, Paul (1886–   ), internationally known French conductor. He met Lili Boulanger when she was at the Villa Medici in 1914. He won the Prix de Rome in composition in 1911.

Piel, Jules (1882–   ), French engraver who won the Prix de Rome in 1910. He became a good friend of Lili Boulanger at the Villa Medici, and in 1915 she corrected the harmony exercises that he sent her from the trenches, while he was fighting in World War I.

Piré, Miki (Madame Miki Paronian) (1892–1973), French-Russian pianist and student of Raoul Pugno; later a nurse. She was Lili Boulanger's closest friend, and introduced her to the Jammes poems the composer set to music as *Clairières dans le Ciel.* "Elle est gravement gaie" was dedicated to her. A multilingual world traveler, poet, and art collector, she was the author and illustrator of *En Recueillement,* a collection of poems written in memory of Lili Boulanger. Until her death she remained a very close friend of Nadia Boulanger.

Pollain, Fernand (1879–1955), French cellist known for trio work with Pugno and Ysaye; toured America with Mary Garden, and edited old violin music. He was a member of the Gargenville group.

Pugno, Raoul (1852–1914), noted as a collector of rare books, art, and artifacts, this French piano virtuoso, organist, and professor at the Conservatoire was famous for his chamber music recitals with Eugène Ysaye, as well as for solo work and for his compositions such as *La Ville Morte,* written in collaboration with Nadia Boulanger (1911). He and his family were very close friends of the Boulangers, and it was at his invitation that the Boulangers joined the Gargenville circle. He was the dedicatee of *Soir sur la Plaine.*

Ricordi, Tito (1865–1933), Italian music publisher who made an exclusive contract with Lili Boulanger just after she won the Prix de Rome in 1913. "Si tout ceci n'est qu'un pauvre rêve" was dedicated to him.

Samain, Albert (1858–1900), French moderate Symbolist poet. Lili Boulanger set his *Soir sur la Plaine* as part of her *concours d'essai* for the Prix de Rome Competition of 1913.

Schmitt, Florent (1870–1958), French composer, fellow-student of Nadia Boulanger in Fauré's composition class at the Conservatoire, winner of the Prix de Rome in 1900. Nadia played the organ at the premiere of his *Psalm 47* (1904), and Lili attended rehearsals for the premiere faithfully.

Scribe, Eugène (1791–1861), prolific French dramatist and librettist. Between 1810 and 1861 more than 400 of his plays were produced in Paris, and his librettos included those for Meyerbeer's *Les Huguenots* (1836) and *Le Prophète* (1849). He was a friend of Ernest Boulanger as well as the librettist for *Le Diable à l'École.*

Silvestre, Armand Paul (1838–1901), minor Parnassian poet, author of *Rimes neuves et vieilles* (1862) ; novelist and playwright. Lili Boulanger set his "Renouveau."

Sue, Marie-Joseph, called Eugène (1804–1857), French writer of long novels such as *The Wandering Jew* (*Le Juif errant*). He was a friend of Ernest Boulanger.

Tournier, Marcel (1879–1951), French harpist and composer who studied with Hasselmans, Caussade, and Lenepveu at the Conservatoire. Winner of the Second Grand Prize in the Prix de Rome Competition of 1909, he replaced Hasselmans as professor of harp at the Conservatoire in 1912. He was one of Lili Boulanger's harp teachers.

Valéry, Paul (1871–1945), French poet in the Symbolist tradition of Mallarmé. His family belonged to the Gargenville circle, and his wife, Jeanne, took piano lessons from Raoul Pugno.

Verhaeren, Émile (1855–1916), Belgian Symbolist poet, member of the Gargenville group. He wrote in free verse. Part of his poetic cycle *Les Heures Claires* (1896) was set to music by Nadia Boulanger and Raoul Pugno.

Vidal, Paul (1863–1931), French pianist and composer. He first taught Nadia Boulanger (1900) in his accompaniment class at the Conservatoire. Later, Lili became a student in his composition class (1912–1913). He lived in the same apartment house in Paris as the Boulangers, and was also a member of the Gargenville circle. Lili Boulanger dedicated *Renouveau* to him. His family also were close friends of the Boulanger family.

Vierne, Louis (1870–1937), although blind, became one of the foremost French organist-composers of his day. His compositions were influenced by Franck. He was Nadia Boulanger's professor of organ in 1899, and Lili often audited his classes. Vierne was also a member of the Gargenville group.

Vuillermoz, Émile (1878–1960), one of the most influential French critics, studied composition under Fauré at the Conservatoire, but later abandoned composition for criticism. He was an active proponent of the modern French school. In 1911 he became Editor-in-Chief of the *Revue Musicale S.I.M.*, and contributed to the *Mercure Musicale, Comoedia, Éclair, Le Temps, Excelsior,* and *La Revue Musicale*. In his reviews he expressed a high regard for Lili Boulanger's music.

Warren, Whitney (1884–1943), American architect and diplomat who studied at the École des Beaux-Arts in Paris. He designed Grand Central Station and the Ritz-Carlton and Biltmore Hotels in New York City, among others. During World War I, he became the president of the Comité Franco-Américain du Conservatoire National de Musique et de Déclamation, which Nadia and Lili had formed, and of which they were the secretaries.

Widor, Charles-Marie (1845–1937), famous French organist, composer, and pedagogue, who replaced Théodore Dubois as professor of composition at the Conservatoire. Nadia Boulanger studied with him there, and Lili often audited his classes.

Ysaye, Eugène (1858–1931), internationally famous Belgian violinist, conductor, and composer. Between 1896 and 1914, he was known for his chamber music recitals with Raoul Pugno, and for his trio performances with Raoul Pugno and Fernand Pollain. Ysaye was also a member of the Gargenville circle.

Notes

Notes to Chapter 1

1. I.e., the fifth year of the French Revolution. Under the nonrevolutionary calendar, the date would be October 24, 1797.

2. "La Distribution des prix du Conservatoire. . . ," *La Décade philosophique,* Oct. 24, 1797, pp. 244–45.

3. Ibid., pp. 246–47.

4. Ibid., "Au Citoyen Frédéric BOULANGER [*sic*], âgé de 19 ans, né en **Saxe,** élève de C. Levasseur. *Prix, un Violoncelle.*"

5. Constant Pierre, comp., *Le Conservatoire National de Musique et de Déclamation. Documents Historiques et Administratifs* (Paris: Imprimerie **Nationale,** 1900), p. 439.

6. Ibid., pp. 405, 715.

7. This was probably Marc-Antoine Desaugiers, the songwriter and popular singer.

8. Frédéric Boulanger, "Stances/Sur la Mort de S.A.R. Monseigneur/le Duc de Berry./ Paroles de Mr Desaugiers/Mises en Musique/ Avec Accompagnement de Piano et Dédiées à Madame la Baronne Eugenie [*sic*] de Margueritte Par Mr Frédéric Boulanger/ Artiste de la Chapelle du Roi et Professeur à l'Ecole Royale de Musique./ A Paris, Rue de Richelieu, No 78." The copy in the Music Division of the Bibliothèque Nationale in Paris is autographed by the composer.

9. Pierre, *Le Conservatoire,* pp. 705, 520, 576.

10. François J. Fétis, *Biographie universelle des Musiciens et Bibliographie générale de la Musique* (Paris: Firman Didot Frères, Fils, 1866), p. 41. "Douée d'une fort belle voix, et possédant une exécution vocale brillante et facile."

11. Fétis, *Biographie universelle,* p. 41. "Rappelée, à grands cris après la représentation, elle fut ramenée sur la scène . . . pour recevoir les bruyants témoignages de la satisfaction du public. Tel fut l'empressement des habitants de Paris à l'entendre que l'administration du théâtre prolongea ses débuts pendant une année entière."

12. Nadia Boulanger to Léonie Rosenstiel, June 8, 1972.

13. Robert Baldick, *The Life and Times of Frédérick Lemaître* (London: Hamish Hamilton, 1959), p. 46.

14. Nadia Boulanger to Léonie Rosenstiel, June 8, 1972.

15. Fétis, *Biographie universelle,* p. 41.

16. On December 10, 1825, Mme Boulanger took part in the premiere of Boïeledieu's *La Dame blanche* in the role of Jenny. Her participation in this introduction of a work which never left the repertory for over seventy-five years, is also duly recorded in Félix Clément and Pierre Larousse, *Dictionnaire des Opéras* (Paris: Librairie Larousse, 1904), p. 286.

17. Ministère de l'Intérieur, Conservatoire de Musique, *Distribution des Prix pour le cours de l'Année 1835.* His age was listed as twenty, probably because it was computed as of the time he received the prize officially and publicly (i.e., November 15, 1835) rather than when he won it (i.e., July of the same year). Had they used his age at the time he won the prize, he would have been listed as nineteen, since his twentieth birthday came in September of 1835.

18. "Discours de M. le Duc de Choiseul," *Moniteur universel,* no. 320, Nov. 16, 1835 (reporting his speech of the preceding day): ". . . les élèves du Conservatoire en donneront la preuve, et cette année même nous offre plus que des espérances."

19. Ibid. Both Frédéric and Marie-Julie Boulanger were well-known and respected musicians in France at that time.

20. The Prix de Rome has been awarded annually since 1663 by the Académie des Beaux-Arts, in the fields of architecture, engraving, musical composition, painting, and sculpture. For further information see Henry Lapauze, *Histoire de l'Académie de France à Rome,* 2 vols. (Paris: Plon, 1924). See also chaps. 3 and 4.

21. Lapauze, *Histoire de l'Académie,* 2 (1802–1910): 244.

22. The French Ambassador

23. Lapauze, *Histoire de l'Académie,* 2: 244.

24. Ibid.

25. Jean Bonnassieux, the sculptor

26. Lapauze, *Histoire de l'Académie,* 2: 245. The *pensionnaires* had been required to leave their passports with the Director of the Villa on arrival, and not to travel without his express permission.

27. Lapauze, *Histoire de l'Académie,* 2: 245–46.

28. Fétis, *Biographie universelle,* p. 41

29. His brooding, romantic aspect is quite evident in the portrait done of him about 1840, which has been attributed to Thomas Couture. It is in the possession of Mlle Nadia Boulanger.

30. Mme Miki Paronian, Interview, Nice, July 6, 1973. This source will hereafter be referred to as Mme Paronian.

31. Jules Martin, *Nos Auteurs et compositeurs dramatiques* (Paris: Ernest Flammarion, 1897), p. 75.

32. Fétis, *Biographie universelle,* p. 41. Other dictionaries all agree on the date of her death, but only Fétis adds any particulars.

33. Currently available sources have so far revealed no information on the date of death or place of burial of Frédéric Boulanger.

34. This friendship was to last for three generations. His son, Pierre Barbier, and later, his granddaughter, Simone de Meyenbourg (née Barbier), remained close to the Boulanger family. For further discussion of Mme de Meyenbourg, see chap. 2.

35. Martin, *Nos Auteurs,* p. 76

36. Ibid., p. 75.

37. Ibid.

38. Nadia Boulanger to Léonie Rosenstiel, June 8, 1972.

39. Mme Paronian, Interview, Nice, July 4, 1973.

40. Mme Paronian, Interview, Nice. July 4, 1973.

41. Nadia Boulanger, Interview, Paris, Nov. 18, 1973.

42. Nadia Boulanger to Léonie Rosenstiel, Jan. 13, 1974. The date that appears in the Catalogue of the Exposition Lili-Boulanger issued by the Bibliothèque Nationale (Paris: 1968), p. 1, gives the year of this marriage as 1875. (A diplomatic facsimile of the original marriage certificate is in the possession of the author.)

43. Nadia Boulanger, Interview, Paris, Nov. 18, 1973.

44. Ibid. The Gonet family remained close to the Boulangers. One of Henri Gonet's other daughters, closer in age to Ernest Boulanger's own children, had a daughter whose daughter now lives in France, and, from a later marriage, a son who is now a godchild of Nadia Boulanger. It was a grandniece of Henri Gonet who oversaw the performance of several works of Lili Boulanger in Marseille in 1972. For further relations between the two families, see chap. 2.

45. Contrary to what Fétis has reported, *La Cachette* was most certainly not the last opera that Ernest Boulanger wrote.

46. P. 991.

47. Martin, *Nos Auteurs*, pp. 75–76.

48. "Une gaieté franche et une mélodie facile." Clément and Larousse, *Dictionnaire des Opéras*, p. 356.

49. "La musique est aussi vieille que la pièce," p. 112. This is no small problem, since the "play" is *The Barber of Seville*.

50. ". . . a tout ce qu'il faut pour aller rejoindre les autres oeuvres de M. Boulanger." Edouard Noël and Edmond Stoullig, eds., *Annales du Théâtre et de la Musique* (1875), p. 112.

51. Nadia Boulanger, Interview, Fontainebleau, July 23, 1973. William Bouwens later became Lili Boulanger's godfather and tutor. See chap. 2.

52. The child's name on her tombstone is given as "Nina Juliette."

53. Nadia Boulanger, Interview, Paris, Nov. 18, 1973.

Notes to Chapter 2

1. Nadia Boulanger to Léonie Rosenstiel, June 8, 1972.

2. The original photographs are in the possession of Mlle Nadia Boulanger. Copies are in the possession of the author.

3. Nadia Boulanger, Interview, Paris, Nov. 18, 1973. "Avec des yeux comme ça elle va vous donner ou beaucoup de joie ou beaucoup de souci."

4. Ibid.

5. Mme Paronian, Interview, Nice, July 6, 1973.

6. Nadia Boulanger, Interview, Fontainebleau, July 23, 1973, and Nadia Boulanger, letter to Léonie Rosenstiel, Oct. 18, 1973.

7. Nadia Boulanger to Léonie Rosenstiel, June 8, 1972, and *Grand Larousse Encyclopédique* (1960 ed.), s.v. "Bernard, Étienne."

8. Nadia Boulanger, Interview, Fontainebleau, July 23, 1973.

9. Ibid., Paris, Nov. 18, 1973.

10. Mme Paronian, Interview, Nice, July 4, 1973.

11. Nadia Boulanger, Interview, July 23, 1973.

12. In 1898 a fourth daughter, Marie Louise, was born to Ernest and Raïssa Boulanger, but she died soon after birth.

13. Nadia Boulanger to Léonie Rosenstiel, June 8, 1972.

14. Nadia Boulanger, Interview July 23, 1973.

15. Ibid., Nov. 23, 1973.

16. See chap. 1.

17. Nadia Boulanger, Interview, Paris Nov. 18, 1973.

18. Ibid., and Mme Paronian, Interview, July 6, 1973: "la bonté en personne."

19. Nadia Boulanger, Interview, Fontainebleau, July 23, 1973.

20. Ibid.

21. Ibid., Paris, Nov. 24, 1973, and unnumbered, undated composition book (no pagination).

22. Nadia Boulanger to Léonie Rosenstiel, June 8, 1972.

23. Nadia Boulanger, Interview, Paris, Nov. 18, 1973.

24. Ibid., Nov. 19, 1973.

25. She was basically a teacher of French.

26. Nadia Boulanger to Léonie Rosenstiel, June 8, 1972, and Nov. 21, 1972.

27. Nadia Boulanger to Léonie Rosenstiel, June 8, 1972 and July 12, 1972.

28. See chap. 4.

29. Nadia Boulanger to Léonie Rosenstiel, June 8, 1973.

30. This is the "Schlummerlied," from the *Albumblätter,* Op. 124. The original programs are in the possession of Mlle Nadia Boulanger. Copies are in the possession of the author. Lili may, in fact, have participated in other student performances as well, for which no programs remain.

31. Mme Paronian, Interview, Nice, July 6, 1973.

32. Nadia Boulanger to Léonie Rosenstiel, June 8, 1972.

33. See chap. 4.

34. Nadia Boulanger to Léonie Rosenstiel, June 8, 1972.

35. See above.

36. Nadia Boulanger to Léonie Rosenstiel, June 8, 1972, and November 21, 1972.

37. Nadia Boulanger to Léonie Rosenstiel, June 8, 1972.

38. Ibid., Aug. 14, 1973.

39. Mme Paronian, Interview, July 6, 1973, and Mme Apostol, Interview, Nov. 21, 1973.

40. Nadia Boulanger to Léonie Rosenstiel, Aug. 14, 1973.

41. Mme Paronian, Interview, Nice, July 6, 1973, and Mme Apostol, Interview, Paris, Nov. 21, 1973.

42. Nadia Boulanger, Interview, Paris, Nov. 18, 1973.

43. To d'Annunzio's poem *La Città Morte,* in 1911.

44. Mme Delavrancea had played in the same 1904 recital of Mme Chaumont's students as Lili had.

45. Mme Paronian, Interview, Nice, July 4, 1973.

46. Mlle Dieudonné to Léonie Rosenstiel, Sept. 12, 1973.

47. Mme Paronian, Interview, Nice, July 4, 1973.

48. Nadia Boulanger, Interview, Paris, Nov. 18, 1973.

49. Ibid., Nov. 16, 1973.

50. He later married Agathe Valéry.

51. The whole area is now considered "Gargenville." Hanneucourt was absorbed into it, and is now known as "Hanneucourt par Gargenville."

52. Nadia Boulanger to Léonie Rosenstiel, Mar. 27, 1972.

53. Ibid., June 8, 1972.

54. See Appendix F.

55. Nadia Boulanger to Léonie Rosenstiel, June 10, 1973.

56. Nadia Boulanger, Interview, Paris, July 23, 1973.

57. Ibid.

58. Nadia Boulanger to Léonie Rosenstiel, Jan. 28, 1974. The Boulangers had had a harmonium in their apartment on rue La Bruyère.

59. Mme Apostol, Interview, Paris, Nov. 21, 1973.

60. Nadia Boulanger to Léonie Rosenstiel, June 8, 1972.

61. Nadia Boulanger, Interview, Paris, Nov. 18, 1973.

62. Mme Paronian, Interview, Nice, July 4, 1973.

63. Ibid., and Mme Apostol, Interview, Paris, Nov. 21, 1973.

64. Nadia Boulanger, Interview, Paris, Nov. 19, 1973.

65. Lili Boulanger to William Bouwens, Jan. 1, 1906. This letter is in the possession of Mlle Nadia Boulanger. A copy is in the possession of the author.

66. Nadia Boulanger to Léonie Rosenstiel, June 8, 1972.

67. Nadia Boulanger, Interview, Paris, Nov. 19, 1973.

68. Nadia Boulanger to Léonie Rosenstiel, June 8, 1972.

69. Ibid., Feb. 1, 1972, and Interview, Paris, Nov. 19, 1973.

70. Ibid.

Notes to Chapter 3

1. Nadia Boulanger, Interview, Fontainebleau, July 23, 1973.

2. Mme Paronian, Interview, Nice, July 4, 1973. Nadia had received the Second Grand Prix in 1908, a situation some felt at the time reflected the jury's prejudice against women more than it did Nadia's abilities as a composer.

3. Nadia Boulanger, Interview, Fontainebleau, July 23, 1973.

4. One example of this type of thinking may be seen in a recent article by Bernard Gavoty in *Rives d'Azur* (Sept. 1967), p. 44, which carries the subtitle, "Lili: Chef-d'oeuvre de Nadia," and states, "Nadia Boulanger renonça très vite et de bon coeur à la composition et se voua à l'enseignement. Second grand prix de Rome, elle s'offre la joie de préparer sa soeur à la récompense suprême."

5. Nadia Boulanger, Interview, Paris, Nov. 19, 1973.

6. Nadia Boulanger to Léonie Rosenstiel, June 8, 1973.

7. Mme Paronian, Interview, Nice, July 4, 1973.

8. The first lesson in the first counterpoint notebook is dated "13 Avril 1910."

9. These are in the possession of Nadia Boulanger.

10. Inside the front cover of Counterpoint III notebook.

11. Mme Paronian, Interview, Nice, July 4, 1973, and *idem*, to Léonie Rosenstiel, Aug. 10, 1973.

12. Nadia Boulanger, Interview, Paris, Nov. 18, 1973.

13. Nadia Boulanger to Léonie Rosenstiel, June 8, 1973.

14. Nadia Boulanger to Léonie Rosenstiel, June 8, 1972.

15. Mme Paronian, Interview, Nice, July 4, 1973.

16. Nadia Boulanger, Interview, Fontainebleau, July 23, 1973. This postcard is in the possession of Nadia Boulanger.

17. Mme Apostol, Interview, Paris, Nov. 21, 1973.

18. Nadia Boulanger, Interview, Paris, Nov. 18, 1973.

19. Mme Apostol, Interview, Paris, Nov. 21, 1973.

20. These pictures are in the possession of Nadia Boulanger.

21. Nadia Boulanger, Interview, Paris, Nov. 18, 1973, and Nadia Boulanger to Léonie Rosenstiel, Jan. 25, 1974.

22. All workbooks and sketchbooks discussed are in the possession of Mlle

Nadia Boulanger. The pages are not numbered. It is impossible to cite any identifying indications, since they are fragments, and are not in chronological order. Apparently Lili was in such haste to write down and thus preserve her ideas that she failed to observe the same care that is evident in her harmony, counterpoint, and fugue notebooks.

23. This manuscript is in the possession of Mlle Boulanger.

24. The first line reads, "Il est ainsi de pauvres coeurs."

25. Mme Apostol, Interview, Paris, Nov. 21, 1973.

26. See chaps. 4 and 5.

27. Nadia Boulanger, to Léonie Rosenstiel, November 20, 1971.

28. Nadia Boulanger, Interview, Paris, November 18, 1973.

29. Nadia Boulanger to Léonie Rosenstiel, Nov. 20, 1971.

30. Ibid.

31. See chap. 5.

32. Composition II/Sous Bois.

33. The manuscript is in the possession of Mlle Nadia Boulanger.

34. Nadia Boulanger, Interview, Paris, Nov. 9, 1973.

35. See chap. 4.

36. Both *Renouveau* and *Les Sirènes* were later published. See chap. 5.

37. Conservatoire National de Musique et de Déclamation, Certificate of Admission, Jan. 10, 1912.

38. March 30, 1912, p. 99.

39. A copy of this program, dated March 19, 1912, is in the possession of Mlle Nadia Boulanger.

40. March 21–28.

41. "Mélodie—Attente de Maeterlinck." This was Lili Boulanger's customary form for indicating that she was working on a piece. The date of composition of *Attente* has been cited in various sources as 1910, e.g., Jacques Chailley, "Boulanger, Lili" in MGG, *142./143 Lieferung/Supplement: BIA-GRU;* Claude Chamfray, "Lili Boulanger," *Le Courrier musical de France*, no. 31, 3d Trimester, 1970, n.p. and the Ricordi edition of 1918. However, the precise date is indicated in Lili Boulanger's notebook—April 18, 1912, and would support the conclusion that this composition was completed two years later than is generally supposed.

42. Nadia Boulanger, Interview, Paris, July 23, 1973.

43. Since she was not admitted to the final round, the manuscripts for these works—the fugue and the chorus *La Source*, have remained in the possession of the Conservatoire National and have never been published.

44. See Figure 18 for 1913 receipt.

45. "Nouvelles Diverses: Revus et Départements," *Le Ménéstral*, May 11, 1912, no. 19, p. 150.

46. Conservatoire National de Musique et de Déclamation, *Année Scholaire 1912–1913. Tableau des Classes du 1er octobre au 30 septembre. Classe de P. Vidal* (unnumbered pages) : "malade à l'examen."

47. Conservatoire National, *Examens semestriels. Rapport des Professeurs. 1912– 1913* (unnumbered pages). Pièce 113, "très douée," and "travaille avec succès."

48. "Nouvelles Diverses: Paris et Départements," *Le Ménéstral*, Saturday, May 18, 1912, no. 20, p. 158.

49. Albert Spalding, *Rise to Follow: An Autobiography* (New York: Henry Holt and Company, 1943) , p. 160.

50. Ibid., p. 159.

51. This had been part of the *concours d'essai* for 1888.

52. Mme Paronian, Interview, Nice, July 6, 1973.

53. Ibid., July 4, 1973.

54. Lili Boulanger to Miki Piré, Sept. 11, 1912.

55. This was probably Dr. Cuche. Mme Paronian, who was also a nurse, was convinced that this problem was a symptom of the fact that Lili's illness had spread to her bones, and likened Lili's condition to that of her own younger brother, who had been similarly afflicted some time before. (Mme Paronian, Interview, Nice, July 6, 1973).

56. Ironically, Lili wrote this letter in phonetic Russian. (Lili Boulanger to Miki Piré, Sept. 11, 1912). As of July 1973, the original was in the possession of Mme Paronian.

57. Nadia Boulanger, Interview, Paris, Nov. 18, 1973.

58. The notation for October 28, for example, reads: "28 octobre—4:40–5:40 leçon."

59. Other entries in this notebook exploring various fugal techniques and procedures are dated November 1, 3, 5, 8, 10, 12, 14, 15, 17, 24, 26, and 27, 1912.

60. See chap. 3.

61. Lili Boulanger to Miki Piré, Nov. 27, 1912.

62. Lili Boulanger to Miki Piré. The date reads, "Vendredi 29 nov. 1912," but, based on the evidence in the previous letter, and the fact that this one mentions having arrived in Berck the preceding day, the correct date should be November 30. Once again, this letter is written mostly in phonetic Russian. As in the previous instance, this letter was translated for me by Mme Paronian, on July 6, 1973.

63. This hotel was also in Berck-Plage.

64. Probably Katia. See chap. 2.

65. Lili Boulanger to Miki Piré, Dec. 10, 1912.

66. Ibid., December 18, 1912.

67. Lili Boulanger to Miki Piré, Dec. 18, 1912, letter no. 2.

68. Mme Paronian, Interview, Nice, July 6, 1973.

69. Lili Boulanger to Miki Piré, Dec. 25, 1912.

70. Conservatoire National, *Examens Semestriels. Rapport des Professeurs.* 1912–1913. Pièce 188, "Nature non Aigue [sic]./ Mauvaise santé, hélas! travail très intelligent"

71. The original is in the possession of Mlle Nadia Boulanger.

72. The tenor soloist for *Pour les Funérailles* was M. Ghasne; the Chorale des Auditeurs Moderne et le Cercle Choral Parisien was under the direction of M. Maxim Thomas. The soloists for *Renouveau* were Mlles Brothier and Sanderson and MM. Capitaine and Tordo. *Le Guide du Concert (Hebdomadaire musical illustré)* IVe Année, no. 18. Feb. 8, 1913, p. 268. A copy of this program is in the possession of Mlle Nadia Boulanger.

73. No. 6, Saturday, Feb. 8, 1913, p. 48.

74. There is no date on this letter, but the postmark on the envelope indicates it was mailed from the post office across the street from the Boulanger apartment at rue Ballu on Feb. 6, 1913. As of July 1973, this letter was in the possession of Mme Paronian.

75. The program for this event is in the possession of Mlle Nadia Boulanger. *Les Sirènes* was performed by the women's chorus with Mlle Van de Putte and Mme Guillemot as soloists. The soloist for the *Hymne au Soleil* was Mlle Hoock. In both instances, the piano accompaniment was played by Mme Stoecklin.

76. Nadia Boulanger to Léonie Rosenstiel, Dec. 11, 1973.

77. Mme Paronian, Interview, Nice, July 6, 1973.

78. For further observations about the contents of this notebook, see above.

79. Nadia Boulanger to Léonie Rosenstiel, Dec. 11, 1973.

80. Conservatoire National, *Examens Semestriels. Rapports des Professeurs. 1912–1913*, MS, Pièce 264, "Nature hors de pair/ Santé précaire, malheureusement."

81. Institut de France. Académie des Beaux-Arts, "Concours de Rome de 1913 . . . Composition musicale," *Concours, Années 1905–1927*, n.p., MS, Archives of the Académie des Beaux-Arts.

82. "Le Prix de Rome," *Le Monde Musical*, no. 9, May 15, 1913, p. 146. See Appendix G.

83. In 1913, Lili Boulanger was assigned to the same loge she had occupied the preceding year—no. 19.

84. Institut de France, Académie des Beaux-Arts, "Concours de Rome de 1913. Composition musicale," *Concours, Années 1905–1927*, n.p., MS, Archives of the Académie des Beaux-Arts.

85. One of these visiting cards is in the possession of the author.

86. "Rêvant au Grand Prix de Rome, Mlle Lily [*sic*] Boulanger," *La Vie Heureuse*, June 13, 1913, p. 150.

87. This point of view contrasts sharply with that current in the United States today, which lays its primary stress on the achievements of the individual while ignoring, denying, or at least minimizing, any contributions that family background may have made to his or her success.

88. "Les Logistes du Prix de Rome" (no. 129) .

89. Claude Delvincourt, the second youngest, was born in 1888.

90. This manuscript is in the possession of Mlle Nadia Boulanger.

91. Nadia Boulanger, Interview, Paris, Nov. 19, 1973.

92. Lili Boulanger to Miki Piré, May 30, 1913. As of July 1973, this postcard, and the envelope in which it was sent, were in the possession of Mme Paronian.

93. Lili Boulanger to Miki Piré, June 24, 1913. As of July 1973, this letter was in the possession of Mme Paronian.

94. Probably the public performance of the cantatas at the final judging

95. Lili Boulanger to Miki Piré, June 24, 1913.

96. As of July 1973, this postcard was in the possession of Mme Paronian.

97. Institut de France. Académie des Beaux-Arts, "Concours de Rome de 1913. . . ."

98. Mme Paronian, Interview, Nice, July 4, 1973.

99. Nadia Boulanger to Léonie Rosenstiel, June 8, 1972. "L'audition des cantates eut lieu dans la grande salle des Séances de l'Institut, où, en plus des membres du jury, était admis un certain numbre d'auditeurs ne faisant pas partie de l'Institut."

100. Those present were: Dubois, Fauré, Charpentier, Paladilhe, and Widor of the Music Section; MM. Besnier, Dagnan-Bouveret, and Roujon—President, Vice-President, and Permanent Secretary, respectively; MM. Bruneau Wormser and Hüe, supplementary jurors. (Institut de France, Académie des Beaux-Arts, *Procès Verbal, 1913–1914*, July 5, 1913, p. 65. See also idem "Concours de Rome de 1913. . . .")

101. No. 131, p. 153.

102. Nadia Boulanger to Léonie Rosenstiel, June 8, 1972.

103. Institut de France, Académie des Beaux-Arts, *Procès Verbal, 1913–1914*, July 5, 1913, p. 65. "Intelligence du sujet. Justesse de la déclamation. De la sensibilité et de la chaleur. Sentiment Poétique. Orchestre intelligent et coloré. Cantate remarquable."

104. Ibid. "En conséquence, le Ier Grand Prix est décerné à Mlle BOULANGER (Marie-Juliette) élève de M. Paul VIDAL, née à Paris, le 21 Août 1893."

105. Ibid., May 10, 1913, pp. 42–43.

106. Ibid., July 5, 1913, p. 65.

107. "Le Prix de Rome," *Le Monde Musical*, nos. 13 and 14, July 15 and 30, 1913, pp. 208–9.

108. Institut de France. . . , July 5, 1913, p. 65.

109. July 15 and 30, 1913 (nos. 13 and 14) , p. 173.

110. **Ibid.**

Notes to Chapter 4

1. "Girl Wins Prix de Rome," *New York Times*, July 7, 1913, p. 3; "Art et Curiosité: Académie des Beaux-Arts, Le Grand-prix [*sic*] de Rome de Musique," *Le Temps* (Paris) , July 7, 1913, p. 5. (Postcard to Lili Boulanger, Nov. 28, 1913.)

2. Renée de Marquein to Léonie Rosenstiel, Sept. 30, 1972.

3. In 1913 this prize was also shared by MM. Delvincourt, Delmas, Mignan, and Dupré. Mlle J. Robert (Curator of the Library of the Conservatoire) to Léonie Rosenstiel, Feb. 27, 1973.

4. Conservatoire National, *Année 1912–1913. Distribution des Prix. Séance Publique Annuelle du Samedi 12 Juillet 1913*, p. 18, "à un jeune musicien ayant produit dans l'année une oeuvre quelconque remarquable."

5. "Lili Boulanger," July 12, 1913 (no. 286) , n.p.

6. **Ibid.**

7. There are two small errors of fact in this caption. First, it states that Lili was "hardly nineteen" when, in fact, she would be twenty in August 1913. The second error is in the report of the voting at the Institut as thirty-two out of thirty-six, when it was actually thirty-one out of thirty-six.

8. "Mlle Lily [*sic*] Boulanger, Grand Prix de Rome pour la Musique," July 15, 1913 (no. 300) , p. 375.

9. "Le Concours du Prix de Rome," July 20, 1913 (no. 20) , p. 936.

10. The latter is on the verso of the unnumbered page facing p. 212.

11. 25 (no. 5) : 115.

12. The original is in the possession of Mlle Nadia Boulanger.

13. Nadia Boulanger, Interview, Fontainebleau, July 23, 1973, and Paris, November 23, 1973.

14. Nadia Boulanger to Léonie Rosenstiel, Nov. 21, 1972.

15. Renée de Marquein to Léonie Rosenstiel, Sept. 4, 1972.

16. Ibid., Oct. 23, 1972.

17. Nadia Boulanger to Léonie Rosenstiel, Dec. 11, 1972.

18. Institut de France, Académie des Beaux-Arts, "Séance Publique Annuelle du Samedi 8 novembre 1913" (Paris: Firmin-Didot et Cie., 1913) , p. 1

19. Ibid., "Disbursement Table," Nov. 8, 1913. MS, Archives of Académie des Beaux-Arts.

20. No. 22, Nov. 30, 1913, p. 323.

21. Having twice won the Prix de Rome himself—the Second Grand Prize in 1883 and the First Grand Prize in 1884—Debussy was well acquainted with the inner workings of this competition.

22. "La Musique espagnole. Faust et Hélène par Lili Boulanger," *La Revue*

S.I.M., Dec. 1, 1913, pp. 43–44. This passage has been reprinted in *Claude Debussy. Monsieur Croche et autres écrits,* François Lesure, ed. (Paris: Gallimard, 1971), pp. 246–47.

23. I.e., the day after the success of *Faust et Hélène* at the Concerts Colonne.

24. "Salles diverses. Gala Nadia et Lili Boulanger," *Le Monde Musical,* Nov. 30, 1913, p. 326.

25. A copy of the original program for this occasion is in the possession of Mlle Nadia Boulanger.

26. Nadia Boulanger to Léonie Rosenstiel, December 11, 1973.

27. Copies of all the programs mentioned above, as well as the gold brocaded box, are in the possession of Mlle Nadia Boulanger. This medallion was later used on the cover of the premiere recording of Lili Boulanger's works. See Figure 52.

28. "Faust et Hélène de Mlle Lili Boulanger," no. 23, 1913, p. 350. The piano-vocal score of this composition was republished by Durand in 1970.

29. This information is contained in entries for January 3, 13, and 14, 1914, on pages from Lili Boulanger's Journal in the possession of Mlle Nadia Boulanger.

30. Nadia Boulanger, Interview, Paris, Nov. 23, 1973.

31. Ibid., Nov. 20, 1973.

32. Institut de France, Académie des Beaux-Arts, *Statuts et Règlements* (Paris: Firmin-Didot, 1908), p. 157.

33. Dr. Paul Chiron, Medical Certificate, Jan. 20, 1914. Archives of the Académie des Beaux-Arts, Paris.

34. Institut de France, Académie des Beaux-Arts, *Procès Verbal, 1913–1914,* n.p., MS, Archives of the Académie des Beaux-Arts.

35. Léon Boudouresque, "Deux femmes—Qui l'eût dit?" *Le Miroir,* July 5, 1914, p. 6.

36. I am indebted to the late Mme Paronian for pointing out this fact to me. The letter was in her possession in July 1973.

37. No envelope is extant for this letter, which was in the possession of Mme Paronian in July 1973.

38. This program, which took place at the Salle Érard, included Lili Boulanger's *Pour les Funérailles d'un Soldat.* A copy of this program is in the possession of Mlle Nadia Boulanger.

39. Mme Paronian, Interview, Nice, July 4, 1973, and Nadia Boulanger to Léonie Rosenstiel, Dec. 11, 1973.

40. Nadia Boulanger to Léonie Rosenstiel, June 8, 1972.

41. Francis Jammes, "Tristesses," *Clairières dans le Ciel* (Paris: Mercure de France, 1902–6), pp. 23–49.

42. Mme Paronian to Léonie Rosenstiel, Oct. 10, 1972, and *idem,* Interview, Nice, July 4, 1973.

43. Nadia Boulanger to Léonie Rosenstiel, June 8, 1972, "fusion entre la jeune fille évoquée par Francis Jammes . . . et elle-même."

44. Mme Paronian, Interview, Nice, July 4, 1973, and Nadia Boulanger to Léonie Rosenstiel, June 8, 1972. A rough translation of *tristesses* would be "sorrows," and of *clairières dans le ciel* would be "illuminations in the sky."

45. Institut de France, *Statuts et Règlements,* p. 157

46. Lili Boulanger to Miki Piré, Mar. 9, 1914. As of July 1973, the original was in the possession of Mme Paronian.

47. Ministère de l'Instruction Publique. Académie des Beaux-Arts, Letter to Albert Besnard, Jan. 31, 1914. Archives of the Villa Medici, Rome.

48. Académie de France à Rome, *Situation des Pensionnaires,* n.p. MS, Archives of the Villa Medici, Rome.

49. Albert Besnard, Letter to the President of the Académie des Beaux-Arts, March 13, 1914. Archives of the Académie des Beaux-Arts.

50. Mme Boulanger had hired Nina Scarpellini to work in this capacity. Nadia Boulanger to Léonie Rosenstiel, June 8, 1972. .

51. Institut de France, *Statuts et Règlements,* p. 158. Chap. 1, Art. 7, "Pendant leur séjour à Rome, les pensionnaires sont tenus d'habiter le palais de l'Académie et d'y prendre leurs repas à une table commune."

52. Albert Besnard, Letter of March 13, 1914.

53. Lili Boulanger to Miki Piré, Mar. 15, 1914 (postmarked March 16). In July 1973 this letter was in the possession of Mme Paronian.

54. Lili Boulanger to Albert Besnard, March 20, 1914. Archives of the Villa Medici, Rome.

55. There were already male servants for the male *pensionnaires.*

56. Institut de France, *Procès Verbal, 1913–1914,* p. 154. MS, Archives of Académie des Beaux-Arts.

57. Lili Boulanger to Miki Piré, March 26, 1914. As of July 1973 this letter was in the possession of Mme Paronian.

58. Mme Paronian, Interview, Nice, July 4, 1973.

59. The records of the Villa Medici show that a chamber maid, Giuseppa Bonini, was already being retained by the Villa for the personal service of Mlle Heuvelmans, the sculptress. In fact, during the months of January and February 1914, the maid spent twenty-four and twenty-eight hours, respectively, doing work for Mlle Heuvelmans, whereas during March—the first month Lili Boulanger was at the Villa—the maid spent fifty-four hours working there. This information is contained in *Albert Besnard, 1913–1921. Comptes 1914,* Exercice 1914, Chap. VIII, Article 3, Bordereau no. 5A, Pièce no. 11. MS, Archives of the Villa Medici.

60. Institut de France, *Procès-Verbal, 1913–1914,* March 28, 1914, p. 157. A careful check of the minutes of all meetings of the Académie des Beaux-Arts from May 1913 to March 1914 reveals no formal deliberations on the question of a maid for Lili. Since there was already a maid to serve Mlle Heuvelmans at the Villa, it is probable that the Boulangers interpreted this to mean that Lili, too, could have a maid of her own. In her weakened condition, Lili was in need of someone who would be constantly available in case of emergency, and the limited amount of time—approximately one-half to three-quarters of an hour per day—that would have been apportioned to her for the services of the maid already in the employ of the Villa would obviously have been totally inadequate for her needs.

61. Lili Boulanger to Miki Piré, n.d. (Postmarked March 30, 1914.) As of July 1973 this letter was in the possession of Mme Paronian.

62. For further details of this letter, see above.

63. Nadia Boulanger to Léonie Rosenstiel, Feb. 1, 1972.

64. Ibid.

65. The original manuscript is in the possession of Mlle Nadia Boulanger.

66. Nadia Boulanger to Léonie Rosenstiel, Feb. 1, 1972.

67. For further discussions of these works, see chap. 6.

68. J. Mathieu to Léonie Rosenstiel, Nov. 2, 1973.

69. These paintings have all been removed from the dining room. With the exception of those of the musicians Berlioz and Debussy, they are now in a store-room on the top floor of the Villa.

70. Nadia Boulanger to Léonie Rosenstiel, June 8, 1972.

71. Ibid., November 21, 1972.

72. Ibid., June 8, 1972.

73. Paul Paray to Léonie Rosenstiel, June 8, 1973, ". . . j'ai d'elle le souvenir d'une exquise camarade, très douée, ayant devant elle une brillante carrière de composition."

74. Jules Piel to Léonie Rosenstiel, Dec. 10, 1972.

75. Nadia Boulanger, Interview, Fontainebleau, July 23, 1973.

76. Boudouresque, "Deux femmes. . . ," pp. 5–6.

77. Ibid.

78. Ibid.

79. Ibid., p. 8.

80. Ibid., pp. 6–7.

81. Mme Paronian, Interview, Nice, July 4, 1973.

82. Lucienne Heuvelmans to Armand Girette, June 7, 1914. MS, Archives of the Villa Medici, Rome.

83. Boudouresque, "Deux Femmes . . ," p. 8. This article was published in July, while the Besnard family was still in France.

84. The fact that there is no evidence of either telegram at the Academy in Paris is somewhat disturbing. It would have been most unusual for a telegram to have been sent in the name of the Academy without due consideration having been given to the circumstances surrounding the request and the reaction to it of the members of the Academy. Normally, this would have taken place during a regular meeting and a mention of it, at the very least, would have found its way into the minutes. M. Besnard's letter, dated June 25, 1914, is in the Archives of the Villa Medici.

85. Armand Girette, "Compte rendu au Directeur, No. 5," June 30, 1914. MS, Archives of the Villa Medici.

86. Nadia Boulanger to Léonie Rosenstiel, Dec. 11, 1973.

87. Lili Boulanger, Telegram to "Monsieur le Secrétaire," July 3, 1914. Archives of the Villa Medici.

88. Mme Paronian, Interview, Nice, July 4, 1973.

89. Nadia Boulanger to Léonie Rosenstiel, June 8, 1972.

90. Mme Paronian to Léonie Rosenstiel, Aug. 10, 1973. These photographs are in the possession of Mlle Nadia Boulanger. Copies are in the possession of the author. They show that Lili Boulanger had decorated the bare rooms with magnificent furnishings, including a Pleyel grand piano, reproductions and original paintings and sculptures, family photographs, an opulent French provincial light fixture, a large punch bowl set, and the Russian icon that had stood at the foot of her bed at home. (See chap. 6.)

91. Mme Paronian, Interview, Nice, July 4, 1973. The Russian baptismal cross has apparently disappeared. The locket was in the possession of Mme Paronian in July 1973. The translation of the original Russian inscription on the cross into French ("sauve et protège") was made by Mme Paronian on July 4, 1973.

92. The original photograph is in the possession of Mlle Nadia Boulanger.

93. Information on the mobilization of the General Secretary and the *pensionnaires* is contained in a note in the *Livre d'Inscription des Pensionnaires ouvert à la Villa Médicis le Premier Octobre Mil Huit Cent Sept*, p. 77. MS, Archives of the Villa Medici:

Le 4 Août 1914, M. Girette (Paul Armand) Secrétaire Général de Académie [*sic*] de France à Rome . . . est mobilisé et part pour la France.

Il n'est pas remplacé dans ses fonctions.

A cette même date, MM. les Pensionnaires [*sic*] dont les noms suivent, Dupas, Piel, Gallon, Mirland, Rénard, Paray, Girodon, Foucault, Maillart, Martial, Lejeune, Séassal, Grégoire et Delvincourt, mobilisés, rejoignent les unités auxquelles ils sont affectés.

94. Albert Besnard to Henri Roujon, Oct. 18, 1914. MS, Archives of the Académie des Beaux-Arts.

95. Institut de France, *Procès Verbal, 1913–1914,* pp. 205–6. Oct. 10, 1914.

96. Académie de France à Rome. *Livre d'Inscription,* p. 77.

97. Albert Besnard to M. Dagnan-Bouveret, Jan. 28, 1915. MS, Archives of the Académie des Beaux-Arts.

98. Mme Paronian, Interview, Nice, July 4 and 6, 1973.

99. Jules Piel to Léonie Rosenstiel, Dec. 10, 1972.

100. Whitney Warren was active in many Franco-American war relief projects during World War I.

101. Jacques Durand, "Quelques Souvenirs. . . ,"pp. 121–22.

102. Nadia Boulanger, Interview, Fontainebleau, July 23, 1973.

103. A copy of this program is in the possession of Mlle Nadia Boulanger.

104. The actual publication of the above scores came after Lili Boulanger's death in 1918.

105. *Soir sur la Plaine* was subsequently published in 1918; *Reflets* remains unpublished.

106. This may have been based on the chorus of the same name, which was the subject of the 1912 *concours d'essai* in the Prix de Rome competition. The work seems to have been either lost or destroyed.

107. This may have been another name for *Cortège.*

108. This may be the *Nocturne,* or perhaps still another lost composition.

109. The original of this list is in the possession of Mlle Nadia Boulanger. A copy is in the possession of the author.

110. This work was published in 1918, but not legally deposited until the following year.

111. The original is in the possession of Mlle Nadia Boulanger. It is undated, but from the same period.

112. This workbook is in the possession of Mlle Nadia Boulanger.

113. Nadia Boulanger to Léonie Rosenstiel, Feb. 1, 1972.

114. Lili and Nadia Boulanger, "Copie Lettre pour Membres Comité d'Honneur," Sept. 23, 1915. The original is in the possession of Mlle Nadia Boulanger. A copy is in the possession of the author.

115. The original is in the possession of Mlle Nadia Boulanger. A copy is in the possession of the author.

116. A copy of this program is in the possession of Mlle Nadia Boulanger.

117. A copy of this program is in the possession of Mlle Nadia Boulanger. Two of the *Clairières,* the *Nocturne,* and *Cortège* had been performed at the *Exposition des Cocardes de Mimi-Pinson* on December 17 under the direction of Francis Casadesus. This program also is in the possession of Mlle Nadia Boulanger.

118. A copy of this issue, as well as all others of the periodical, are in the possession of Mlle Nadia Boulanger. The last number is that for June 1918.

119. Nadia Boulanger to Léonie Rosenstiel, June 8, 1972.

120. Institut de France, *Procès Verbal, 1915–1916*, Feb. 12, 1916, pp. 323–24.

121. République Française. Sous-Secrétariat d'État et des Beaux-Arts. Letter to the President of the Académie des Beaux-Arts. Feb. 18, 1916. MS, Archives of the Académie des Beaux-Arts, ". . . que, bien que leur pension demeure suspendue, elles devront se conformer strictement au Réglement."

122. Institut de France, *Procès Verbal, 1915–1916*, p. 324.

123. Nadia Boulanger to Léonie Rosenstiel, June 8, 1972, "On eût dit qu'elle s'était identifée à la pauvre petite héroïne de Maeterlinck, comme il y avait déjà eu fusion entre la jeune fille évoquée par Francis Jammes dans les 'Clairières' et elle-même."

124. These letters from Maurice Maeterlinck, dated Feb. 16, 18, and 20, 1916, are in the possession of Mlle Nadia Boulanger.

125. The original telegram is in the possession of Mlle Nadia Boulanger.

126. Nadia Boulanger to Léonie Rosenstiel, June 8, 1972.

127. Nadia Boulanger, Interview, Fontainebleau, July 23, 1973.

128. This was the original title of Claudel's famous play *L'Annonce faite à Marie*.

129. Paul Claudel, *Cahiers, Vol. 3. Correspondance Paul Claudel-Darius Milhaud 1912–1953* (Paris: Gallimard, 1961), p. 47. "Lili a eu le prix de Rome. Naturellement elle m'a demandé *La Jeune Fille Violaine*, pour la mettre en musique." The letter is dated Rome, March 18, 1916.

130. Ibid., p. 48. "Elles me l'ont demandée, mais naturellement j'ai refusé. Pas plus elles qu'aucun d'autre." This letter is dated July 5, 1916.

131. She was undoubtedly referring both to Dr. Marchia Fava, who was then treating her, and to Nadia, who had gone to Rome to be with her sister.

132. Lili Boulanger to Miki Piré, April 2, 1916. As of July 1973 this letter was in the possession of Mme Paronian.

133. Albert Besnard, Letter to M. le Président de la Section d'Art de l'Institut, Apr. 10, 1916. MS, Archives of the Académie des Beaux-Arts.

134. Completed works sent back to the Institut in Paris. Required of all Prix de Rome winners during their tenure.

135. Institut de France . . . *Procès Verbal, 1915–1916*, Apr. 15, 1916, p. 332, ". . . de faire le buste de Mlle Boulanger. Ce buste, elle l'exposera parmi ses envois futurs où il sera certainement très apprécié, tant pour sa ressemblance avec son modèle, que pour son exécution."

136. Nadia Boulanger to Léonie Rosenstiel, Nov. 21, 1972, "Cette grande tragédienne, ayant appris que L.B. était malade, et bien qu'elle même fût déjà âgée et malade, alla voir plusieurs fois L.B. montant les 4 étages de la Villa et lui portant des roses."

137. Ibid., ". . . des histoires extraordinaires, très spirituelles et d'un air absolument imperturbable."

138. Nadia Boulanger, Interview, Fontainebleau, July 23, 1973, and Mme Paronian, Interview, Nice, July 6, 1973.

139. Both were published by Durand et Cie. after her death; *Psalm 24* in 1924, *Psalm 129* first in a transcription for voice and piano in 1921 and, in 1924, in its full original version.

140. A picture of Lili, dressed in white, leaving this audience, with Mme Boulanger and Nadia in the background, is in the possession of Mlle Nadia Boulanger. A copy is in the possession of the author.

141. Mlle Nadia Boulanger has assured me that both she and Mme Boulanger were aware of the gravity of Lili's condition long before this, but were trying to

keep their knowledge from Lili. Apparently they had succeeded.

142. Mme Paronian, Interview, Nice, July 4, 1973.

143. "A ma chère petite collaboratrice Lili Boulanger/qui doit donner à la Princesse Maleine, de par la volonté des dieux de la musique et du Destin [sic], l'âme attendue." The original photograph is in the possession of Mlle Nadia Boulanger.

144. These three restrictions are underlined in the letter, the first once, the last two twice.

145. Lili Boulanger to Miki Piré, June 30, 1916. As of July 1973 this letter was in the possession of Mme Paronian.

146. Nadia Boulanger, Interview, Paris, Nov. 20, 1973.

147. The original autograph manuscript is in the possession of Mlle Nadia Boulanger. It was published by Ricordi in 1919.

148. Nadia Boulanger to Léonie Rosenstiel, Feb. 1, 1972.

149. Lili Boulanger to Miki Piré, Sept. 6, 1916. As of July 1973, this letter was in the possession of Madame Paronian.

150. Société Anonyme des Éditions Ricordi, Contract of Transfer of Author's Rights, Nov. 30, 1916. The original is in the possession of Mlle Nadia Boulanger. A copy is in the possession of the author.

151. Lili Boulanger to Miki Piré, Dec. 31, 1916. As of July 1973 this letter was in the possession of Mme Paronian.

152. The original of this list is in the possession of Mlle Nadia Boulanger. A copy is in the possession of the author. Although there is no date on this list, the quality of the handwriting, the names of the people mentioned, and the activities make such a date the most plausible.

153. Lili Boulanger to Miki Piré, Feb. 14, 1917. As of July 1973 this letter was in the possession of Mme Paronian.

154. This photograph is in the possession of Mlle Nadia Boulanger. ("À ma chère Lili/Bien affectueusement, avec mes/Meilleurs voeux/Un vieil et fidèle ami, Th. Dubois.")

155. This photograph is in the possession of Mlle Nadia Boulanger.

156. This notebook is in the possession of Mlle Nadia Boulanger.

157. Nadia Boulanger, Interview, Paris, November 20, 1973.

158. Lili Boulanger, postcard to Miki Piré, Mar. 23, 1917. As of July 1973 this postcard was in the possession of Mme Paronian.

159. This notebook is in the possession of Mlle Nadia Boulanger.

160. This photograph is in the possession of the author.

161. Copies of both programs are in the possession of Mlle Nadia Boulanger.

162. These are the dates recorded in her composition workbook. The book itself is in the possession of Mlle Nadia Boulanger. It should be noted that, for the entire period she spent at Arcachon, Lili was under the constant care of a nurse, Mlle Sarro.

163. Lili Boulanger to Miki Piré, May 10, 1917. As of July 1973 this letter was in the possession of Mme Paronian.

164. Madame Paronian, Interview, Nice, July 4, 1973.

165. Lili Boulanger to Miki Piré, July 29, 1917. As of July 1973 this letter was in the possession of Mme Paronian.

166. Nadia Boulanger to Léonie Rosenstiel, June 8, 1972; idem, July 12, 1972.

167. Mme Paronian, Interview, Nice, July 4, 1973.

168. Ibid.

169. An opium preparation.

170. Mme Paronian, Interview, Nice, July 4, 1973.

171. Ibid.

172. Renée de Marquein to Léonie Rosenstiel, Sept. 30, 1972.

173. Mme Paronian, Interview, Nice, July 4, 1973.

174. Nadia Boulanger to Léonie Rosenstiel, June 8, 1972.

175. Renée de Marquein to Léonie Rosenstiel, Sept. 4, 1972, "Lorsqu'elle est devenue malade, sa gaieté a disparu, pour revenir pourtant de temps à autre, mais elle a vécu sa maladie avec beaucoup de courage et de lucidité . . . elle était très croyante et je pense que cela lui a été un secours."

176. Mme Paronian, Interview, Nice, July 6, 1973, quoting a letter from the former Simone Plé, who was present at that audition.

177. Nadia Boulanger to Léonie Rosenstiel, June 8, 1972.

178. Nadia Boulanger, Interview, Paris, Nov. 23, 1973.

179. Lili Boulanger to Miki Piré, September 27, 1917. As of July 1973 this letter was in the possession of Mme Paronian.

180. The above photographs are in the possession of Mlle Nadia Boulanger. Copies are in the possession of the author.

181. I am indebted to Mme Paronian for pointing this fact out to me. This original snapshot is now in the possession of the author.

182. After Lili's operation, Mme Boulanger visited her sick room less often than before. Part of the reason may have been the strong perfume, "Jasmin de Siam," of which Mme Boulanger was so fond. Such a heavy odor would not have been soothing to Lili at that point. Mme Paronian, Interview, Nice, July 4 and July 6, 1973.

183. Lili Boulanger to Miki Piré, Oct. 10, 1917. As of July 1973 this letter was in the possession of Mme Paronian.

184. See chap. 2.

185. Lili Boulanger, Postcard to Miki Piré, Oct. 15, 1917. As of July 1973 this postcard was in the possession of Mme Paronian.

186. The original manuscript is in the possession of Mlle Nadia Boulanger.

187. Nadia Boulanger, Interview, Paris, July 23, 1973.

188. A copy of this program is in the possession of Mlle Nadia Boulanger.

189. Entries for these dates are to be found in her workbook.

190. Nadia Boulanger to Léonie Rosenstiel, June 8, 1972, ". . . elle continuait toujours de travailler, se faisant porter au piano de temps en temps." Lili was "carried to the piano" because she was no longer strong enough to walk, and had to be carried wherever she wanted to go.

191. The manuscript copy in the possession of Mlle Nadia Boulanger contains the notation "indication, nuances/ complétés [sic] par NB."

192. Nadia Boulanger to Léonie Rosenstiel, June 8, 1972, "quand elle ne pût plus écrire, elle dictait note par note, ligne par ligne . . . l'oeuvre qui s'était conçue intérieurement."

193. The only extant evidence of a previous sketch for this work is the "Amen."

194. The original is in the possession of Mlle Nadia Boulanger.

195. Nadia Boulanger to Léonie Rosenstiel, June 8, 1972. "Les bombardements devenant de plus en plus rapprochés, Madame Boulanger décida de quitter Paris avec ses filles, et Lili Boulanger fut transportée à Mézy."

196. Nadia Boulanger, Interview, Paris, Nov. 19, 1973, and Nadia Boulanger, Letter to Léonie Rosenstiel, Feb. 3, 1974.

197. Mme Paronian, Interview, Nice, July 4, 1973.

198. Ibid.

282

199. Annette Dieudonné to Léonie Rosenstiel, Sept. 12 and Sept. 25, 1973, and Mme Apostol, Interview, Paris, Nov. 21, 1973.

200. Mme Paronian, Interview, Nice, July 4, 1973.

201. Ibid.

202. Mme Apostol, Interview, Paris, Nov. 21, 1973.

203. Mme Paronian, Interview, Nice, July 4, 1973. A photograph of the body of Lili Boulanger in this dress, laid out on her deathbed, was in the possession of Mme Paronian as of July 1973, and was shown to the author at that time.

204. Nadia Boulanger to Léonie Rosenstiel, June 8, 1972.

205. Mme Paronian, Interview, Nice, July 4, 1973.

Notes to Chapter 5

1. *Attente.* See chap. 3.

2. Of the thirteen compositions written before this, none has survived intact. All traces of every piece except *La Lettre de Mort* seem to have vanished, and even that work remains only in the form of a sketch. For further information on these early works, see chap. 2.

3. This composition remains in the possession of Mlle Nadia Boulanger, but was not made available to the author for an analytical examination. It is interesting to note that Eduard Reeser lists this as a work for chorus and piano which was well along toward being orchestrated. ("Lili Boulanger," *De Muziek* 7 (1933): 216–17). The autograph manuscript seen by the author in November 1973 was for chorus and orchestra, however, and was completed. No manuscript version of this piece for chorus and piano was to be found at that time.

4. For further discussion of the sequence of events and dates in this regard, see chap. 1.

5. If this really was Lili Boulanger's second cantata, then either *Bérénice* or *Maia*—for which there are entries in her very first composition notebook—was not completed. It would have been most uncharacteristic for Lili to have been inaccurate about such a detail.

6. This composition was not made available to the author for detailed analysis. The separate manuscript containing Scene I indicates—in Lili's own handwriting—that it was completed on Saturday, September 23, 1911, and the workbook that contains sketches for the entire cantata lists as a final entry October 3, 1911. It is most probable that, in trying to prepare for the Prix de Rome competition, Lili would have tried to simulate as nearly as possible the conditions of the competition itself. Therefore, if she had begun work on *Frédégonde* in mid-September, she would almost certainly have tried to finish it by mid-October. That would have meant that she would have completed the piano-vocal score at about the time of the last entry in her workbook, and have spent the last week or two orchestrating the composition, just as she would be expected to do at Compiègne. Reeser's date of 1913 for this work does not agree with either the original manuscript or the original workbook, since neither carries this year as that of composition (Reeser, "Lili Boulanger," p. 216). Both the last scenes of *Frédégonde* and the orchestral score are now missing.

7. New York: G. Ricordi and Company, 1918, and Paris: Société Anonyme des Éditions Ricordi, 1918.

8. See *D'un Matin de Printemps*, for example. See also chap. 6 below.

9. The only available copy of this score is a much later one in Nadia's hand, seemingly written around 1950, since a notation on the bottom of the first page of the score indicates both the first copyright date by Ricordi (1918) and the fact that the copyright was renewed in 1950.

10. Because of the limitations imposed by the pianist's two hands and the resources of the instrument, this contrast between the two accompanying textures would have been impossible to produce in the violin-piano version.

11. See, for example, "Au pied de mon lit," chap. 6.

12. At the time of its initial publication by Ricordi in 1918, this piece was dedicated to Paul Vidal, who had been Lili's composition professor at the Conservatoire. This dedication reflects Lili Boulanger's desire to thank her teacher for his help and encouragement. The dedication reads, "To my dear teacher and friend/Paul Vidal/in respectful gratitude and sincere affection," and is signed with her monogram, L. B. ("A mon cher Maître [sic] et Ami [sic]/Paul VIDAL [sic]/en respectueuse gratitude et/sincère affection.")

13. (Paris: Ricordi, 1918). Dedicated to Mme Jane Engel Bathori. See Appendix U.

14. Maurice Maeterlinck, *Serres Chaudes* (Brussels: P. Lacomblez, 1890).

15. The best evidence presently available dates this work sometime during 1911 (Nadia Boulanger to Léonie Rosenstiel, Feb. 1, 1972). Until the original manuscript is found, no more precise dating than 1911 is possible. (The Ricordi edition of 1919 carries the indication that the piece was completed in Gargenville in 1916, but that date seems unlikely to be correct.)

16. At the end of her fourth composition notebook, Lili indicates she was to make corrections on *Soleils de Septembre*. No date is given for this, but it was most probably in December 1911.

17. This manuscript appears not to have survived.

18. Lili Boulanger's sketches for *La Princesse Maleine* were not made available for detailed analysis.

19. Lili Boulanger was familiar with Debussy's music, and had heard *Pelléas and Mélisande* before its formal premiere. See chap. 2.

20. The chorus *Soir d'Été* was composed for this purpose. Neither sketches nor finished manuscripts for it can now be found.

21. Her first harmony lesson took place in December 1909.

22. Lili took her first lesson in fugal techniques on June 15, 1911.

23. Her first work that constituted part of this preparation was *Frédégonde*.

24. Neither of these pieces has ever been published. Apparently, there is no extant piano-vocal score for *La Source*.

25. Published by Ricordi in 1918, at which time it was dedicated to Count San Martino e Valperga, whom Lili had met in Paris.

26. *Le Paria;* see chap. 2.

27. For further discussion of this work, see chap. 3. The orchestration is no longer to be found. This piece was composed between July 21 and July 28 at Gargenville.

28. No sketches or manuscripts exist for this work, but it is fairly safe to assume that it was another chorus in preparation for the *concours d'essai:* Lili Boulanger did not identify it by genre, and she seems to have finished it in less than three weeks' time. By August 21, 1912, her fourth fugue notebook indicates that she had already completed it and was working on the final corrections.

29. The original manuscript can no longer be found. There is no stylistic reason to assume that the date of composition given at the end of the Ricordi

edition of 1918 is inaccurate. Assuming that both the date and place of composition are reliable in this case, and given the fact that Lili did not return to Paris until mid-October—at which time she was busy working on *Pour les Funérailles d'un Soldat*—she must have composed this piece between August and early October of 1912.

30. "Comme à travers la brume."

31. The text is taken from Act IV, Scene I. Alfred de Musset, *Oeuvres Complètes. I. Poésies* (Paris: Charpentier, 1866), pp. 283–84.

32. Mme Paronian, Interview, Nice, July 6, 1973.

33. This piece was orchestrated early in 1913. See chap. 3.

34. "Nous voulons au tombeau, porter le capitaine,/ Il est mort, en soldat sur la terre chrétienne."

35. This work was published by the New York branch of Ricordi in 1918, a full year before it appeared in Europe. The American version, however, was a piano reduction of the original orchestration, and contained an English translation by Frederick H. Martens. The French edition carries the dedication, "To my dear teacher and friend/ Georges Caussade/ in deep gratitude, in sincere affection." ("A mon cher Maître et ami Georges Caussade,/ en profonde reconnaissance/ en sincère attachement.") The French edition has a cover designed by Jacques Débat-Ponsan.

36. *Soir sur la Plaine* was published by Ricordi in a piano-vocal score only in 1918. The original manuscript of the orchestral score is in the possession of the Bibliothèque Nationale in Paris. A copy is in the possession of the author.

37. Mme Paronian, Interview, Nice, July 4, 1973.

Notes to Chapter 6

1. Reeser, for instance, lists this as an unfinished work ("Lili Boulanger," pp. 216–17).

2. Unfortunately, this work was not made available to me for detailed analysis.

3. It is not possible to substantiate the existence of such an arrangement of *Cortège* by referring to written records in the possession of the company. All such records, correspondence, etc., were returned to Mlle Nadia Boulanger some years ago, and many seem to have disappeared. The contract that Lili signed with Ricordi on January 29, 1918, mentions specifically only two versions of *Cortège*: violin and piano, and piano solo.

4. This work was dedicated to Lily Jumel, whose mother had a political salon. Lily Jumel had been a student of Henri Dallier and was a good friend of the Boulanger family.

5. Nadia Boulanger to Léonie Rosenstiel, Feb. 1, 1972.

6. For further discussion of the Symbolist aesthetic, see chap. 7.

7. It was not until years later that the mystery was resolved. The parents of the young lady had prevented Jammes from marrying her. See *Francis Jammes et André Gide, Correspondance, 1893–1938* 3d ed. (Paris: Gallimard, 1948), pp. 211–12.

8. Her baptismal names were Olga, Marie, Juliette. However, she always referred to herself as "Lili," using the diminutive of Juliette along with her family name.

9. Mme Paronian, Interview, Nice, July 4, 1973, and Nadia Boulanger, Interview, Paris, Nov. 24, 1973.

10. *Clairières dans le Ciel* was published twice: first by Ricordi in 1919, later by Durand et Cie. in 1970. The feeling tone of this cycle has also been compared by Chailley ("Boulanger, Lili") to that of Robert Schumann's *Frauenliebe und Leben.*

11. Nadia Boulanger to Léonie Rosenstiel, Nov. 20, 1973.

12. These dedications—in addition to those to her closest friends—read like a Who's Who of intellectuals and artists. The first song is dedicated to Gabriel Fauré; the third to Fernand Francell; the fourth to Yvonne Brothier; the sixth to Tito Ricordi; the seventh to Henri Albers; the ninth to Rodolphe Plamondon; the eleventh to David Devriès; the thirteenth and last to Roger Ducasse. Of these thirteen songs, the first, fifth, sixth, seventh, tenth, eleventh, and thirteenth were later orchestrated by the composer.

13. Sketches for both go back at least to September 1915. The melodic line for *Psalm 129* has also been traced as far back as a composition book Liili used in 1910–1913. The division of the present consideration of her works into those completed before and after the Prix de Rome is based on two factors. After the prize was hers, Lili Boulanger was on her own. There was no one to tell her at that point which genres to work in, or which texts to choose. Also, she was no longer compelled to practice any special techniques or to use every technique in every piece if her own artistic judgment dictated otherwise. These conditions evidently led her to bring to fruition a number of projects she had been working on sporadically but had been prevented by her other obligations from completing earlier.

14. Nadia Boulanger, Interview, Paris, Nov. 19, 1973.

15. Neither of these works was published during the composer's lifetime. *Psalm 24,* dedicated to the Boulanger family's old friend, Jules Griset, was published in both versions in 1924 by Durand. *Psalm 129* was published in both reductions in 1921, but it was not until 1924 that the orchestral score was published by Durand.

16. This composition, dedicated to Claire Croiza, was published by Ricordi in 1918, but not legally deposited until the following year.

17. Reeser, "Lili Boulanger," p. 217. This work was first published by Durand in 1925.

18. This work is dedicated to the composer's father. It was not published until after Lili Boulanger's death. *Psalm 130* was published by Durand in both orchestral score and piano reduction in 1925.

19. Nadia Boulanger, Interview, Paris, Nov. 23, 1973.

20. Mauclair, "Lili Boulanger," p. 152, for example.

21. Venerable Kosgoda Sobhita to Léonie Rosenstiel, Jan. 26, 1972. A copy of the Sinhalese version and his transliteration of it are to be found in Appendix R. Other translations of this same text appear in Walpola Rahula, *L'Enseignement du Bouddha d'après les Textes les plus anciens* (Paris: Éditions du Seuil, 1961) , pp. 130–31. F. Max Müller, ed., *Sutta Nipata, The Sacred Books of the East,* vol. 10, pt. 2 (London: Oxford University Press, 1898) : 24–25.

22. The piano reduction was published by Durand in 1921, the orchestral score in 1925.

23. Nadia Boulanger, Interview, Paris, Nov. 19, 1973 and Nadia Boulanger to Léonie Rosenstiel, Nov. 12, 1975.

24. Reeser, "Lili Boulanger," p. 269, mentions an unfinished symphonic poem begun by the composer in 1915–1916, but Mlle Nadia Boulanger states (Interview, Paris, Nov. 23, 1973) that no such work exists. I myself saw no sketches for any composition fitting this description during my detailed examination of the com-

poser's notebooks and sketchbooks.

25. Reeser, "Lili Boulanger," p. 270.

26. *D'un Soir triste* has never been published. The trio version was deposited with the Société des Auteurs, Compositeurs et Éditeurs de Musique, according to their stamp on the title page, on Feb. 3, 1919, under their number 221,569. The flute and piano and violin versions of *D'un Matin de Printemp*s were published by Durand in 1922. The orchestral and trio versions have remained unpublished. (Cécile Armagnac to Léonie Rosenstiel, April 20, 1976.) As of 1975, *D'un Soir triste* was being edited for publication (Nadia Boulanger to Léonie Rosenstiel, Nov. 12, 1975).

27. The version for organ, harp, string quartet, and voice was first published by Durand in 1922. The organ reduction was not published by Durand until 1924.

Notes to Chapter 7

1. Lili Boulanger's compositions in the larger forms—the *Psalms*, the *Pie Jesu* and *D'un Soir Triste* and *D'un Matin de Printemps* had not yet been performed in public. In fact, the composer herself had never heard them before her death. His knowledge of her work was, therefore, limited to her cantata *Faust et Hélène*, some of the *Clairières dans le Ciel*, perhaps *Renouveau*, *Les Sirènes*, her early songs, and *Nocturne* and *Cortège*.

2. P. 3

3. R. Crussard, "Lili Boulanger," *Journal des Ouvrages de Dames*, June 1, 1918 (no. 363), p. 119.

4. "Lili Boulanger," *France-Aviation. Revue Technique, industrielle et littéraire*, August 1918, pp. 50–52.

5. "À la Villa Médicis," *Excelsior*, May 3, 1918, p. 3.

6. Nadia Boulanger, Interview, Fontainebleau, July 23, 1973.

7. "Music," *New York Times*, Dec. 4, 1918, p. 11.

8. "Music: A Gala French Concert," *New York Times*, Dec. 27, 1918, p. 9.

9. Ibid.

10. Ministère de l'Instruction publique et des Beaux-Arts. Conservatoire National de Musique et de Déclamation, *Distribution des Prix pour le Cours d'Études de l'Année 1917–1918. Séance publique annuelle du dimanche 13 octobre 1918* (Paris: Imprimerie Nationale, 1918), p. 24. Roussel had been a classmate of Lili's at the Conservatoire.

11. The programs for these performances are in the possession of Mlle Nadia Boulanger.

12. All programs are in the possession of Mlle Nadia Boulanger.

13. "Lili Boulanger," *The Musician* 24 (Feb. 1919): 43.

14. The full title reads: *En Recueillement: Composé et Orné par Miki Piré. Préface de Camille Mauclair.*

15. Madame Paronian, Interview, Nice, July 6, 1973.

16. Albert Spalding, *Rise to Follow*, p. 160, and Mme Paronian, Interview, Nice, July 4, 1973.

17. Jean Macdonald, *Song Recital*, Mar. 18, 1920. This program is in the possession of Mlle Nadia Boulanger.

18. This program is in the possession of Mlle Nadia Boulanger.

19. The works are not named on the program, but they probably were *D'un*

Soir triste and *D'un Matin de Printemps,* which were frequently played as companion pieces. The program is in the possession of Mlle Nadia Boulanger.

20. "Vous m'avez regardé," "Deux ancolies," "Au pied de mon lit," "Si tout ceci," and "Je garde une médaille d'elle."

21. These programs are in the possession of Mlle Nadia Boulanger.

22. "Les Concerts," August 1, 1921 (no. 10), pp. 163–64.

23. June 14, 1921.

24. "La Musique au Concert," June 17, 1921, p. 2.

25. June 21, 1921, p. 2.

26. Feb. 4, 1923, p. 4.

27. "Audition des Envois de Rome de Lili Boulanger," *Comoedia,* Jan. 18, 1923, p. 3, and "Au Conservatoire," *Le Gaulois,* Jan. 21, 1923, p. 4.

28. One of these programs is in the possession of the Bibliothèque Nationale, Paris. A copy is in the possession of the author. Ministère de l'Instruction Publique et des Beaux-Arts, *Audition des Envois de Rome: Programme—Oeuvres de Lili Boulanger,* Jan., 1923.

29. These programs are in the possession of Mlle Nadia Boulanger.

30. Léon Jéhin to an unnamed friend, Mar. 16, 1924. This letter is now in the possession of Mlle Nadia Boulanger. A copy is in the possession of the author.

31. Léon Jéhin to Mme Boulanger, Apr. 5, 1924. The original is in the possession of Mlle Nadia Boulanger. A copy is in the possession of the author.

32. April 15, 1924, pp. 891–93.

33. Nadia Boulanger, Interview, Paris, Nov. 24, 1973.

34. These programs are in the possession of Mlle Nadia Boulanger.

35. A copy of the New York Symphony Orchestra program is in the possession of the author. All original programs are in the possession of Mlle Nadia Boulanger.

36. Feb. 9, 1925, p. 12, "C'est avec plaisir que nous enrégistrons le grand succès remporté par cet ouvrage, récemment édité."

37. "Théâtres," *Le Temps,* July 3, 1927, p. 5.

38. There are at least three surviving programs for this concert. The first is in the possession of Mlle Nadia Boulanger, the second in the Lili Boulanger Memorial Fund archives, the third in the Bibliothèque Nationale, Paris. A copy is in the possession of the author.

39. Lili Boulanger Memorial Fund, Inc., Brochure (Boston, 1971), n.p.

40. Everest LPBR 6059 and stereo SDBR 3059. It was reissued in 1967 by EMI under the number CVA 919 (stereo).

41. "On Records: Stereo Eastertide," Apr. 10, 1960, p. 5.

42. "Music's Other Boulanger," *Saturday Review,* May 28, 1960, p. 60.

43. Blitzstein, "Music's Other Boulanger," p. 60. The EMI reissue did include some information by Claude Rostand, but it is imprecise.

44. Académie du Disque Français, *Palmarès du Grand Prix National du Disque pour 1960–61,* n.p.

45. "Music: Nadia Boulanger," Feb. 17, 1962, p. 10.

46. Ibid.

47. Paul Henry Lang, "Music. New York Philharmonic," *Herald Tribune,* Feb. 17, 1962, p. 6; Irving Kolodin, "Music to My Ears: Nadia Boulanger. . . ," *Saturday Review,* Mar. 3, 1962 (vol. 45, no. 9), p. 25; Harriett Johnson, "Words and music. Boulanger leads Philharmonic," *New York Post,* Feb. 17, 1962, p. 14.

48. "At Carnegie Hall. 'Birthday,'" *New York Journal American,* Feb. 17, 1962, p. 8. (*Psalm 130* had preceded *Psalms 24* and *129* on the Philharmonic program.)

49. Nadia Boulanger to Léonie Rosenstiel, June 8, 1972.

50. Ibid.

51. Les Amis de Lili Boulanger, Circular (Paris: Mazarine, n.d.), n.p.

52. CVC 2077 (Paris: E.M.I., Stereo, 1968). This record has never been released in the United States.

53. Bibliothèque Nationale, Département de la Musique, *Lili Boulanger (1893–1918)* (Paris: n.p., 1968). An 8mm silent film of this exhibit was made by Antoine Terrasse.

54. The exhibit itself was moved on to Brussels and then to Oxford later that same year.

55. Clarendon (pseud. of Bernard Gavoty), "A la Mémoire de Lili Boulanger," *Le Figaro*, Mar. 28, 1968, p. 2.

56. Jacques Bourgeois, "La Musique: Le Mythe de Lili Boulanger," *Le Nouveau Journal*, Mar. 30, 1968, p. 4.

57. Mme Paronian, Interview, Nice, July 6, 1973, and Nadia Boulanger to Léonie Rosenstiel, Aug. 14, 1973.

58. The speakers were Igor Markevitch, Gabriel Kaspereit (Secretary of State for Small and Medium Sized Businesses and Handicrafts), and M. Gerville-Réache.

59. W. H. Johnstone to Léonie Rosenstiel, Oct. 30, 1971.

60. Present at this ceremony were: Louis Martin (Inspecteur Principal de la Musique, representing André Malraux, the Minister of Cultural Affairs), Gaston Kaspereit, Raymond Colibeau (Vice-President of the Council of Paris), M. Gerville-Réache, and Igor Markevitch.

61. Many reports of this ceremony appeared in the papers, among them: "Gargenville a inauguré la place Lili-Boulanger," *Le Parisien* (édition de Mantes), June 13, 1972, p. 1; "Tout Hanneucourt a participé à l'inauguration de la place Lili-Boulanger," *Paris-Normandie*, June 14, 1972, p. 1, and "Une place Lili-Boulanger inaugurée à Hanneucourt," *Le Courrier* (Mantes), June 14, 1972, pp. 1, 7.

62. "Le Souvenir de Lili Boulanger," *Le Journal* (Paris), Mar. 14, 1939, p. 2.

63. After the death of Mme Boulanger in 1935, the Mass was held in commemoration of the death of both Lili and her mother.

64. Jeanne Mercier, "Observations of a Great Musician," *Ethos*, Jan. 1940, p. 33.

65. Frédéric Boulanger was born in 1777. See chap. 1.

66. See chap. 5.

67. Friedrich Herzfeld (Frankfurt-Berlin: Verlag Ullstein, 1968), p. 82.

68. *La Musique française* (Paris: Éditions A. et J. Picard, 1970), p. 378.

69. Ibid., p. 390.

70. Marc Honegger, ed. (Paris: Bordas, 1970), 1: 133.

71. (New York: Scribner's Sons, 1971), pp. 140–41.

72. Ibid., p. 184.

73. "Lili Boulanger (1893–1918) ou 'Musique pour une Éternité,' " no. 9, n.p.

74. Ibid.

75. See chapters 3–6 above.

76. "Boulanger," *MGG 142/143* . . . (Kassel, Basel, Tours, and London: Bärenreiter, 1971), pp. 1006–7.

77. Nadia Boulanger to Léonie Rosenstiel, Nov. 1, 1975, p. 4.

78. Vol. 23, no. 2 (Feb. 1973): 48.

79. Ibid., p. 52.

80. See chap. 3 and Figures 14, 18, 20, and 23 for a description of the competition and proof that Lili Boulanger's participation was public knowledge.

81. See chap. 4.

82. See chap. 3.

83. Léonie Rosenstiel to The Editor, *High Fidelity*, January 31, 1973.

84. Kenneth Furie to Léonie Rosenstiel, March 9, 1973.

85. See below.

86. (New York: Charles Scribner's Sons and London: The Hutchinson Publishing Group, 1973), pp. 132–33. Some of the data in his "Lili Boulanger," *The Musical Times*, March 1968, pp. 227–28, are in error, however.

87. The last such work was Edward Burlingame Hill's *Modern French Music* (Boston and New York: Houghton Mifflin Company, 1924), pp. 343–47.

88. Flore Wend to Léonie Rosenstiel, n.d. (1974), and "Lili Boulanger Concert March 19," *Peabody notes. Peabody Conservatory of Music,* 27, no. 3 (March 1974): 1, 2.

89. March 21, 1974, p. B12.

90. *Premiere: Recorded performances of Keyboard Works by Women* (Hollywood, Calif.: Avant Records, 1974). The short biographical note on Lili Boulanger is accurate.

91. Nancy Fierro to Léonie Rosenstiel, Nov. 11, 1973.

92. "Women: From Silence to Song," vol. 24, no. 1: 6.

93. "The Boulanger Sisters," *Country Life* (London) 157, no. 4056 (Mar. 27, 1975): 778.

94. Marcel Mihalovici to Nadia Boulanger, Mar. 25, 1975. A copy of the letter is in the possession of the author.

95. "Women Composers: Reminiscence and History," vol. 15: 32.

96. Janet Knight, "For the First Time on the Great Stage," vol. 4, no. 5: 93.

97. Marnie Hall, Interview, New York, Oct. 13, 1975.

98. Marnie Hall (comp.), *Woman's Work* (New York: Gemini Hall Records, 1976), and idem, "Lili Boulanger," ibid., pp. 26–27.

99. Norma Davidson and Joyce Strong, Interview with Robert Sherman and Donna Handly, Interview with Léonie Rosenstiel, Oct. 24, 1975. On her broadcast Ms. Handly corrected two errors about Lili Boulanger that had appeared in *Ms.*: that she had won the Prix de Rome through submission of an anonymous composition, and that she was denied entry to the competition in 1918 because no women were allowed to compete.

100. Donna Handly, Interview, New York City, Oct. 24, 1975.

101. Nadia Boulanger to Léonie Rosenstiel, Jan. 27, 1976, p. 1.

102. "Young French Women Winning Honors," *Musical Leader* 26, no. 5 (July 31, 1913), p. 117.

103. "Young French Women Winning Honors," *The Sun,* Section 3, p. 5.

104. "Notes on the Program: 'Faust et Hélène,' " Nov. 1975, p. 16.

105. Ibid., p. 27.

106. Joseph McLellan, "A Woman's Place Is on the Podium," *Washington Post,* Nov. 12, 1975, pp. B10, B12, and Richard Dyer, "Sarah Caldwell, female composers make history," *Boston Globe,* Nov. 11, 1975, p. 13, for example. Although Rosalyn Tureck had also conducted the Philharmonic, she had done so from the keyboard, which is not quite the same thing.

107. "Philharmonic Concert Misfires," *Long Island Press,* Nov. 11, 1975, p. 16.

108. "Celebrating women composers," Nov. 12, 1975, p. 40.

109. Bob Micklin, "Celebrating the women," *Newsday,* Nov. 11, 1975, p. 9a.

110. "Music: Two 'Firsts' for Sarah Caldwell," Nov. 12, 1975, p. 48.

111. "Sarah Caldwell's Baton Debuts in N.Y.," Nov. 11, 1975, p. 39.

112. William Bender "Sarah's Women," *Time,* Nov. 24, 1975, p. 88 and Herbert

Saal, "The Sound of Women," *Newsweek*, Nov. 24, 1975, pp. 83, 85.

113. "Ladies' Night," Nov. 24, 1975, p. 151.

114. "Philharmonic Concert Misfires."

115. See chapters 3–4.

116. Léonie Rosenstiel, "Lili Boulanger, 1893–1918," *Woman's Work* (New York: Gemini Hall Records, 1976), pp. 25–27.

117. "The Listening Room," February 23 and 24, 1976.

118. See above.

119. Léonie Rosenstiel, "Letters," vol. 4, no. 9: p. 4.

120. Léonie Rosenstiel, "Lili Boulanger: Myths and Realities," March 3, 1976.

121. Virginia Gifford, Interview, Poughkeepsie, N.Y., March 4, 1976.

122. "Ladies' Day at the Turntable," vol. 30, no. 11: 124.

Selected List of Sources

1. *List of Abbreviations*

AABA	Archives of the Académie des Beaux-Arts, Paris
ANP	Archives Nationales, Paris
AVM	Archives of the Villa Medici, Rome
BNP	Bibliothèque Nationale, Paris
CNP	Conservatoire National, Paris
MPC	Miki Paronian Collection, Nice
NBC	Nadia Boulanger Collection, Paris

2. *Published Sources: Books*

Académie du Disque Français. *Palmarès du Grand Prix du Disque pour 1960–1961*. Paris: n.p., 1961.

Les Amis de Lili Boulanger. Circular. Paris: Mazarine, n.d.

Baldick, Robert. *The Life and Times of Frédérick Lemaître*. London: Hamish Hamilton, 1959.

Bibliothèque Nationale. Département de la Musique. *Lili Boulanger (1893–1918)*. Paris: n.p., 1968.

Claudel, Paul. *Cahiers*. Vol. 3: *Correspondance Paul Claudel-Darius Milhaud 1912–1953*. Paris: Gallimard, 1961.

Clément, Félix and Larousse, Pierre. *Dictionnaire des Opéras*. Paris: Larousse, 1904.

Delavigne, Jean François Casimir. *Le Paria*. Paris: n.p., 1833.

Duforcq, Norbert. *La Musique française*. Paris: Éditions A. et J. Picard, 1970.

Durand, Jacques. *Quelques Souvenirs d'un Éditeur de Musique.* 2ᵉ Série (1910–1924). Paris: A. Durand, 1925.

Fétis, F. J. *Biographie universelle des Musiciens et Bibliographie générale de la Musique.* Paris: Firmin Didot, 1866.

Grand Larousse Encyclopédique, 1960 ed. S.v. "Bernard, Étienne."

Hall, Marnie. *Woman's Work.* New York: Gemini Hall Records, 1975.

Herzfeld, Friedrich. *Ullstein Lexikon der Musik.* Frankfurt-Berlin: Verlag Ullstein, 1968. S.v. "Boulanger, Nadia."

Hill, Edward Burlingame. *Modern French Music.* Boston and New York: Houghton Mifflin Company, 1924.

Honegger, Marc, ed. *Dictionnaire de la Musique.* Vol. 1. Paris: Bordas, 1970.

Institut de France. Académie des Beaux-Arts. *Statuts et Règlements.* Paris: Firmin-Didot, 1908.

Jammes, Francis. *Clairières dans le Ciel.* Paris: Mercure de France, 1902–1906.

Lapauze, Henry. *Histoire de l'Académie de France à Rome.* Vol. 2: 1802–1910. Paris: Plon, 1922.

Lili Boulanger Memorial Fund. Concert Program: Symphony Hall, Boston. Boston: n.p., March 6, 1939.

──────. Brochure. Boston: n.p., 1971. Archives of the Lili Boulanger Memorial Fund, Boston.

Maeterlinck, Maurice. *Théâtre I: La Princesse Maleine.* 24th ed. Brussels: Paul Lacomblez, 1911.

Martin, Jules, ed. *Nos Auteurs et Compositeurs dramatiques; Portraits et Biographies.* Paris: Ernest Flammarion, 1897.

Müller, Max, trans. and ed. *The Sacred Books of the East.* Vol. 10, Part 2: *Sutta Nipata.* London: Oxford University Press, 1898.

Musik in Geschichte und Gegenwart, 1971 supplement. "Boulanger, Marie-Julie . . . Ernest-Henri-Alexandre . . . Nadia (Juliette) . . . und Lili (Marie-Juliette). . . ," by Jacques Chailley.

Musset, Alfred de. *Oeuvres Complètes.* Vol. 1: *Poésies. La Coupe et les Lèvres.* Paris: Charpentier, 1866.

Palmer, Christopher. *Impressionism.* New York: Charles Scribner's Sons and London: The Hutchinson Publishing Group. 1973.

Pierre, Constant, ed. *Le Conservatoire National de Musique et de Déclamation. Documents historiques et administratifs recueillis ou reconstitués par Constant Pierre, Sous-chef du Secrétariat, Lauréat de l'Institut.* Paris: Imprimerie Nationale, 1900.

Piré, Miki. *En Recueillement: Composé et Orné par Miki Piré. Préface de Camille Mauclair.* Paris: Floury, 1920.

Rahula, Walpola. *L'Enseignement du Bouddha d'après les Textes les plus anciens.* Paris: Éditions du Seuil, 1961.

Rosenstiel, Léonie. "Lili Boulanger, 1893–1918." In *Woman's Work,* edited by Marnie Hall. New York: Gemini Hall Records, 1976. (Program booklet for the record album of the same name. See also under *Published Sources: Recordings.*)

Slonimsky, Nicholas. *Music Since 1900.* 4th ed. New York: Scribner's Sons, 1971.

Spalding, Albert. *Rise to Follow: An Autobiography.* New York: Henry Holt, 1943.

3. *Published Sources: Periodicals*

"A la Villa Médicis." *Excelsior,* April 3, 1918, p. 3.

"A Remarkable Young French Woman Prize Winner." *The Musical Leader,* Thursday, July 31, 1913, p. 115.

"Art et Curiosité: Académie des Beaux-Arts." *Le Temps* (Paris), July 7, 1913, p. 5.

Belt, Byron. "Philharmonic Concert Misfires." *Long Island Press,* November 11, 1975, p. 16.

Bender, William. "Sarah's Women." *Time,* November 24, 1975, p. 88.

Blitzstein, Marc. "Music's Other Boulanger." *The Saturday Review,* May 28, 1960, p. 60.

Borroff, Edith. "Women Composers: Reminiscence and History." *College Music Symposium* 15 (Spring 1975) : 32.

Boudouresque, Léon. "Deux femmes—Qui l'eût dit?" *Le Miroir,* July 5, 1913, pp. 5–8.

Bourgeois, Jacques. "La Musique: Le Mythe de Lili Boulanger." *Le Nouveau Journal* (Paris), March 30, 1968, p. 4.

Ceillier, Laurent. "Faust et Hélène de Mlle Lili Boulanger." *Le Monde Musical,* December 15, 1913, p. 1.

Charpentier, Raymond. "Audition des Envois de Rome de Lili Boulanger." *Comoedia,* January 18, 1923, p. 3.

———. "Les Concerts." *L'Avenir* (Paris), June 14, 1921, p. 2.

Clarendon (Pseud. of Bernard Georges Gavoty). "A la Mémoire de Lili Boulanger." *Le Figaro* (Paris), March 28, 1968, p. 2.

"Les Concerts du Conservatoire royal de musique de Bruxelles." *Comoedia,* February 9, 1925, p. 4.

Crussard, R. "Lili Boulanger." *Journal des Ouvrages des Dames,* June 1, 1918, p. 110.

Debussy, Claude. "La Musique espagnole. Faust et Hélène par Lili Boulanger." *La Revue S.I.M.,* December 1, 1913, pp. 43–44. Reprinted in *Claude Debussy. Monsieur Croche et autres écrits.* Edited by François Lesure. Paris: Gallimard, 1971.

Delaquys, Georges. "Le Souvenir de Lili Boulanger." *Le Journal* (Paris), March 14, 1939, p. 2.

"Discours de M. le Duc de Choiseul." *Moniteur universel*, (no. 320, November 16, 1835).

"La Distribution des Prix du Conservatoire." *La Décade philosophique,* October 24, 1797, pp. 244–47.

Dyer, Richard. "Sarah Caldwell, female composers make history." *Boston Globe,* November 11, 1975, p. 13.

"L'Examen des Classes de composition musicale." *Le Ménéstral,* no. 6 (February 8, 1913), p. 48.

Fleming, Shirley. "Notes on the Program: 'Faust et Hélène.'" *Lincoln Center,* November 1975, p. 16.

"Gargenville a inauguré la place Lili-Boulanger." *Le Parisien* (Mantes edition), June 13, 1972, p. 1.

Gavoty, Bernard. "Hommage aux 80 ans de Nadia Boulanger." *Rives d'Azur,* September 1967, pp. 43–44.

Gazette des Classes de Composition du Conservatoire (Lili Boulanger and Nadia Boulanger, eds.). December 1915 to June 1918. NBC

"Girl Wins Prix de Rome." *New York Times,* July 7, 1913, p. 3.

Green, Miriam. "Women: From Silence to Song." *American Music Teacher* 24, no. 1 (September–October 1974): 6.

Henahan, Donal. "Music: Two 'Firsts' for Sarah Caldwell." *New York Times,* November 12, 1975, p. 48.

Huneker, James Gibbons. "Music." *New York Times,* December 4, 1918, p. 11.

———. "Music: A Gala French Concert." *New York Times,* December 27, 1918, p. 9.

Jenkins, Speight. " A Ms-ical Celebration!" *Lincoln Center,* November 1975, p. 27.

Johnson, Harriett. "Words and music. Boulanger leads Philharmonic." *New York Post,* February 17, 1962, p. 14.

Julien, Adolphe. "Les Envois de Rome." *Le Journal des Débats* (Paris), February 4, 1923, p. 4.

Kastendieck, Miles. "At Carnegie Hall. 'Birthday.'" *New York Journal American,* February 17, 1962, p. 8.

Knight, Janet. "For the First Time on the Great Stage." *Ms.* 4, no. 5 (November 1975): 93.

Kolodin, Irving. "Music to My Ears: Nadia Boulanger . . ." *Saturday Review* 45, no. 9 (March 3, 1962) : 25.

Kresh, Paul. "Ladies' Day at the Turntable." *Stereo Review* 30, no. 11 (May 1976) : 124.

Kupferberg, Herbert. "On Records; Stereo Eastertide." *New York Herald Tribune,* April 10, 1960, p. 5.

Landormy, Paul. "Lili Boulanger." *Musical Quarterly* 16 (October 1930) : 510–15.

Lang, Paul Henry. "Music. New York Philharmonic." *Herald Tribune,* February 17, 1962, p. 6.

"Lili Boulanger." *Les Hommes du Jour,* no. 286 (July 12, 1913), n.p.

"Lili Boulanger." *The Musician* 24 (February 1919) : 43.

L[indenlaub], Th[éodore]. "Nécrologie: Mlle Lili Boulanger." *Le Temps* (Paris), March 18, 1918, p. 3.

————, Th[éodore]. "Théâtres." *Le Temps* (Paris), July 3, 1927, p. 5.

Loisel, Paul. "Le Concours du Prix de Rome." *Comoedia Illustré,* no. 20, July 20, 1913, p. 936.

McLellan, Joseph. "A Woman's Place Is on the Podium." *Washington Post,* November 12, 1975, pp. B10, B12.

"Mlle Lily [*sic*] Boulanger, Grand Prix de Rome pour la Musique." *Femina,* (no. 300), July 15, 1913, p. 375.

Mangeot, Auguste. "Soirées et Auditions diverses." *Le Monde Musical,* March 30, 1912, p. 99.

Martineau, Paul. "Concerts Colonne, Concert de Musique française: Franck, La Cantate de Mlle Lili Boulanger, A. Bruneau, Debussy, Berlioz. 16 Novembre." *Le Monde Musical,* no. 22, November 30, 1913, p. 323.

Mauclair, Camille. "La Vie et l'oeuvre de Lili Boulanger." *La Revue Musicale,* no. 10, August 1, 1921, pp. 147–55.

Mercier, Jeanne. "Observations of a Great Musician." *Ethos* (January 1940), pp. 32–35.

Méry, Jules. "Lili Boulanger." *Rives d'Azur,* no. 167, April 15, 1924, pp. 891–93.

Micklin, Bob. "Celebrating the women." *Newsday,* November 11, 1975, p. 9a.

Migot, Georges. "Les Concerts." *La Revue Musicale,* no. 10, August 1, 1921, pp. 163–64.

Ministère de l'Instruction Publique et des Beaux-Arts. Conservatoire National de Musique et de Déclamation. *Distribution des Prix.* 1913 and 1918, n.p.

Ministère de l'Intérieur. Conservatoire de Musique. *Distribution des Prix pour le Cours d'études de l'année 1835,* n.p.

Moullé, Edouard. "Salles diverses. Gala Nadia et Lili Boulanger." *Le Monde Musical,* no. 22, November 30, 1913, p. 326.

Noël, Edouard and Stoullig, Edmond, eds. *Annales du Théâtre et de la Musique.* Paris: n.p., 1875.

"Nouvelles Diverses: Paris et Départements." *Le Ménéstral,* no. 20, May 18, 1912, p. 158.

"Nouvelles Diverses: Revus [*sic*] et Départments." *Le Ménéstral,* no.

19, May 11, 1912, p. 150.

Palmer, Christopher. "Lili Boulanger." *The Musical Times,* March 1968, pp. 227–28.

———. "The Boulanger Sisters." *Country Life* (London) 157, no. 4056 (March 27, 1975) : 778.

"Une Place Lili-Boulanger inaugurée à Hanneucourt." *Le Courrier* (Mantes), June 14, 1972, pp. 1, 7.

Porter, Andrew. "Ladies' Night." *New Yorker,* November 24, 1975, p. 151.

"Le Prix de Rome." *Le Monde Musical,* no. 9, May 15, 1913, p. 146.

Reeser, H. Eduard. "Lili Boulanger." *De Muziek* 7 (1933) : 210–21, 264–79.

"Rêvant au Grand Prix de Rome, Mlle Lily [*sic*] Boulanger." *La Vie Heureuse,* June 13, 1913, p. 150.

Rosen, Judith. "Why Haven't Women Become Great Composers?" *High Fidelity* 23, (February 1973) : 52.

Rosenstiel, Léonie. "Letters." *Ms.* 4, no. 9 (March 1976) : 4.

Rubin-Rabson, Grace. "Why Haven't Women Become Great Composers?" *High Fidelity* 23, no. 2 (February 1973) : 48.

Saal, Herbert. "The Sound of Women." *Newsweek,* November 24, 1975, pp. 83, 85.

Schneider, Louis. "Au Conservatoire: Audition des Envois de Rome de Mlle Lili Boulanger." *Gaulois* (Paris), January 21, 1923, p. 4.

Schonberg, Harold. "Music: Nadia Boulanger." *New York Times,* February 17, 1962, p. 10.

"Tout Hanneucourt a participé à l'inauguration de la place Lili-Boulanger." *Paris-Normandie.* June 14, 1972, p. 1.

Trieu-Colleney, Christiane. "Lili Boulanger (1893–1918) ou Musique pour une éternité." *Jeunesse et Orgue,* no. 9 (Noël 1971), n.p.

United Press International (U.P.I.). "Sarah Caldwell's Baton Debuts in N.Y." *Evening Bulletin* (Philadelphia,) November 11, 1975, p. 39.

Vuillemin, Louis. "La Semaine musicale." *La Lanterne* (Paris), June 21, 1921, p. 2.

Vuillermoz, Émile. "La Guerre en Dentelles." *Musica,* no. 131, August 1913, p. 153.

———. "Lili Boulanger." *France-Aviation. Revue Technique, industrielle et littéraire* (August 1918), pp. 50–52.

"Young French Women Winning Honors." *The Sun* (New York), July 20, 1913, Section 3, p. 5.

"Young French Women Winning Honors." *Musical Leader* 26, no. 5 (July 31, 1913) : 117.

Zakariasen, Bill. "Celebrating women composers." *Daily News* (New York), November 12, 1975, p. 40.

4. Published Sources: Recordings

Boulanger, Lili. "Cortège" and "D'un vieux Jardin." *Premiere: Recorded performances of Keyboard Works by Women.* Hollywood, Calif.: Avant Records, 1974.

Boulanger, Lili. "Nocturne" and "Clairières (nos. 1, 2, 8 and 9)." *Woman's Work.* New York: Gemini Hall Records, 1975.

Boulanger, Lili. *Trois Pièces pour violon et Piano . . . Clairières dans le Ciel.* Paris: EMI (Stereo, CVC 2077), 1968.

Boulanger, Lili. *World Première Recording: Works of Lili Boulanger.* Paris: Everest (Mono, LPBR 6059; Stereo, SDBR 3059), 1960. Reissued as *Lili Boulanger. Du Fond de l'Abîme, Psaume 24, Psaume 129, Vieille Prière Bouddhique, Pie Jesu.* . . . Paris: EMI (CVA 919), 1967.

Boulanger, Nadia. *Nadia Boulanger, Professeur de Musique.* Collection: Français de Notre Temps No. 83. Paris: Réalisations sonores Huges Desalle, 1973.

5. Published Sources: Scores

Boulanger, Frédéric. *Stances sur la Mort de S.A.R. Monseigneur le Duc de Berry. Paroles de M^r. Desaugieres Mises en Musique Avec Accompagnement de Piano et Dédiées à Madame la Baronne Eugenie de Margueritte par M^r. Frédéric Boulanger, Artiste de la Chapelle du Roi et Professeur à l'Ecole Royale de Musique.* Paris: Aug. Le Duc, n.d.

Boulanger, Lili. *Attente.* Paris: Ricordi, 1919.

———. *Clairières dans le Ciel.* Paris: Ricordi, 1919. Republished by Durand, 1970 in new edition by Nadia Boulanger. (Version for voice and piano only.)

———. *Cortège.* Paris: Ricordi, 1919.

———. *Dans l'immense tristesse.* Paris: Ricordi, 1918. (Legally deposited, 1919).

———. *D'un Jardin Clair.* Paris: Ricordi, 1918.

———. *D'un Vieux Jardin.* Paris: Ricordi, 1918.

———. *Faust et Hélène.* Paris: Ricordi, 1913. Reissued by Durand, 1970. Orchestral score, Ricordi, 1921.

———. *Hymne au Soleil.* Paris. Ricordi, 1919. (Piano-vocal score.)

———. *Pie Jesu.* Paris: Durand, 1922. (Reduction for voice and organ, 1924.)

———. *Pour les Funérailles d'un Soldat.* Paris: Ricordi, 1919. (Full score.) Preceded by: *For a Soldier Burial* (text translated by Frederick H. Martens) . New York: Ricordi, 1918. (Piano reduction only.)

———. *Psaume 24.* Paris: Durand, 1924.

———. *Psaume CXXIX.* Paris: Durand, 1921.

———. *Psaume "Du Fond de l'Abîme."* Paris: Ricordi, 1925.

———. *Renouveau.* Paris: Ricordi, 1919.

———. *Le Retour.* Paris: Ricordi, 1918.

———. *Les Sirènes.* Paris: Ricordi, 1919. (Piano-vocal score only.)

———. *Soir sur la Plaine.* Paris: Ricordi, 1918.

———. *Vieille Prière Bouddhique: Prière quotidienne pour tout l'univers.* Paris: Durand, 1921–1925. (Piano-vocal score, 1921; orchestral score, 1925.)

6. *Unpublished Sources: Documents*

Académie de France à Rome. Albert Besnard, 1913–1921. Comptes 1914. AVM.

———. *Livre d'Inscription des Pensionnaires ouvert à la Villa Médicis le Premier Octobre Mil Huit Cent Sept.* AVM.

———. *Situation des Pensionnaires. March, 1914.* AVM.

Armagnac, Cécile. To Léonie Rosenstiel. April 20, 1976

Besnard, Albert. To Armand Girette. June 25, 1914. AVM.

———. To M. Dagnan-Bouveret. January 28, 1915.

———. To M. Henri Roujon. October 18, 1914. AABA.

———. To M. le Président de l'Académie des Beaux-Arts. March 13, 1914. AABA.

———. To M. le Président de la Section d'Art de l'Institut. April 10, 1916. AABA.

Bibliothèque publique Municipale de Perm (Russia). To Lili Boulanger. November 28, 1913. NBC.

Boulanger, Lili. To Miki Paronian: (MPC)

	September	11,	1912
	November	27,	1912
	November	29,	1912
	December	10,	1912
	December	18,	1912 (A)
	December	18,	1912 (B)
	December	25,	1912
(postmarked)	February	6,	1913
	May	30,	1913
	June	24,	1913
	June	27,	1913

(postmarked)	December	6, 1913
(undated)	January	1914
	March	9, 1914
	March	15, 1914
	March	26, 1914
(postmarked)	March	30, 1914
	April	2, 1914
	June	30, 1914
	September	6, 1914
	December	31, 1916
	February	14, 1917
	March	23, 1917
	May	10, 1917
	July	29, 1917
	September	27, 1917
	October	10, 1917
	October	15, 1917

————. To William Bouwens van der Boijen. January 1, 1906. NBC.

————. Telegram to Monsieur le Secrétaire. July 3, 1914. AVM.

————. To Albert Besnard. March 20, 1914. AVM.

Boulanger, Nadia. To Léonie Rosenstiel:

November	20, 1971
February	1, 1972
March	27, 1972
June	8, 1972
July	12, 1972
November	21, 1972
December	11, 1972
June	10, 1973
August	14, 1973
October	18, 1973
December	11, 1973
January	13, 1974
January	28, 1974
February	3, 1974
November	1, 1975
November	12, 1975
January	27, 1976

Chiron, Dr. Paul. Medical Certificate. January 20, 1914. AABA.

Conservatoire National de Musique et de Déclamation. *Année Scholaire 1912–1913. Tableau des Classes du 1er octobre au 30 septembre. Classe de P. Vidal.* ANP.

————. Certificate of Admission to the Conservatoire for Lili Boulanger. January 10, 1912. NBC.

————. *Examens semestriels. Rapports des Professeurs. 1912–1913.* ANP.

Dieudonné, Annette. To Léonie Rosenstiel:

> September 12, 1973
> September 25, 1973
> March   22, 1976

Fierro, Nancy. To Léonie Rosenstiel. November 11, 1973.

Furie, Kenneth. To Léonie Rosenstiel. March 9, 1973.

Girette, Armand. "Compte rendu au Directeur No. 5." June 30, 1914. AVM.

Grandjany, Marcel. To Léonie Rosenstiel. June 18, 1973.

Heuvelmans, Lucienne. To Armand Girette. June 7, 1914. AVM.

Institut de France. Académie des Beaux-Arts. *Concours, Année 1905–1927.* AABA.

————. *Procès Verbal, 1913–1914, 1915–1916.* AABA.

Invitation to the Funeral of Lili Boulanger. March 19, 1918. NBC.

Maeterlinck, Maurice. To Lili Boulanger: (NBC)

> February   16, 1916
> February   18, 1916
> February   20, 1916

Jéhin, Léon. Telegram to Mme Ernest Boulanger. April 5, 1924. NBC.

————. To an Unnamed Friend. March 16, 1924. NBC.

Johnstone, W. H. To Léonie Rosenstiel. October 30, 1971.

Marquein, Renée de. To Léonie Rosenstiel:

> September 4, 1972
> September 30, 1972
> October   23, 1972

Mathieu, J. To Léonie Rosenstiel. November 2, 1973.

Mihalovici, Marcel. To Nadia Boulanger. March 25, 1975.

Miki Paronian Collection: Lili Boulanger Memorabilia, Nice.

Ministère de l'Instruction Publique. Académie des Beau-Arts. To Albert Besnard. January 31, 1914. AVM.

Nadia Boulanger Collection: Lili Boulanger Memorabilia, Paris.

Paray, Paul. To Léonie Rosenstiel. June 8, 1973.

Paronian, Miki. To Léonie Rosenstiel:

> October 10, 1972
> August   10, 1973

Piel, Jules. To Léonie Rosenstiel. December 10, 1972.

République Française. Sous-Secrétariat d'État et des Beaux-Arts. To

M. le Président de l'Académie des Beaux-Arts. February 18, 1916. AABA.

Robert, J. To Léonie Rosenstiel. February 27, 1972.

Rosenstiel, Léonie. "Lili Boulanger: Myths and Realities." Lecture delivered for the Vassar College Women's Studies Symposium, Poughkeepsie, N.Y., March 3, 1976.

Sobhita, Kosgoda, Venerable. To Léonie Rosenstiel. January 26, 1972.

———. Transliteration of Maitrī Bhāvanāva. January 26, 1972.

Société Anonyme des Éditions Ricordi. Contract of Transfer of Author's Rights. November 30, 1916. NBC.

———. Contract of Transfer of Author's Rights. January 29, 1918. NBC.

Terrasse, Antoine. Film of the Exposition Lili-Boulanger. Paris, 1968.

7. *Unpublished Documents: Interviews*

Apostol, Mireille. Interview, Paris, November 21, 1973.

Boulanger, Nadia. Interviews, Fontainebleau:

> July 26, 1971
> July 19, 1971
> July 23, 1973

———. Interviews, Paris:

> November 18, 1973
> November 19, 1973
> November 20, 1973
> November 21, 1973
> November 22, 1973
> November 23, 1973
> November 24, 1973

Davidson, Norma, and Strong, Joyce. Interview with Robert Sherman (WQXR-FM), "The Listening Room," November 6, 1975.

Gifford, Virginia. Interview, Poughkeepsie, N.Y., March 4, 1976.

Grandjany, Marcel. Telephone Interview. New York. June 7, 1973.

Hall, Marnie. Interview, New York City, October 13, 1975.

Handly, Donna. Interview, New York City, October 24, 1975.

Paronian, Mme Miki. Interviews, Nice:

> July 4, 1973
> July 6, 1973

8. *Unpublished Sources: Autograph Scores*

Boulanger, Lili. *Choeur. Concours de Rome. 1888. Hymne au Soleil.* 1912. NBC.

———. *Clairières dans le Ciel* (nos. 1, 5, 6, 7, 10, 11, 12, and 13.) n.d. NBC. (Orchestral scores with vocal solo.)

———. *Dans la Sombre tristesse.* August 24, 1916. NBC.

———. *D'un Matin de Printemps.* 1917–18. NBC. (Violin or flute and piano.)

———. *D'un Matin de Printemps.* 1917–18. NBC. (Trio score.)

———. *D'un Soir triste.* n.d. NBC. (Orchestral score.)

———. *D'un Soir triste.* n.d. NBC. (Cello and piano score.)

———. *D'un Soir triste.* 1917–18. NBC. (Trio score.)

———. *Faust et Hélène.* June 21, 1913. NBC. (Piano-vocal score.)

———. *Fugue. Concours d'Essai,* 1912. CNP.

———. *Fugue. Concours d'Essai,* 1913. BNP.

———. *Morceau pour Piano: Thème et Variations.* June 13, 1914. NBC.

———. *Nocturne.* n.d. NBC. (Orchestral score.)

———. Notebooks, Sketchbooks and Workbooks:

> Composition Books (7 volumes)
> 1906–1918
> Counterpoint Notebooks (3 volumes)
> April 1910–September 1911
> Fugue Notebooks (7 volumes)
> June 1911–December 1913
> Harmony Notebooks (9 volumes)
> January 1911–October 1911

———. *Pièce courte pour flûte et piano.* October 1911. NBC. (Identical to *Nocturne* for violin or flute and piano.)

———. *Pièces en Trio.* (See *D'un Soir triste* and *D'un Matin de Printemps.*)

———. *Pour les Funérailles d'un Soldat.* October 13, 1912. NBC. (Piano-vocal score.)

———. *Pour les Funérailles d'un Soldat.* January 30, 1913. NBC. (Orchestral score.)

———. *Psaume 129.* Rome, 1916. NBC. (Orchestral score.)

———. *Psaume 130. De Profundis.* n.d. NBC.

———. *Reflets;* n.d. NBC. (Orchestral score.)

———. *Soir sur la plaine.* May 1913. NBC. (Orchestral score.)

———. *La Source. Concours D'Essai,* 1912. CNP. (Orchestral score.)

Index

Italicized numbers represent pages on which illustrations or musical examples are found.

305

WQXR-FM, 231, 233. *See also* Sherman, Robert

Wagner, Richard, 37, 139, 164, 179, 187, 222

Warren, Whitney, 113, 114, 116, 265, 279 n. 100

Warren, Mrs. Whitney, 116

Washington Post, 228

Wend, Flore, 228

Widor, Charles-Marie, 43, 60, 114, 116, 265–66, 274 n. 100

Wolf-Ferrari, Ermanno, 205

Wood, James, 229

Wuorinen, Charles, 213

Ysaye, Eugène, 39, 40, 266

Zakariasen, Bill, critical review, 232